The Dark Matter of Words

The
Dark
Matter
of Words

• • •

Absence, Unknowing, and Emptiness
in Literature

Timothy Walsh

Southern Illinois University Press
Carbondale and Edwardsville

Library of Congress Cataloging-in-Publication Data

Walsh, Timothy, 1958–
The dark matter of words : absence, unknowing, and emptiness
in literature / Timothy Walsh.
p. cm.
Includes bibliographical references and index.
1. Nothingness in literature.
2. Nothing (Philosophy)
3. Sunyata.
4. Literature—History and criticism.
I. Title.
PN56.N69W35 1998
809'.9338—dc21   98-18307
ISBN 0-8093-2172-6 (cloth : alk. paper)   CIP

Dedicated
with love
to my father
JOHN EVANGELIST WALSH
a true writer's writer
and to my mother
DOROTHY WALSH
(née Przybyszewska)
whose creativity
manifests itself in many ways

Contents

Plates

Preface

In *The Literary Mind and the Carving of Dragons*, a beguilingly titled work of Chinese literary theory dating back some 1,500 years, Liu Hsieh identifies the two essential elements of literary effort as *feng-ku*, or "the wind and the bone." Roughly translated, "wind" represents the source of ideas and their animating, vital spirit, while "bone" represents the creative, inspired structuring of that vital spirit in language. As Liu explains, "When expressions are organized on the right principles, literary bone is there; and when the emotion and vitality embodied are swift and free, there we find the purity of the literary wind" (313).

Sometimes Liu uses *feng-ku* as a single term, implying that in practice the two elements are so mutually intertwined and interpenetrating that they comprise a single dynamic entity (rather like the particle/wave nature of light).

Liu's sage advice to not be "thin in ideas and fat in words" like the pheasant that "with all its colorful feathers, is limited in scope of flight to a hundred paces because it is fat-fleshed and has little or no vigor" (315) is a timely warning for anyone venturing to write literary theory in an era when academic discourse has seemingly drifted far from the ideal of *feng-ku*. In what follows, I have done my best to ensure that the animating spirit remains vital, while cast in language that is supple yet strong, in the hope that this effort may soar farther than a hundred paces.

In his discussion of beauty, Liu also distinguishes between the *recondite* and the *conspicuous*, explaining that

> [t]he beauty of the recondite lies in its mystery, and that of the conspicuous in its startling transcendency. . . . The recondite, as a form, suggests ideas which are beyond linguistic expression and are comprehended indirectly through abstruse overtones, which unobtrusively reveal hidden beauty. (415)

In this book about the obscure workings of absence in literature, I attempt to explore the recondite by means of the conspicuous, a procedure that is a significant departure from the more familiar deconstructive methods that often seek to fathom the recondite through a discourse that itself is self-consciously recondite.

As Liu puts it, "vigorous roots foster conspicuous branches" (415). It would be a fatal mistake to assume that there really are no living roots simply because none are visible. Going to the other extreme and uprooting the tree to examine the roots directly would inevitably kill the tree. So I proceed under the assumption that it is by the conspicuous branches that we can best know the vitality and condition of the recondite roots.

For their constant support, understanding, and encouragement during the years I've worked on this book, I must thank most of all my wife, Barbara, and my son, Andrew. During many fruitful conversations, Barbara helped me distill and clarify my ideas while Andrew insisted on simple and direct explanations that forced me to strip away all nonessential encumbrances.

I remember one spring morning I was walking along with my son amid seas of dandelions, the bright gold discs set against deep green lawns newly reawakened from a hard winter.

"What do you notice about that yard?" I asked Andrew, pointing at one particular plot of land.

"Nothing," he said. "I don't see anything."

"Look again," I encouraged.

"Oh," he realized in a flash. "There are no dandelions there."

It was a lesson in how it is more difficult—though not impossible—to see what is *not* there (as well as a lesson in the overuse of pesticides).

I also owe a debt to basketball. There is a certain zen quality to a game of spinning balls and empty hoops. Basketball is a game that forces you to approach the recondite by way of the conspicuous. After all, playing basketball consists of deftly and gracefully hitting a marked circle of emptiness with a twirling globe. The ball is the world; the empty hoop is the void. The art is to send that spinning world through the opening to emptiness as often as possible.

The quieting of the mind necessary to play basketball well, clearing away all verbal chatter and foreseeing the arc of your shot falling softly through a zone of emptiness bounded by a steel ring, was often the best prelude for the writing of these pages. So behind these words you can envision a hoop encircling nothing, a net (itself a mesh of emptiness) directing the flow through emptiness, and a spinning globe that, through subtle arts, can inhabit that space.

Phillip Herring at the University of Wisconsin–Madison provided just the right amount of constructive criticism during all stages of the project. The initial idea for this book was hatched years ago in David Hayman's memorable seminar on literary sublimina. Hayman generously read the manuscript and made several helpful comments.

Eric Rothstein and Richard Begam also read the manuscript, providing valuable criticisms and suggestions. Jay Clayton provided some key advice during the formative stages, and Martin Nystrand encouraged new perspectives in his seminar on composition theory. Tracey J. Sobol, my editor at Southern Illinois University Press, helped immensely in the many details involved in bringing this book to press. Thanks also to Carol Burns, managing editor, and Alexandria Weinbrecht, who very ably copyedited the manuscript.

For lively discussion of the topic, I must also thank my father, John Evangelist Walsh; my mother, Dorothy Walsh; my brothers John and Matthew; my sister Mandy; and friends Michael Heinz and John Heasley. Responsibility for the views expressed is, of course, entirely mine.

An earlier version of chapter 2 appeared in *Mosaic* 25.2 (Spring 1992) entitled "The Cognitive and Mimetic Function of Absence in Art, Music, and Literature." Dr. Evelyn J. Hinz, editor of *Mosaic*, provided many helpful comments and suggestions, which improved not only that chapter but the entire book.

I gratefully acknowledge the copyright holders for permission to reprint the following material:

Excerpt from a letter by Robert Frost from *Selected Letters of Robert Frost* edited by Lawrance Thompson, © 1964 by Lawrance Thompson. Reprinted by permission of Henry Holt and Company, Inc.

Selected lines from "Mending Wall" by Robert Frost from *The Poetry of Robert Frost* edited by Edward Connery Lathem, © 1958 by Robert Frost, © 1967 by Lesley Frost Ballantine, Copyright 1930, 1939, © 1969 by Henry Holt and Company, Inc.

Selected lines from *Tao Te Ching*, translated by Gia-Fu Feng and Jane English. Copyright © 1972 by Alfred A. Knopf, Inc.

Selected lines from *The Coral Sea* by Patti Smith. Copyright © 1996 by Patti Smith. Reprinted by permission of W. W. Norton & Company, Inc.

Selected lines by Shiqi Xinyue from *A Tune Beyond the Clouds* edited and translated by J. C. Cleary. Copyright © 1990 by Asia Humanities Press.

Selected lines from "Of Lucifer" by R. P. Blackmur from *Poems of R. P. Blackmur*. Copyright © 1977 by Princeton University Press.

"Love Poem" by Bill Kemmett from *Yankee* (1990). Copyright © 1990 by Bill Kemmett.

"A Note to the Difficult One" and selected lines from "Malcolm Mooney's Land" by W. S. Graham from *Selected Poems* by W. S. Gra-

Part One

•

An Aesthetics of Absence

This world is made of clouds and shadows of clouds. It is made
of mental landscapes, porous as air, where men and women
are as trees walking, and as reeds shaken by the wind.

—John Cowper Powys, *Wolf Solent*

Thirty spokes share the wheel's hub;
It is the center hole that makes it useful.
Shape clay into a vessel;
It is the space within that makes it useful.
Cut doors and windows for a room;
It is the holes which make it useful.
Therefore profit comes from what is there;
Usefulness from what is not there.

—Lao-tsu, *Tao Te Ching*

1
Seeing What Isn't There

> On a divide between two watersheds I came upon the scene
> of a battle between a moose and three wolves. The story was
> written plainly in the snow at my feet. . . . What might have
> been silence, an unwritten page, an absence, spoke to me as
> clearly as if I had been there to witness it. I have imagined a
> man who might live as the coldest scholar on earth, who fol-
> lowed each clue in the snow, writing a book as he went.
>
> —John Haines, *The Stars, the Snow, the Fire*

A signet ring pressed into wax leaves us with a form that tells us all we need to know about the ring's shape and design, even if the ring itself were lost. Similarly, many other things are known indirectly through what they leave behind, by their lingering effects on whatever remains in their absence: love, perhaps, and happiness—but such examples will seem too sentimental. Raccoons, then, shall we say, who vanish with the dawn and whose unmistakable signature is an overturned garbage can and litter strewn across your yard. But this is perhaps too rustic.

Light itself may be the most obvious example. Light is so central to our lives that we seldom pause to consider it. The fact is that the world of light is always an old story. What light reveals to us is inevitably a view of things that have already happened, whether a microsecond or a millennium ago. It is strange to think that light itself has a history: sunlight, which is always eight minutes old when it reaches earth; or moonlight, which is a mere tick of a watch old; or the evanescent light of stars, which is nothing less than the living heat of the past reverberating through the present.

Like tracks in the snow that reveal so much to the alert observer, starlight speaks eloquently of what has gone before. Speeding across the vastness of the universe, the light from stars takes thousands, millions, or billions of years to reach us, so gazing into the night sky is really an unobstructed view into the past. The "lookback time" of quasars, for example, is thought to be about ten to fifteen billion years (since they are ten to fifteen billion light-years away), so we are seeing them now as they were shortly after the formation of the universe. Similarly, when the earth was treated to the magnificent supernova of 1987, the events we witnessed had actually occurred more than 150,000 years ago (the amount of time it took the light from the explosion to reach us).

There is, in fact, scarcely a year in our distant past that we cannot "see," since, of all the billions upon billions of stars, we can always find one the requisite distance away to allow a glimpse back in time. It is not without a touch of irony that humankind often feels trapped in the present, irrevocably cut off from the past, since by simply venturing outside at night we can watch the sky above us replay the entire history of the universe.

Conversely, some of the stars we now see in the night sky are no longer there, but we will all be long dead by the time their light speeds across mind-boggling distances to bring the news of their demise. For these reasons, astronomers and cosmologists have to become particularly comfortable in dealing with absence. What they see is always what is no longer happening, artifacts of ancient events, figurative tracks in the snows of time.

But while the light from stars has a story to tell, it is the nature of the black "void," of the "aether" between them, as Aristotle would call it, that has become the more fascinating concern. Today, the issue of the "dark matter" of the universe is central to astrophysics. Even to understand the nature of the problem is a daunting task: All the visible matter of the universe, all of the stars and planets and interstellar dust, the aggregate of everything in the universe we have come to know as "matter," accounts for no more than 5 to 10 percent of the total mass of the cosmos. In other words, 90 to 95 percent of the universe seems to be composed of something invisible and undetectable that we were previously comfortable in calling nothing itself, yet a "nothing" that accounts for nine-tenths of the mass of creation.

As with the wax impression that can inform us about the features of a lost signet ring, we know of the "missing matter" only through the impression it leaves on the visible and detectable segment of reality: the known continually implicates the unknown, just as the conspicuous perpetually leads us toward the recondite. As Lawrence Krauss remarks in *The Fifth Essence*, a study of dark matter, "there is unquestionable evidence that the formation of everything we see is governed by that which we cannot" (xv). So upon the frontiers of science, the outriders have adopted hypotheses concerning this dark matter that are as enchanting as they are aesthetically pleasing.[1]

Though this book is concerned with literature and language rather than deep space, the dramatic re-emergence of the unknown in astrophysics can prove instructive. For it is only by means of a tentative and admittedly imperfect sense of the total picture and of the state of learning across the disciplines that we can appreciate the full significance of any individual contribution. So in a study about the workings of absence in literature, it seems vital to recognize connections between the domain of words and the realm of worlds, acknowledging that the lacunae at the heart of life inevitably impress themselves upon all facets of existence, from the most fleeting of sensations to the grandest artistic endeavors.

It is desirable, for instance, that we be able to recognize the correspondence between tracks in the snow and starlight, between tracks in the snow and those other impressions upon a white background we call words, and perhaps even between the missing words marked by an ellipsis at the end of a paragraph and the "missing" dark matter of the universe. Long after you have risen in the morning, the pillow bears silent testimony to the fact of your sleep, and that bowl-like impression in a pillow becomes yet another clue to your existence—just as an empty holster speaks of a gun and a single discarded glove reveals much about the anatomy of the human hand. So from a simple impression in a pillow, we could deduce where someone has slept and even confirm the existence of a resident where before there may have been doubt (which perhaps explains the ancient injunction to smooth one's bed upon rising).

What I propose to look for across the pages of books are similar kinds of impressions that can speak volumes about what is missing, the figurative signets and sleepers that press upon our stories and then depart. Like tracks in the snow that tell us only about what is not there and alert us to the "partialness" and time-boundedness of our perceptions, the patterns of absence in literary works also leave behind characteristic footprints. By following the visible trail of absences through a story, we begin to better appreciate exactly how what is not said relates to what is, sensing in the shadows of words those other whispers that go unheard.

Just as all physical creation now seems to implicate a greater, unseen realm of dark matter, so too do our words continually implicate the wordless. As Thomas Carlyle proposed in an essay on Sir Walter Scott,

> There is a great discovery still to be made in Literature, that of paying literary men by the quantity they *do not* write. Nay, in sober truth, is not this actually the rule in all writing; and,

moreover, in all conduct and acting? Not what stands above ground, but what lies unseen *under* it, as the root and subterrene element it sprang from and emblemed forth, determines the value. Under all speech that is good for anything there lies a silence that is better. Silence is deep as Eternity; speech is shallow as Time. (404)

By insisting upon the nascent fecundity of silence, Carlyle sounds a note in harmony with countless others, from Lao-tzu to John Cage, from Jalaluddin Rumi to D. H. Lawrence. It is also worth emphasizing here that this sense of silence as a kind of looming immanence is very different from the concept of nothingness postulated by some modern philosophers and bandied about all too easily in classrooms. As Eugene Goodheart succinctly puts it, "Absence implies presence, the opposite of nothingness" (9).

Silence is experienced as an absence, but since silence itself is something perceived, this absence also becomes palpably present to our consciousness. In one sense, silence is a negative quality; in another it is a positive force. Paradoxically, we register absence as a felt quality that engages a definite response. This seeming contradiction is at the heart of Carlyle's observation, where silence is felt to be far "deeper" than speech and is thereby figured as an entity with measurable attributes. It is also the central insight in Henri Bergson's discussion of the "idea of nothing," not to mention the Buddhist sense of Emptiness, "Void" (*sunyata*), and "Suchness" (*tathata*), all of which will be taken up later.

Words are undeniable presences upon the page, so when they attempt to body forth absences, they tend to be embarrassed by their own corporeality. The labyrinthine twistings that language must therefore undergo in order to accommodate our transactions with absence, silence, and emptiness are a primary focus of this study. Whenever we try to discuss silence, the ineffable, or nothingness, we inevitably employ phrases that are bent to our use, sometimes violently hammered into shape and jury-rigged, and such tropes often reveal more than the ostensible content of a passage. Conversely, the varieties of felt absences that influence our stories often result in textual fissures that serve to mark the juncture of the word encountering the wordless.

This may all seem like suggestive but weightless speculation, so a few preliminary instances will serve to set the scene. In a chapter about painting in *The Meaning of Culture*, John Cowper Powys writes:

> Upon some hill-top the trees mass themselves in a certain way as we watch the scenery through a train window, or we catch a glimpse of a group of straw-stacks huddled in the corner of a field; and we respond to an organized harmony in this chance-

thrown pattern of light and shade and find that it answers some secret need of our natures with startling reciprocity.

But in the greatest pictures this instinct in us which inevitably reacts to formal pattern finds its comfort in this abstract design heightened by something else. This something seems an irreducible, ultimate quality evoked by the original imagination of the artist, working upon the structural mysteries of the universe. (70)

What is especially interesting in this passage, besides Powys' acuity regarding the essence of visual art, is the way its very grammar and syntax are made to mirror and rehearse in microcosm the principle being articulated. Since the "irreducible, ultimate quality" inhering in great paintings is unnameable and immune to discursive representation, it becomes a force registered in absentia. Paradoxically, this kind of active and vibrant perception exposes a gap in our conceptual knowledge, revealing a shortcoming in our analytic resources as well as a limitation in our language. We necessarily must acknowledge it without being able to define or describe it in any satisfactory way: it is a registered presence that exposes an absence. In this same way, the perception of any undefined or hidden presence can strike us as an absence.

To convey an insight so vaporous and elusive, Powys allows the full weight of his observation to rest on a phrase, "something else," that is as empty of meaning as words can be. "Something else" hollows out a space at the heart of the statement, which is a way of importing the "irreducible, ultimate quality" being described directly into the description. As with the great paintings that are his subject, Powys' sentences orbit around a central "something else" that can be felt but not named.

This manipulation of lexically "empty" items as a way of mirroring or perhaps crystallizing our discourse on emptiness and absence is heightened considerably in *The Wings of the Dove*, Henry James's intricate masterpiece. Here is a description of Kate Croy's first meeting with Merton Densher:

She had had originally her full apprehension of his coerced, certainly of his vague, condition—full apprehensions often being with her immediate; then she had had her equal consciousness that within five minutes something between them had—well, she couldn't call it anything but come. It was nothing to look at or to handle, but was somehow everything to feel and to know; it was that something for each of them had happened. (89)

The chain of empty husks assembled here ("something . . . anything . . . nothing . . . everything . . . something") is a virtuoso exercise in avoidance replete with intimations of some recondite realization that, while always barely glimpsed, is never finally revealed. Furthermore, the wider context of this passage does nothing to lessen the inscrutable uncertainty of these boldly contentless phrases. While bristling with suggestive implications, these words lack anything but the most nebulous antecedents, so that we find ourselves stymied if we attempt to pin down their meaning in any precise way.

In *Nil*, Robert Adams's study of the "literary conquest of void," one is continually stumbling over these kinds of suggestive constructions. Regarding Flaubert, Adams notes that "cosmic void, as it gives man reason to doubt his own intellect and sense his own diminished proportions, has about it something aseptic and soothing" (70). While "something aseptic and soothing" affirms the potentially comforting effect of the encounter with cosmic emptiness, the accent here is on "something," stressing that the reasons for this reaction remain mysterious. In this sense, "something" functions within the sentence as a domesticated "cosmic void," a syntactic pothole that analogically reinforces the idea while Adams is in the process of shaping it.

All these deferrals to shadow-language and pregnant "somethings" may not seem troubling at first, nor particularly arresting, but I would suggest that this is simply because we have largely inoculated ourselves against their special significance. The very omnipresence of such concessions to what cannot be captured in language has rendered them as invisible as the unnameable regions toward which they point. In attempting to approach this shadowy threshold, please note that I am likewise regularly forced to adopt the very same stylistic strategies in phrases like "what cannot be captured in language," which delineates by default something tangibly before us that we cannot quite grasp with our tools of logic and language. The regularity with which we come across this dark matter in language, where vagueness is pressurized to the bursting point, testifies to the fundamental nature of these encounters with boundaries beyond which language cannot venture but across which our deepest sensibilities can sometimes vault.

Although language is surely the most crucial development in human evolution as well as our most wonderful resource, language does not encompass the full range of human experience, nor does it provide access to our highest moments of enlightenment. This perspective is in complete opposition to the prevailing tenets of poststructural literary theory, which maintains that we can never be privy to authentic and unifying knowledge because all human cognition is mediated by language—language which itself is ultimately ungrounded in any "transcendental presence" but is a shifting "tracery of difference." Language is our birthright, the current wisdom goes, but language remains self-enclosed and self-reflexive, bestowing knowledge not of the outside world but only of its own inner workings. The gifts of language are always relative, fraught with undecidability, and we are forever trapped within its yawning abysses. . . . Such a myopic viewpoint, so obviously out of step with the actual conditions of daily life, could only have arisen within the cloistered and artificial atmosphere of academic intellectualism, which itself does sometimes seem self-enclosed and self-reflexive.

The problem with such a train of thought is that it refuses to recognize any other mode of knowing besides the linear and linguistic—other ways of knowing that, in fact, always supplement our discursive faculties. Moments of genuine wordless enlightenment, of mystical rapture and sublime transport, are authentic and irreducible human capacities that have been celebrated and portrayed by artists for as long as art has existed. Such modes of awareness cannot be completely housed in words or translated directly into another medium. They cannot be exhaustively analyzed or even successfully argued. They vanish whenever we try to pin them down. But they are nevertheless real.

Literary theorists are understandably wary of handling such ethereal experiences in sober discussions. However, increasingly in the past few decades academic theorists have not only assumed such visionary states to be counterfeit or contrived, but openly attack them, preferring to "demystify" all such moments by laying bare the sublimated discourses of power, psychological or political, that supposedly underlie them.

Yet it is obvious to an unjaundiced eye that many of our greatest works of art have been erected around such transcendent moments. When we turn from Dante to Garcia Marquez, from Novalis to Virginia Woolf, or from Milarepa to Emily Brontë, this is the single indestructible thread binding together these otherwise quite different artists. Often the heart of their work, the dynamic pulsing energy living on within otherwise inanimate pages, derives its vitality from such searing and profoundly wordless moments of insight.

When in the sixth century Dionysius the Aeropagite expounded on the illusory nature of all human language, his insight was not necessarily less incisive than that of a Jacques Derrida. But unlike most current theorists, Dionysius the Aeropagite went beyond a mere consideration of the limitations of language to an affirmation of what subsists beneath and beyond words, urging us to cultivate the wordless vision within ourselves. The same observation might be made regarding the authors of the voluminous corpus of Sanskrit poetics, the Taoist poets of T'ang, or the Sufi poets of Islam, not to mention the followers of the Symbolist movement of Nerval, Rimbaud, and Mallarmé—all of whom are thoroughly mindful of the entanglements and instabilities of language, while also realizing that the arts ultimately have their fullest impact on a wider realm of knowing and a higher plane of perception.[2]

It has become a common feeling among working poets and creative writers that academic literary theory has evolved into something completely out of sympathy with both the process and ultimate significance of its purported object of attention. In its flight into political and social theory, philosophical and psychological methodologies, and the resulting professionalized specialization, literary theory too often fails to engage with literary art *as art*. Cynthia Ozick's understandable complaint that "College teachers were never so cut off from the heat of poets dead or alive as they are now" (3) is typical of the kind of exasperated response the current state of affairs inspires.

In the profession today, we tend to see literary art simply as a manifestation of this or that ideology, or as a convenient field of action to demonstrate the workings of our latest psycho-social obsessions. We have seemingly forgotten that art has its own concerns and its own significance, its own *power*—that art partakes more of magic than the museum, more of spiritual alchemy than the archaeological dig. We have seemingly forgotten that the ultimate aim of true art has more to do with the transformation of consciousness than with the reflection of particular cultural ideologies or socio-political constructs. If art is a living force (as it surely is), then fundamentally it must be seen as experiential and transformational.

A great poem or short story or novel is, like a bicycle, first and foremost something that *works*, and it is also, like a bicycle, something to be ridden. It is a conveyance, a mode of transportation that requires no license but literacy. The question is how do we help potential riders get started, as well as provide experienced riders with advanced instruction.

A treatise on the socio-political significance of the bicycle in a capitalist state, on the self-deconstructing dualisms of bicycle advertising in a motorized age, or on the gender prejudices of the bicycling bourgeois may be of interest, but such studies will not help you understand how a bicycle actually works, and they certainly will not teach you how to ride one.

In this book, I have tried to keep the focus, figuratively speaking, on how the bicycle works in order to help interested riders ride better, while perhaps conveying some insight on the questions of why it is we ride and where we get to. For this reason, I do not propose to demystify artistic works in this study, but rather to participate as fully as possible in their mystery. A close examination of rhetorically successful devices for communicating the incommunicable will set the stage for a more searching consideration of the place and purpose of absence, unknowing, and emptiness in the literary arts.

Such an approach is not exhaustive or comprehensive and is not meant to be the last word on such matters (since there really can be no last word). What is "last" I do not pretend to know, but it is certainly not a word and cannot be packed into language. At the least, this book will illuminate certain interesting aspects of literary art, particularly as it reconnoiters the borderlands where what can be humanly known in the deepest sense runs up against the limitations of language and the fetters of biophysical necessity.

Whether it be tracks in the snow or starlight, the pangs of love lost, or an ingenious deferral to "something," the various vehicles for seeing what isn't there, for sampling the infinitely shifting aftertastes of absence, press upon us from all sides, so that we too easily forget how a large part of our consciousness is formed in response to encountered absences and thwarted expectations. In the following pages, the vaporous quarry pursued through literary works will be the pointed use of absence, emptiness, and blankness, focusing particularly on the sometimes peculiar, sometimes provocative varieties of uncertainty that the encounter with absence can produce.

Consequently, there will be much to say about silence and void, inexpressibility and ineffability, the unsayable and unspeakable, as well as the unnameable and unknowable. Merely listing a string of such terms may cause some readers to draw back, suspecting perhaps a warm and fuzzy journey through maddeningly insubstantial esoterica. So I hasten to add that even the most stratospheric flights of sympathetic commentary are anchored in concrete, demonstrable examples, wherein the visionary is grounded in the actual.

Periodically, we will return to a certain core of the most representative examples, not, I hope, to suggest that others would be hard to find, but simply because the various chapters approach the subject from different angles. By applying new insights incrementally to a familiar core of examples, a fuller picture will begin to emerge.

Most recent accounts of indeterminacy and undecidability in literature stress those moments of latent ambiguity or instability of which the author was presumably unaware but toward which the critic can turn a more perceptive eye. This is the root of Paul de Man's notion of "blindness" and is a basic presumption of most deconstructionist approaches. While there is no doubt a grain of validity to such a perspective, it completely ignores the vastly larger and more central fields of action wherein an author has consciously deployed strategic uncertainties, intentionally weaving complex webs of interlacing lacunae that individually and collectively radiate a vital force through almost any work of literature of lasting value.

Deconstruction as a self-sufficient methodology has largely fallen by the wayside as literary theorists and critics have gravitated to culture studies, the new historicism, and feminist and gender studies. But the lasting legacy of deconstruction—still alive in the carry-on baggage of the recently tenured and the commodious attics of the academic mind—is the notion of linguistic indeterminacy, of *aporia* and undecidability, as the ultimate ground of all human language. Not only is language figured as an unfathomable abyss, but (and here is the most damaging misconception of most poststructuralist theory) language is assumed to be what we are and all we are.

Despite many premature obituaries, deconstruction is hardly dead, as the continuing stream of books defending, extending, recuperating, or revivifying deconstruction testify.[3] In literary theory, the current conception of the nature and role of absence, void, indeterminacy, and undecidability still bears an unmistakable deconstructionist stamp.[4] While there is no need to rehearse the many objections to the deconstructionist "project," since these have been admirably set forth in a number of incisive studies, such as Alexander Argyros's *A Blessed Rage for Order*, John Ellis's *Against Deconstruction*, Richard Poirier's *The Renewal of Literature*, and George Steiner's *Real Presences*, among others,[5] what is needed is an alternative perspective on the nature and function of absence. It is therefore crucially important to revisit this moonlit terrain to survey it and map it anew from a fresh vantage point.

Contrary to the deconstructionist tendency to see absence as a condition "always already" underlying all texts and evenly distributed through all language, the examples of absence examined in what follows are important and interesting precisely because there is something "more missing" in them than in their relatively more stable surrounding context. The examination of such conspicuous absences (as in a mystery writer's withholding of vital information or even in a simple pronoun without an antecedent) thus represents a categorically different approach than the looser critique of "presence" still ubiquitous in literary circles today due to the zealous advocacy and playfully obscurantist methods of some recent theorists.

If, as these critics insist, language always and inevitably gives rise to a radically indeterminate "free play" of meaning, then everything from an Horatio Alger novel to *Finnegans Wake* must be seen as equally "incoherent." Since I am confident that any literate reader knows intuitively that this is not the case, that there are, in fact, categorical differences between a Hardy Boys novel and the writings of Gertrude Stein, a primary aim of this study will be to illuminate the repertoire of techniques whereby writers engender a sense of perceived absence in order to bring about specific effects.

Such a task is obviously easier to imagine than to accomplish. As Robert Adams notes regarding Baudelaire, "the use of void within individual poems as technique rather than subject-matter fills them with a negative energy which is easy to feel but hard to define" (124). The same thing might be said regarding the paintings of Caspar David Friedrich, the sculpture of Henry Moore, or the music of Charles Valentin Alkan: It is impossible not to feel the negative energy at work, to register the dynamic element of absence, but it is difficult to describe and seemingly impossible to reach any generalizing conclusions.

Duly cautioned, but confident that the allure of blankness and empty immensity are familiar enough to us all to provide at least a tentative foundation, our expedition will set out toward the heart of darkness to search for the sources of this "negative energy" flowing through literature.

2
Orchestras of Shadow

The sea was dense as a Rothko, prosaic, unbroken. But the shadows, they seemed to be everywhere; invading every hollow, every secret place, as a flapping of wings, where there were no birds, not even a gull.

—Patti Smith, *The Coral Sea*

Music is at its best when it carries you along at a level deeper than the music itself and forces you to live in its spaces as well as its notes.

—Keith Jarrett, *Eyes of the Heart*

When Alice tells the White King in *Through the Looking Glass* that she sees nobody on the road, the White King remarks that she must indeed have sharp eyesight to be able to see nobody ("And at that distance too!"). As usual, there is considerable wisdom behind Carroll's drollery. The ability to recognize what is not there, to "see" what is missing, is a basic though easily overlooked component of cognition and of consciousness. Like a woodsman warned by a sudden silence in a forest, we are all attuned in myriad ways to sense significant absences.

Too often these days, the uncertainty arising from the many forms of absence in literary works has been seen by critics as either debilitating and confusing, or else as a primary symptom of a general bankruptcy of meaning. Contrary to both of these positions, I would suggest that the aesthetic manipulation of absence and uncertainty can be uniquely productive, often playing a very specific role in the overall design of a work. Rather than being a roadblock on the path to meaning or a sign of some radical and suppressed internal contradiction, the aesthetic generation of uncertainty is as legitimate and specific an artistic aim as the desire to evoke sympathy, laughter, or outrage.

Often, critics of a deconstructive bent imply that the purported radical indeterminacy at the heart of language erodes or obliterates any claims to referentiality, destroying the "illusion" that language has anything whatever to do with the external world. A more expansive perspective, however, would suggest that the absences and resulting uncertainties called into play in works of art might more usefully be seen as a subtle facet of mimesis—as corresponding to aspects of the human condition and perhaps even to the structure of the physical universe in which we play our small part.

The parallels between the aesthetic function of absence in literature, art, and music suggest that there is something fundamental about the manipulation of silence, darkness, ellipsis, and other forms of absence within human constructions. The magnificent cathedrals of Europe, for example, are in one sense attempts to enclose emptiness on an unprecedented scale, and they beautifully demonstrate the paradox that to capture the glorious majesty of space one must confine it so that it can more easily be seen. Just as architects exploit the potential of empty space by enclosing it, writers, composers, and artists have likewise developed special strategies for harnessing emptiness, for domesticating Nothing—for, as Theseus put it, giving "to airy nothing a local habitation and a name."

If the *Venus de Milo* had been found intact when it was unearthed on the island of Melos in 1820, it would probably not have excited quite so much attention and lavish praise centering on the statue's mysterious suggestiveness. As soon as it arrived in Paris, speculation about the original position of the missing arms and left foot sparked a controversy that has continued to this day, effectively thwarting the many proposals to restore the statue to a hypothetical original state.

Whether a viewer inclines toward the notion that this Venus was holding a shield to gaze at her reflection, or that she was spinning thread, or that the right arm held the drapery around her hips while the left rested on a pillar, no one can completely escape the residue of tentativeness accompanying this kind of conjecture. The idea that the *Venus de Milo* may originally have been part of a larger group of statues introduces yet another element of uncertainty that casts doubt on the adequacy of any of these simple solutions. Even if we try to reconstruct the statue imaginatively as we view it, we do so without confidence and are constantly thrown back on the actual emptiness residing where the arms once were. Yet it is this very emptiness, this purely negative element, that seems to enhance our perception of the figure's beauty (see plate 1).

Plate 1. *Venus de Milo*. Reproduced from Auguste Rodin,
Venus: To the Venus of Melos (1912).

The example of the *Venus de Milo* thus lends support to a strictly literal application of Ralph Waldo Emerson's precept that a statue is beautiful when it begins to be incomprehensible. Emerson was, of course, referring to finished and complete works of art, but the special case of this most famous of statues becomes something of an acid test for his observations, which seem more true than ever in this instance. The passage from his essay on "Love" continues:

> The statue is then beautiful when it begins to be incomprehensible, when it is passing out of criticism, and can no longer be defined by compass and measuring wand, but demands an active imagination to go with it, and to say what it is in the act of doing. The god or hero of the sculptor is always represented in transition *from* that which is representable to the senses, *to* that which is not. Then first it ceases to be a stone. (105)

With the *Venus de Milo*, the statue has not only ceased to be a stone but has, in part, ceased to be anything at all. This element of nothing-made-visible is therefore only an unusually graphic example of what, as Emerson would have it, is a basic element in all art and the primary prerequisite of beauty.

Since there are so many ancient statues surviving in fragmentary form, it is an interesting question why this one in particular so inflamed the nineteenth-century imagination.[1] A tentative conjecture might be that the intriguing and unprecedented spiraling twist of the torso provokes speculation in a way that a more conventional fragment would not. We wonder what kind of stance, what sort of occupation and context, could possibly account for such a strikingly beautiful position, and so we are moved to a heightened awareness of what is there through the agency of what is not. The absence seems not to disfigure the work, but to enhance it in a strange way.

Writing in 1882 when the statue was still widely regarded as possibly the finest in existence, Walter Perry focuses on the figure's "pleasing undulation" and explains:

> The attitude of the Goddess is a very peculiar one, not easy to be accounted for. She stands proudly erect, inclining from the waist upwards to the right, but facing slightly round to the left. She rests the whole weight of her stately form on the right leg, while the left foot, which is lost, was raised and rested on some object—a helmet or tortoise. . . . The beautiful rhythm, however, is obscured by the loss of the fine arms which must have belonged to so majestic and superb a figure. (601–2)

As with many other critics, Perry has no difficulty moving from the statue's "peculiar" pose and the uncertainty resulting from its fragmentary state to an assertion of its unique achievement: "The figure is ideal in the highest sense of the word; it is a form which transcends all our experience, which has no prototype or equal in the actual world, and beyond which no effort of the imagination can rise" (602). Implicit in Perry's argument is the idea that the evocative power of this particular work stems at least partly from the fact that it is incomplete, that it shades off suggestively into nothingness, or, conversely, that it seems to take shape amidst a background of emptiness made more than usually palpable.

The idea of a fragmentary statue representing an art "beyond which no effort of imagination can rise" may seem perplexing until one realizes that the ineffable can be effectively approached in art only through some kind of felicitous subtraction, some conspicuous omission that grants emptiness a home and allows it to work its subtle magic. In this case, the absence of the arms both challenges the imagination and highlights the limits of the intellect, preventing any "resolution" of the figure while insuring that a maximum level of uncertainty remains.

In one of the more grandiloquent paeans ever penned about the *Venus de Milo*, Auguste Rodin presses the point even further. Addressing the statue directly, he proclaims, "Mutilated, you remain entire to the eyes. If the ravages of time have been permitted, it is only that a trace may continue of their profane effort and of their impotence" (4–5). Through an ingenious trope, Rodin manages to turn the heavy toll exacted by the passage of centuries into an almost transfigurative victory over time, so that the fragmentary state of the statue paradoxically reinforces our trust in the permanence of art.

For Rodin, what is vital is not simply the tension between presence and absence made graphic by the statue's fragmented form but the still subtler interplay of light and shadow over the incomplete statue's exquisitely modeled features. Stressing from the outset the propitious way the figure is exhibited in the Louvre, where (again directly addressing the statue) "the twilight deepens in the room that you may be more clearly seen" (3), Rodin holds forth on the "ineffable passages of light into shadow" (21) that make the Venus seem to breathe:

> The shadows, the divine play of shadows on antique marbles! One might say that shadows love masterpieces. They hang upon them, they make for them adornment. I find only among the Gothics and with Rembrandt such orchestras of shadows. They surround beauty with mystery; they pour peace

over us to hear without trouble that eloquence of flesh that ripens and amplifies the spirit. (20)

The necessity of incorporating "vigorous shadows" (3) within works of art is, in this case, directly allied with the statue's mutilated state—two versions of blankness and darkness that reinforce and intensify one another, so that Rodin, like Perry, must defer to the statue's "incomprehensible magic" (12).

Once again, the aesthetic equation proposed by Rodin—that art aspires to darkness, shading off into invisibility, that it is most intense when half-perceived—is not as eccentric as it may at first appear. On a more general note, Rodin explains: "The expression of life, in order to keep the infinite suppleness of reality, must never be stopped or fixed. The dark element, essential to the effect, must then be carefully contrived" (24–25; see plate 2). The manipulation of shadow and the incorporation of lacunae, ellipses, and other forms of conspicuous absence are vital to any work of art. Such lapsing into darkness, wordlessness, and silence engenders a necessary fluid quality, preventing a work from lapsing into a static finality and insuring that a living quality of uncertainty and untapped, unrealized potential resonates perpetually around the work.

Plate 2. *Meditation*, 1885, by Auguste Rodin. Reproduced by permission of The Rodin Museum: Philadelphia. Gift of Jules E. Mastbaum.

The exploitation of emptiness allied to a purposely cultivated unfinished quality are also essential elements of Chinese landscape painting. In *Taoism: The Road to Immortality*, John Blofeld, whose writings on Taoism and Buddhism are especially insightful in this regard, explains that

> [t]he Taoist artist deliberately leaves his work unfinished, that the viewer may complete it from his own intuition. Just as, in Ch'an (zen), an apparent nonsensical set of words or a sudden action may bring about an extraordinary communication from mind to mind, so do paintings of this kind sometimes cause an illuminating blaze of intuition to leap into the beholder's mind, and he is conscious of being touched by the flow of cosmic energy communicated by the painting. (8)

In *The Idea of the Holy*, Rudolph Otto likewise credits darkness, silence, and emptiness as being the only direct methods for rendering the numinous in art, explaining that the "darkness must be such as is enhanced and made all the more perceptible by contrast with some last vestige of brightness, which it is, as it were, on the point of extinguishing" (68). Yet, while Otto is no doubt correct, we must not confine the virtues of these negative methods to any narrow conception of the numinous or of only the most obvious gestures toward the sublime. As Rodin's more general remarks suggest, the use of absence—of darkness, silence, shadow, and void—is more likely a basic constituent of all enduring art.

The final proving ground for Rodin's aesthetic principles can be found, appropriately enough, in his own incomparable masterpieces, many of which are left intentionally "incomplete" or "mutilated." The infamous *Man Walking*, for example, headless and armless, created a scandal when it was first exhibited (see plate 3). There are dozens of other examples, such as the similarly headless and armless *Cybele*, or the armless *Meditation* of 1897, whose twisting torso seems to owe something to the *Venus de Milo*. There are so many examples, in fact, that one critic has aptly described Rodin as an "advocate of fertile incompletion" (Taillander 16) and another as "a sculptor who grasped the implications of the fragment as a work of art in its own right" (Sutton 34).

Such observations would apply equally well to the endlessly fascinating sculpture of Henry Moore, where forms are perpetually on the verge of becoming, vitalized by a dynamic harnessing of absence. The genesis of his *Draped Torso* of 1953 is especially instructive, since this work was literally subtracted and recast as a separate entity from a previous "complete" work, the *Draped Reclining Figure* of 1952–53 (see plates 4 and 5).

Plate 3. *Man Walking* (*L'Homme Qui Marche*) by Auguste Rodin. All rights reserved. Reproduced by permisssion of The Metropolitan Museum of Art, Gift of Miss G. Louise Robinson, 1940. (40.12.4)

Plate 4. *Draped Reclining Figure* by Henry Moore. Reproduced by permission of the Henry Moore Foundation.

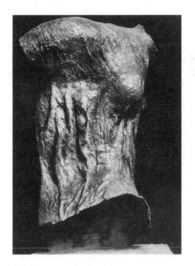

Plate 5. *Draped Torso* by Henry Moore. Reproduced by permission of the Henry Moore Foundation.

Moore explains:

> A large work like the *Draped Reclining Figure*, has to be cast
> in several pieces which are then welded together. That figure
> was cast in about five sections—the head, two arms, the torso,
> and the legs. I have to see, of course, the sections in wax
> before they are cast and when I saw the torso part, separate
> from the rest, even I, who had done it, was very struck by its
> completeness and impressiveness just as a thing on its own. It
> was then that I thought of making that part, a work in its
> own right, as I pictured it a piece standing on my own lawn.
> So after the whole figure had been cast in bronze I asked the
> foundry to make a wax of the torso part alone, cut off at just
> what points I thought out as most satisfactory. I then worked
> on the wax for quite a time and made some modifications.
> The design of it as a fragment (just where to end the arms,
> neck, etc., and deciding on their angle), and the poising of
> the torso upright, were all a problem to make it completely
> satisfactory in itself. (Philip James 239)

The problem of making a once-complete, now intentionally fragmentary form "completely satisfactory in itself" might seem almost
unfathomably mysterious until we realize that the expertly structured
engagement with *what is not there* is an essential element of aesthetic
satisfaction.

In this regard, Rodin's and Moore's work can be placed within the
larger tradition of the *non finito*, the deliberately unfinished work whose
lasting effect depends heavily on its seeming to be incomplete or fragmentary. The dynamic potential of the unfinished—torsos, literary fragments, sketches, or even ruins—enkindles in us a compensatory response,
so that while we try to flesh out what is not there, we are seemingly
brought within the aesthetic construct itself as a participant. In this way,
the energy latent in the unfinished can often seem more "alive" and vital
than anything more neatly fashioned.[2]

In his early study of Rodin, Rainer Maria Rilke focuses on this paradox of vitality and wholeness inhering in fragments, remarking that "com-
pleteness is conveyed in all the armless statues of Rodin; nothing necessary
is lacking. One stands before them as before something whole. . . . There
are among the works of Rodin hands, single, small hands which, without belonging to a body, are alive" (26–27).

Implicit in such a formulation, as with Perry's and Rodin's related
remarks, is an admittedly unquantifiable intuition that the aesthetic uncertainty arising from such graphic absences functions as a kind of ca-

thartic analog to the experiential uncertainties we are all subject to in an epistemological sense. To appear real and whole, the art work, like the "real" object, must retain an element of irreducible mystery.

The positing of such a confluence of aesthetics and epistemology based on the central role of absence is, in fact, a fundamental assumption of Bruce Kawin's groundbreaking study of "reflexive fiction and the ineffable." In *The Mind of the Novel*, Kawin suggests that "author, text, and readers participate in the creation of meaning and confront the limits of their levels of awareness in response to the challenge of the ineffable, and that opening to the ineffable is an experience not of vacuity but of something recognized as irreducibly authentic" (xii). Later, referring to Beckett's *The Unnamable*, Kawin makes the point more directly: "Beckett's reader confronts a system whose limits are analogous to those of his or her own verbal consciousness" (7).

Fundamental to this aesthetics of absence is an awareness that we ourselves are born into uncertainty, that, epistemologically speaking, uncertainty is the mother of everything as well as the limit toward which everything converges. As Philip Wheelwright suggests in his ruminations on "Man's Threshold Existence," the human condition can best be described as fundamentally "liminal" in nature, as a suspended state of "radical incompleteness" where we are "always on the borderland of a something more" (18).

According to such a view, uncertainty is what our consciousness awakens to and what we will die amidst; it is what we grapple with in countless daily travails, and what occupies our consciousness while gazing into the night sky. As Robert Frost aptly put it, "the background is hugeness and confusion shading away from where we stand into black and utter chaos" (Thompson 419). It follows quite naturally from such a perspective, from such a birthright, that art, our most powerful and complex mode of expression, should of necessity embody this fluid and unfixed state where potential is never arrested and never completely fulfilled.

The absences and lacunae in our artistic endeavors can therefore be understood as attempts to replicate the real and inescapable limits of human experience beyond which we cannot see. Whether in a novel, a painting, or a symphony, gaps and silence function as the principal means by which the limitations of human consciousness are encoded. We can know our own limitations, we can even anatomize the physical mechanisms by which we exist, but we cannot comprehend in any discursive or rational way what it is that lies beyond them.

In *The Tangled Wing*, an intriguing study of the "biological constraints on the human spirit," Melvin Konner shows how we are constantly striving to transcend our biological and biochemical limits, whose very mechanisms are responsible for both producing the desire to overstep them and preventing such liberating flights from taking place. Thus expressed, we would seem to be caught in either a vicious or a miraculous circle—or both. While engaged in the kind of metaphysical mind games that attempt to totalize the flotsam and jetsam of our short lives into theory, it is always worth reminding ourselves what we really are. As Konner sees it,

> Anatomy may not be destiny, but it is all we bring into this world and all we can take away with us when leaving. . . . in this intricate, dense, moist web of cells we carry around with us (and not in any airy thing attached to it) lies the substance of all the love and hate, joy and grief, hardheaded analysis and excited imagination we experience during our sojourn on this planet. And it is only because certain cells make signals, chemical and electrical, to communicate with each other, that we are able to think and feel at all. (59)

Boundaries, however, tend to imply the unbounded. Just as the Berlin Wall had always been associated with what was on the other side—either greener fields or a bleaker and regimented existence—so frontiers of all sorts inevitably imply something beyond, perhaps even create that something beyond. Likewise, in recognizing our own human limitations, we do, in a sense, verify the existence of something beyond them—unknowable and mysterious—but inexorably there.

Long before Kurt Gödel demonstrated that human systems of logic must establish their validity by appealing to something outside that system, Ralph Waldo Emerson was wrestling with a similar paradox. In his seminal essay "Circles," he observes that "Every ultimate fact is only the first of a new series. Every general law only a particular fact of some more general law presently to disclose itself. There is no outside, no enclosing wall, no circumference to us." With regard to the evolution of the individual consciousness, Emerson describes the process even more incisively as a "self-evolving circle" that "rushes on all sides outwards to new and larger circles, and that without end" (181).

Fundamental to Emerson's paradigm of ever-expanding, ever-evolving circles of consciousness is the idea that we are always subject to human limitations of some form and that we are always conscious of these boundaries, especially during those transitional phases when we are attempting to break through to a wider circle.

Insofar as works of art are necessarily born of the limited consciousness of a human creator, they must inevitably reflect and incorporate these inherent limitations. In this sense, the aesthetic use of blankness, darkness, silence, and shadow is both natural and indispensable, figuratively suggesting that the "wholeness" of artistic vision paradoxically includes an awareness of its own incompleteness—that it is, like us, finite amid infinitude.

From a technical perspective, the most basic device for fabricating this living quality, this aura of ungraspable mystery, is simply to leave something out. By creating puddles of darkness, by injecting gaps and breaks, or by creating a context for silence, an artist can both engage and entangle an audience with that minimum of effort known in mathematics as elegance. Constructing the plot of a detective story, for instance, consists primarily in deciding what aspects to leave in darkness, just as the element of mystery essential to any narrative depends on consciously manipulated suppressions.

An aesthetics of absence may seem to reduce the complexities of form to a formula, but the art of leaving things out does not proceed according to any recipe, and there is no guarantee of success. As Thoreau remarks in *Walden*, "You will pardon some obscurities, for there are more secrets in my trade than in most men's, and yet not voluntarily kept, but inseparable from its very nature" (20). These secrets of the trade, these obscurities inseparable from aesthetic effort, are not simply stock effects injected into a work, but arise from within as inexorable by-products of creative endeavor. Moreover, the endless possibilities regarding what is left out and how this is accomplished are the very stuff of creativity. The difference between the lacunae in an Ellery Queen mystery and those in *The Golden Bowl*, for example, demonstrate the gradations of power exerted by conspicuous absence, varying from the wooden fill-in-the-blank of conventional whodunits to the dynamic and volatile sense of the numinous in art, brought on by deftly managed instabilities.

Whether it be a twenty-second gap in a presidential tape or the "mystic blue flower" of Novalis, forever sought but never attained, absence often commands an attention that far surpasses the potential of anything present. Once an absence has been made conspicuous, once it has been "implicated" in some fashion, we are forced to accommodate some degree of uncertainty in our interactions with that larger entity of which the absence is a part.

In speaking of absence as "conspicuous," I am assuming a necessary distinction between those absences that directly impinge on our sensibility and "pure" absence (if such a thing is possible to conceive). When we say, for example, that a politician is "conspicuous by his absence" at some event, the absence is registered only because certain events generate at least a tentative expectation that certain persons be present: of all the millions of people not present at any given event, only a few can be conspicuously absent. Conversely, there are innumerable events that certain politicians will not attend, but only a limited few from which they will be conspicuously absent.

Generally speaking, absence can be registered only when the expectation of something is thwarted or deferred. To cogitate on absence prior to or apart from expectation may be possible, but such exercises belong to the mystic or the saint and cannot be embodied discursively. A crude analogy can be made by contrasting the example of the *Venus de Milo* with the much more nebulous sense we might conjure up of other ancient statues that still lie buried, never to be rediscovered. While we can entertain the notion of such hypothetical lost statues, such speculation can never engage the intense acts of attention that the *Venus de Milo* provokes, where what exists generates an anxious expectation, a palpable desire, for what is missing.

During the act of reading, to move to another medium, there is a submerged awareness that the words we scan are inscribed on a larger blankness, on sheer whiteness, which, as Melville has so eloquently shown, can represent either absence or plenitude, nothingness or wholeness. In the same way that we "read" the constellations against the vast blackness of the night sky, written words present themselves as islands of coherence rising out of a fundamentally unintelligible background. This is even more apparent in the field of music where the printed score emblematizes the interplay of sound and silence through the relationship of the black notes, the "sounds," inscribed on the white "silence" of the page. In music, the fact that the printed notes must be performed before acquiring any meaning is obvious, though the same is also true of literature, where words remain inert until "performed" by a reader.

There is, however, an important difference between the ambient blankness of a page and the more pointed sense of absence that can be created through the deft use of words. The sense of conspicuous absence that can lead to productive uncertainty can be achieved only by manipulating these islands of coherence themselves.

In James Joyce's "The Dead," for instance, what is arguably the most significant moment in the story is little more than an artful deferral to blankness. Gabriel's chance encounter with his wife, who is standing in shadow at the top of a staircase "listening to something," produces an epiphany that, while passing quickly, lingers in the reader's mind long afterward:

> He stood still in the gloom of the hall, trying to catch the air that the voice was singing and gazing up at his wife. There was a grace and mystery in her attitude as if she were a symbol of something. He asked himself what is a woman stand-

ing on the stairs in shadow, listening to distant music, a symbol of. (210)

Gabriel cannot answer this question, nor can the reader, and this
momentary suspension, this deferral to absence, becomes paradoxically
pregnant with unuttered significance.[3] Everywhere in this passage the
drift is toward darkness, stasis, and blankness: Gretta, frozen like a statue,
stands in shadow while Gabriel looks on from amid the gloom, straining
unsuccessfully to hear what has so entranced his wife. All this together
becomes a strange and moving "symbol of something," a central vortex
of the story signaling Gabriel's new but still flawed reawakening toward
his wife. The key phrase that bears the full weight of this flickering awareness, "a symbol of something," is little more than a palpable gap—like
the missing arms of the *Venus de Milo*. Nevertheless, it is upon this
phrase, a phrase with little or no assignable meaning, that the story finds
its balance point.

Of course, nothing could be more appropriate than to situate such a
conspicuous absence within a story that is, after all, specifically about
absence—about "the memory of those dead and gone great ones," about
Gretta's long-dead former love who mysteriously returns in a remembered melody, and the "vast hosts of the dead" that the gently falling
snow seems to unite with the living. The remembered dead are undoubt-
edly one of the most conspicuously absent yet still resonant forces in our
lives, and so it is singularly appropriate that the narrative structure of
this tale mirrors the thematic content by resting so solidly upon absence.

To cite just one further example, a similar "empty" phrase is used in
a related manner in Faulkner's *The Bear*. Near the end of the story, Ike
McCaslin returns to the fast-dwindling hunting grounds of his youth
and encounters a very old and large rattlesnake. Surprisingly, it is the
odor of the snake that affects him most profoundly: "he could smell it
now: the thin sick smell of rotting cucumbers and something else which
had no name, evocative of all knowledge and an old weariness and of
pariah-hood and of death" (110).

Once again, the deferral to blankness, to "something else which had
no name," generates a pregnant uncertainty: the odor is similar to rotting cucumbers and yet different. It is "evocative of all knowledge"—a
puzzling and nearly impossible analogy—and is somehow related to
"pariah-hood." In short, this is an odor that no marshaling of words or
images can approximate; hence the disclaimer that it is "something else
which had no name." Yet even as we struggle with Faulkner's impossible
equation, we are forced to credit the fact that the odor, whatever it really
was like, did conjure up these mysterious associations in Ike's mind. The
uncertainty concerning the odor itself as well as the logic of its associa-

tions feeds into the larger and equally productive uncertainties concerning Ike's problematic relationships with his family, society, the land, and the wilderness.

These characteristic deferrals to absence on the part of Joyce and Faulkner, these two varieties of resonant "somethings," represent strategies for "incorporating vigorous shadows," to borrow Rodin's phrase, within the realm of words. "Something" is a word always without specific meaning. It is an "empty" word that, while functioning as a semantic place holder, can also function as something much more—as a means of capturing *what we cannot say* and confining it within inked scratches on a page. Even in context, "something" remains a nebulous quantity. Yet it is a word we cannot do without, a word we depend on at those crucial moments when our purpose is to communicate vagueness in as direct a manner as possible. At such moments, the discursive thread of the narrative fades into shadow and from shadow into darkness—but it is a productive darkness, an "illuminating" darkness. As Rudolf Otto suggests, vagueness is often our only analog to the visionary, the nebulous our only mirror of the numinous.

Within the general slip and slide of meaning that forms the mercurial foundation of language, there may suddenly come a moment where any pretense about the ability to communicate the full nature of certain experiences or states of mind is summarily abandoned, and the reader is forced to accept something on faith alone. Such a moment represents, figuratively speaking, a lapsing into silence, a transient pressure point where the limited resources of language have been exhausted and the only recourse is to allow the eloquence of silence to intercede on behalf of those states of awareness that can find no linguistic equivalent.

In speaking of the potential "eloquence" of silence, however, it is important to remember that this effect can be attained only when the limits of language have been dramatized, and the reader is left on the threshold of some imminent wisdom that is essentially wordless. Attempts to invoke the silent eloquence of visionary states often misfire if they are too easily reached. A poet like W. W. Story may declare confidently that "Of every noble work the silent part is best, / Of all expression, that which cannot be expressed" (308), but the difference between such fluff and a lyric by Novalis or Leopardi is like setting a cardboard statue among those made of marble.

If silence is truly golden, it is most likely because it is our most common experience of how absence can assume palpable form and how "nothing" can be magically transmuted into a looming *something*, pregnant with significance. Silence is, of course, a relative concept since we are never completely without sound. Though we usually tune it out, there is always a background ambiance, always an invisible din ensuring that we never really experience silence in an absolute sense. Even in a sound-proof room, as John Cage is fond of pointing out, there can be no silence. As soon as we step inside, we will be startled by how loud the sound of our own heart has become.[4]

Within systems of organized sound like language or music, however, silence plays a crucial role. In an essay about the remarkable Estonian composer Arvo Pärt, Paul Hillier comments eloquently on this point:

> All music emerges from silence, to which sooner or later it must return. At its simplest we may conceive of music as the relationship between sounds and the silence that surrounds them. Yet silence is an imaginary state in which all sounds are absent, akin perhaps to the infinity of time and space that surrounds us. We cannot ever hear utter silence, nor can we fully conceive of infinity and eternity. When we create music, we express life. But the source of music is silence, which is the ground of our musical being, the fundamental note of life. How we live depends on our relationship with death; how we make music depends on our relationship with silence. (134)[5]

As Hillier makes clear later in his essay, the concept of absolute silence that forms the foundation of musical compositions is allied with the use of relative silence that the composer exploits. Hillier's comments are especially pertinent to Pärt's music, where silence paradoxically assumes a structural and even tonal significance. In a composition like *Tabula Rasa*, long silences regularly become the focus of the work. The brooding, vaguely menacing silences that punctuate the first few bars foreshadow the sublimely peaceful and mysterious silence into which the instruments gradually evaporate at the conclusion. Heard in relation to what is played by the instruments, the periodic silences seem charged with an ineffable, transcendent music. The way the composition finally dies away into utter silence, dissolving like some rare dye dispersed upon ocean waves, makes it seem that silence itself has swelled into the audible.

Silence, the absence of sound, becomes paradoxically a positive force, a state pregnant with unrevealed significance. Like the absences at work in the *Venus de Milo*, or the passages from Joyce and Faulkner, these various non-statements or non-things become almost unaccountably productive in the overall context of the work. Silence thoroughly permeates all music, affecting the way we hear individual passages as well as entire compositions. On the smallest level, there is the performer's use of *tempo rubato* (robbed time), the incorporation of brief pauses or hesitations in shaping the flow of music to establish fleeting pockets of silence before or after the sounding of a note. On a larger scale, to mention just one obvious example, there is Haydn's thousand and one manipulations of rests and pauses, all silences of a sort.[6]

Beyond such local manipulations of silence, the many great musical compositions that were never completed, often cut short by the intercession of death, present us with absences of a different order. When we listen to works like Bach's Art of the Fugue, Mozart's Mass in C Minor, or Schubert's "unfinished" symphony, the cessation of the music leaves us hypersensitive to the enveloping silence. We cannot help focusing on the music that is not there, the missing music suggested and prepared for by the completed sections, the music that might have been but for the whimsy of fate.

Greatest and most mysterious of all such unfinished works is Bruckner's Ninth Symphony in which the musical exploration of oblivion and bodily dissolution is reinforced by the work's incompleteness. As the titanic brass peroration of the Adagio flows into a serene and deeply meditative coda, the listener is carried toward the threshold of non-being, inescapably focused, as the final soft horn call and pizzicato die away, on how the hand of death prevented the completion of the final movement. In a tragic way, Bruckner's Ninth, like the *Venus de Milo*, seems more empowered than diminished by this absence. As the symphony fades into silence, merging with the image of the afflicted composer struggling unsuccessfully to complete the final movement on his deathbed, the fragmentary nature of the work as we now know it strangely enhances its impact. The finale is silence, and this movement-that-is-not becomes more effective aesthetically, perhaps, than any completed movement could hope to be.

In general, the tension between silence and sound in music corresponds roughly with the interplay of light and shadow in the visual arts, and, as the examples from Joyce and Faulkner demonstrate, it is not difficult to find analogs to silence and shadow in literature. Kafka's "unfinished" novels, for example, provide an interesting correlation to Bruckner's Ninth. With a work like *The Trial*, a question arises as to whether or not its fragmentary nature is an integral component of the overall design. Certainly the avoidance of closure intensifies its weirdly shadowed ethos, winding down as it does, like a car out of gas, in random notes and jottings, many of uncertain status, until the story gives a last unceremonious heave and expires.

Adding to the bewilderment of a book without a formal, definite ending is the well-known fact that Kafka had instructed his friend Max Brod to burn his manuscripts, forbidding publication. Never for a moment do we forget that we are reading *ashes*. Despite our awareness that

Brod ignored the instructions, the book has already, figuratively speaking, gone up in smoke, and we are left to sift through the charred remains like a shaman searching for portents. We read as if under a magical dispensation, and every page we turn is invested with a sense of undeserved privilege. It is like reading someone's secret diary, only a thousand times more intense. We feel that we've been allowed to read a book rescued from the other side of silence, from the other side of death.

The effect of reading a book that seems to fall apart in our hands rather than conclude, a book that has risen Phoenix-like from the ashes, is so deliciously provocative that one wonders if perhaps Kafka had really wanted Max Brod merely to announce their intended consignment to flames and then proceed posthaste with publication. Even if such a laudable conspiracy were never openly stated, it is a plausible assumption that Kafka knew Brod would never destroy the manuscripts—a point Brod himself makes, echoed more recently by Charles Bernheimer.[7]

Intentional or unintentional, conscious or unconscious, the abandonment of the novels in a seemingly unfinished state and their symbolic consignment to the flames is a masterstroke—Kafka's master *trope*, one might say. This ultimate and unprecedented turn of the screw, involving as it does the physical state of the book as *artifact*, blurs the distinction between the aesthetic and the "real." The invented world between the book's covers and the "real" world in which the book-as-book exists are thus fused, and this fusion immeasurably magnifies the work's impact.

In this regard, it is interesting to compare the effect of Kafka's works with other gestures of abandonment like Edgar Allan Poe's "Ms. Found in a Bottle." Poe's macabre and fantastic short story of a voyage on a ship peopled with dead souls breaks off, characteristically, just prior to the moment of ultimate revelation. Although the fragment purports to be a manuscript found in a bottle, the title of the story, followed by the author's name, announce that this is purely a narrative device even before the story has begun. Contrary to the situation with Kafka's unfinished works, the fragmentary nature of Poe's story is made a part of the story's exposition. We never really credit the pretense that the story itself, the story-as-story, is incomplete, or that it was actually a manuscript found in a bottle.

Another analog to Kafka's strategy is Chaucer's "Retraction" to *The Canterbury Tales*, where Chaucer disowns and castigates the preceding stories, then dutifully appends the retraction to the foregoing tales. Seen in the light of Chaucer's obviously rhetorical gesture, Kafka's own final instructions seem tinged with an equally strategic motive.

Kafka's blurring of the aesthetic and the real by exploiting the physical, artifactual nature of a work also brings to mind the delicious confusion Jorge Luis Borges caused with his deadpan reviews of non-existent books and obituaries of imaginary people. Other works like Vladimir Nabokov's *Pale Fire* or even Laurence Sterne's *The Life and Opinions of Tristram Shandy* also blur the line between the real and the fictional; but a distinction must be made between obviously novelistic gestures like Nabokov's or Sterne's and the extra-textual manipulation of readers engaged in by Borges and (possibly) Kafka.

It is perhaps worth emphasizing that the point here is not the particular parallels that can be drawn between such fragmentary works in themselves. Rather, the larger purpose is to forge relations between the various manifestations of absence across the arts so that we can better appreciate the affinities between, for example, *The Trial*, Bruckner's Ninth, and the *Venus de Milo*: between the artist's studied use of shadow, the composer's use of silence, and the storyteller's use of expressive vagueness. For it is nowhere but in the masterly evocation of hidden depths imperfectly glimpsed, the numinous sense of *what is not there*, of the ineffable permeating the effable that artists are able to conjure up some semblance of those ineluctable mysteries at the heart of humanity's unalterably liminal condition.

The examples from Bruckner and Kafka might seem like special cases, but they do serve to illuminate on the largest scale what other works attempt within smaller precincts. In D. H. Lawrence's *St. Mawr*, for example, there is no massive blankness like that approached by Bruckner's last symphony or Kafka's novels. Rather, a much more minute dispersion of shadow penetrates all aspects of the unfolding story so that *St. Mawr* seems inhabited more by darkness than light. This periodic lapsing into silence develops into a characteristic rhythm that becomes the most distinctive feature of the novel. Lou Witt's predicament, as well as her mother's, is brought on by her encounter with St. Mawr, a wild and dangerous stallion who seems "to look at her out of another world" (14). St. Mawr functions as a living emblem of non-human otherness, forcing Lou to a new consciousness of what is missing in her own life.

As always in Lawrence, this conflict is anchored in immediate physical relations, but the crisis quickly spreads to the most esoteric and ineffable of concerns: "The visible world, and the invisible. Or rather, the audible and the inaudible. She had lived so long, and so completely in the visible, audible world. She would not easily admit that other, inaudible" (99).

This metaphysical dilemma centers directly on St. Mawr, a fellow creature whose power to disturb and disrupt stems from his very alienness:

> Only St. Mawr gave her some hint of the possibility. He was
> so powerful, and so dangerous. But in his dark eye, that
> looked, with its cloudy brown pupil, a cloud within a dark

fire, like a world beyond our world, there was a dark vitality glowing, and within the fire, another sort of wisdom. (26)

Exactly what this "world beyond our world" is, this invisible and inaudible world in which St. Mawr exists as if in a parallel universe, is never made clear because it simply cannot be penetrated or formalized in human terms. Moreover, the accumulating effect of this story derives from the way Lawrence systematically allows the narrative to retreat into darkness and fade into shadow so that the novel, like Lou's consciousness, seems enveloped in a mysterious haze.

In trying to gesture toward this "world beyond our world," Lawrence is faced with a knotty but quite typical problem: if he delineates this realm too specifically, too lucidly, the all-important other-worldly quality will become domesticated and the story's basic premise will be instantly undone. To escape this, Lawrence cultivates various strategies of avoidance, and partialness becomes the fingerprint of the work. When Lou is overwhelmed with the futility of her present life, it is because "she was aware that something else existed, but she didn't know where it was or what it was" (38). When Lou comes across a dead adder, she is suddenly struck by a troubling vision: "some strange thing had happened, and the vast mysterious force of positive evil was let loose. . . . It was something horrifying, something you could not escape from" (69). "Unless something touches my very spirit," she tells herself later, "the very quick of me, I will stay alone, just alone. Alone and give myself only to the unseen presences, serve only the other unseen presences" (139). Similarly, the flaw she finds in her Mexican manservant can be described only by default: "Something was beyond him. And this something must remain beyond him, never allow itself to come within his reach" (139).

These passages are a small sampling of the frequent and meticulously orchestrated deferrals to nebulous language that crop up continually, page after page, paragraph after paragraph. The long final exchange between Lou and her mother is particularly interesting when Lou tries gropingly and unsuccessfully to explain the nature of the "something else," the "something that matters," the "something bigger" to which she longs to dedicate herself (157–58). Especially marked is the use of "something," in the sense of "something beyond," at precisely those moments when an important revelation seems imminent. On the threshold of truth, the narrative invariably fades into darkness, and there is no disclosure of any definite meaning beyond the bare implication that such a meaning does indeed exist, even if on a level inaccessible to human rationality.

Paralleling Lou's initiation into mystery through St. Mawr is her mother's own awakening through her desire for their groom, Lewis. Lewis is the only character in *St. Mawr* who seems to have some access to the "other world," the primal, non-human world of perception symbolized by the magnificent horse. What so fascinates Mrs. Witt about Lewis is "his seeming to inhabit another world than hers. A world dark and still, where language never ruffled the growing leaves, and seared their edges like a bad wind" (99). Lewis is seen as a member of "the aristocracy of the invisible powers, the greater influences, nothing to do with human society" (119). Mrs. Witt's personal failing is that she comes to identify these mysteries solely with Lewis himself, whereas Lou is able to distinguish between St. Mawr as a horse and the "other worlds" she is able to glimpse through him.

When Lou decides to return to America, the terms of comparison with England are striking, since both places are evaluated in light of the unnameable "somethings" that so obsess her: "And suddenly, she craved again for the absolute silence of America. English stillness was so soft, like an inaudible murmur of voices, of presences. But the silence in the empty spaces of America was still unutterable, almost cruel" (74).

When Lou ultimately decides to remain alone on her ranch where, amid the vast open spaces, "the stillness simply speaks" (154), she is still not able to articulate her reasons in any but the most shadowy and tentative of terms:

> There's something else for me, mother. There's something else even that loves me and wants me. I can't tell you what it is. It's a spirit. And it's here, on this ranch. It's here, in this landscape. It's something more real to me than men are, and it soothes me, and it holds me up. I don't know what it is, definitely. It's something wild. . . . (158)

Like an artist painting pockets of shadow to bring out more forcefully the colors in a picture's lighted regions, Lawrence retreats into opacity at all the critical moments when the story teeters on the brink of some ultimate illumination. This pattern is repeated so often and so conspicuously that the central focus of the story shifts to the shadows themselves and what lies beyond the veil of words—towards that which all these anxious and resonant "somethings" gesture. As in Arvo Pärt's music, where silence becomes a kind of supercharged sound, ultimate meaning is figured as the untapped potential of emptiness.

Fittingly, the novel ends on an indeterminate note. The story simply breaks off with Lou having decided to remain on her ranch amid the vast open spaces, listening to the silence while meditating on the ineffable sense of "something" that must always remain unnamed. Like the *Venus de Milo* or Bruckner's Ninth, *St. Mawr* is, in a sense, another sort of felicitous fragment. As we become more sensitized to what is not there, to what is missing in the story, we are simultaneously brought into tentative contact with the same boundaries to our own consciousness that Lou Witt so desperately longs to surpass. And herein lies the special value of this story and many others like it: they may not be able to say much about exactly what lies beyond the threshold—indeed, we are immediately suspicious of other works that claim to be able to do so without difficulty—but they succeed admirably in conducting readers to a doorstep they may not have otherwise encountered.

A common element in all these various aesthetic uses of darkness—blankness and shadow, silence and emptiness—is the general sense that behind the apparent emptiness is some sort of wonderful and wordless plenitude. Behind the mask of "something," beyond the "end" of *The Trial* or of Bruckner's Ninth, and in that hazy region of unnameable non-things gestured at in *St. Mawr*, there seems to reside marvelous unknown potentialities that always retreat from the verge of revelation, one step ahead of the seeker, into the refuge of darkness and shadow.

As Borges has demonstrated so amazingly in different contexts, the aesthetic phenomenon is centered on what he calls the "imminence of a revelation which does not occur" (188). Though we can posit a hypothetical realm somewhere in the beyond where the *Venus de Milo* exists complete and in absolute perfection, we can never actually visit her there. Moreover, here in our fallen and imperfect world, the fragmentary statue as it now exists speaks most eloquently of the potential forms beyond its present accidental state.

In terms of the aesthetic uses of absence, a work of art can be likened to a net, a pattern of interwoven filaments thoroughly permeated with absences that, while nothing in themselves, are nevertheless circumscribed and made visible by what is there, by the particular patterns spun by the artist. It is worth reminding ourselves that such a description also applies to the architecture of the physical universe, which itself is mostly made up of emptiness. As John Stewart Collis has remarked in speaking of the atomic structure of creation, "everything is chiefly made of holes":

> [T]he volume of space kept clear by the electrons is enormously greater than the total volume of the electrons themselves—the ratio being that of bullets in a battlefield. . . . a solid is not solid but chiefly holes; and water also full of holes; and the air riddled with holes. . . . It is not easy for us to realize the essential hollowness of things, that we are all hollow men. We see a great hulk of material in front of us and we suppose it is massive because of its material. Yet it is massive because it lacks material; it is bulky because it has little

bulk; it is visible because most of it does not exist. This is not immediately obvious. . . . The truth is that emptiness is the norm of the universe. It is almost void of matter. (7)

Drawing a parallel between the function of absence in art and its place in the physical universe is, admittedly, a sweeping generalization, but the point is simply to suggest that the aesthetic use of absence is not only a question of technique, but also a concealed aspect of mimesis.

Our organs of sense are severely limited, and consequently we are often more sharply aware of what we cannot see, hear, or comprehend than what we can. For this reason, we are of necessity attuned to what is not there, to whatever lies beyond the threshold of perceptual and conceptual limits. This sense of the unknown, as it impinges on our limited sensibilities (indeed, the unknown is *created* by these very limitations), is granted a local habitation within works of art through various forms of conspicuous absence, such as shadow, silence, blankness, and fragmentedness. All these types of lacunae, in their subtly varying ways, potentially represent doorways to a "beyond" we can register but cannot know, and they are consequently the artist's best means of faithfully replicating this ineluctable aspect of the human condition.

The aesthetic manipulation of absence, far from heralding a descent into undecidable "free play" as many poststructuralists suggest, is very often suggestively resonant and meaningful if one is attuned to, as T. S. Eliot phrased it, those "frontiers of consciousness beyond which words fail, though meanings still exist" (15). Just as the radical emptiness of the physical world is productive of everything including life itself and our own unique consciousness, the artistic manipulation of emptiness can accomplish effects that are both irreducibly authentic and achievable in no other way. As Meister Eckhart observed long ago, "Clay is fashioned, and thereby the pot is made; but it is its hollowness that makes it useful" (Clark and Skinner 194).

Part Two

•

The Roar on the Other Side of Silence

If we had a keen vision and feeling of all ordinary human life, it would be like hearing the grass grow and the squirrel's heart beat, and we would die of that roar which lies on the other side of silence. As it is, the quickest of us walk about well wadded with stupidity.

—George Eliot, *Middlemarch*

The solitary flute sounds
A tune beyond the clouds
Apart from those who know its voice
Who else recognizes it?

—Shiqi Xinyue ("Stone River")

3
The Wordless Blank and the Gift of Tongues

Poetry is a verbal means to a non-verbal source.

—A. R. Ammons, "A Poem Is a Walk"

In a letter to Bernard of Clairvaux, Hildegard of Bingen, that remarkable twelfth-century visionary, describes an experience that is at once exceptional and, from an aesthetic perspective, probably the most typical dilemma writers have faced for as long as writing has existed. Regarding the sacred visions that have periodically possessed her, she explains to Bernard:

> I am very preoccupied on account of a vision that appeared to me in the mystery of the spirit. . . . I understand the inner sense which touches my heart and soul like a burning flame, teaching me the depths of explanation without, however, giving me literary mastery in the Teutonic language, of which I am deprived, for I can read only in a simple way. . . . (Brunn and Epiney-Brugard 19–20)

While trying anxiously to give some semblance of her mystical experiences, Hildegard also graphically describes her encounter with the limits of language, drawing a sharp distinction between the "inner sense" understood in her heart and soul, and her limited ability to translate this understanding into the imperfect medium of words. In a letter to Guibert of Gembloux, she makes the distinction even clearer: "the words in this vision are not like words uttered by the mouth of man, but like a shimmering flame, or a cloud floating in a clear sky" (Newman 7).

Yet the core of Hildegard's dilemma is that she cannot keep silent. Though she realizes the impossibility of fully conveying her experiences and directly translating her wordless visions into words, she neverthe-less is overwhelmed by the compulsion to do so. As she explains to Ber-nard, "I experience great torments in this vision, not knowing what I must say of the things I have seen and heard. And sometimes, after the vision, I am confined to my bed by terrible sufferings, because I am silent, and I cannot even stand up" (Brunn and Epiney-Brugard 20).

Of course Hildegard, the "Sybil of the Rhine," did go on to record her strange and wonderful visions in such works as *Scivias* and in her morality play *Ordo Virtutum* and, perhaps most perfectly, in the exten-sive collection of music and poetry entitled *The Symphony of the Har-mony of Celestial Revelations*.[1] All through these works, however, there remains a constant tension between the compulsion to capture the expe-rience—to explain and to describe—and the acute perception that the words and language structures employed to this end will always fall short of fully conveying the essence of the vision or of the motivating intention.

In Mary Webb's *Precious Bane*, to move to our own century, Prue Sarn describes a similar predicament in her lilting Shropshire dialect:

> [T]here are some things so hard to write of that even a great scholar might boggle at it, and I, though I can do the tall and the short script, am not anything of a scholar, and words be hard to find for some things. I think, times, that in our mor-tal language there are no words for the things that are of most account. So, when those things come upon us we are struck silent, and can but feel and feel, till our hearts are like a bursting dam. . . . So, if I fail in what I've set out to do, you must pardon what I canna help, and fill up the glats in my speech with the brushwood of your own imagining. (294)

Both Hildegard and Webb make use of what Ernst Robert Curtius has called "inexpressibility topoi," disclaimers, often stylized, declaring the incapacity of language to convey the full import of our deepest percep-tions. This "motif of semantic inadequacy," as George Steiner prefers to call it, has probably been around for as long as language has existed. Its very universality suggests that it conveys a fundamental truth to which we all instinctively respond, namely, that we all do experience levels of awareness that can never be adequately housed in words. As Ann Chalmers Watts succinctly puts it, "Language protesting the failure of language apprehends the sure being of what cannot be expressed" (33).

This conception of language as a pale reflection of something greater than itself is both current today and as old as the wind. The *Tao Te Ching*, for instance, begins "The Tao that can be told is not the eternal

Tao. The name that can be named is not the eternal name," a sentiment echoed eons later by Flaubert when he described human language as a "cracked kettle on which we beat out a tune for a dancing bear, when we hope with our music to move the stars" (188).

Paradoxically, the acknowledged failure of language in its very self-denial often succeeds brilliantly in establishing the validity of nonverbal, paralinguistic spheres of knowing: the masterful use of words leading up to a declaration of inexpressibility upon the brink of some wordless empyrean often brings into being the reality of such states of mind, at least indirectly. They are set squarely before the reader, so to speak, by the declared inability to describe them and are thus left to linger in the reader's mind, richly and vibrantly inchoate.

That we all know of inexpressibility from direct experience and hardly need convincing on this point is amply demonstrated by the simple fact that we find such appeals unproblematic, accepting them at face value without question. More important, however, is the way such inexpressibility tropes make us sharply aware of our usually tacit affirmation of states of mind beyond words—even perhaps confirming the living reality of such states, a point emphasized by Watts in her essay on the subject:

> Paradox, of course, characterizes inexpressibility: words say that words cannot say. Paradox extends further, however, to the realm of epistemology and experience shared by reader and poetic speaker: if the highest poetic words say they cannot say, then what cannot be expressed must exist, must ever maintain a reality outside these verbal and imaginative constructions that say they cannot say. (26)

The urgent and paradoxical drive to recapture in words the essence of what are perceived precisely as visions beyond the reach of words is a recurrent topic in both Webb's and Hildegard's works, as in nearly all mystical and visionary writing. For Hildegard, this compulsion is often described as an all-consuming physical condition, precipitating illness and suffering, and the labor to cast such experiences into words is taken up in full recognition that it will not succeed. For Webb, the physical wasting away that accompanied such strenuous creative effort proved all too literally true.

Without questioning the authenticity of such states of awareness, we can note that such a standpoint gives rise to some very successful rhetorical strategies that periodically reinforce this overarching premise of a foredoomed enterprise that is nevertheless indispensable. For example, in the fifth vision of the second part of *Scivias*, Hildegard relates that "underneath the area where the woman glowed with the reddish color that was similar to the dawn, I saw a darkness that was as dark as that between heaven and earth. This darkness was so horrible that human language cannot even describe it" (104).

Though Hildegard maintains that she cannot possibly convey such perceptions, though this moment is ostensibly presented as little more than a lacuna in the description, the fact is that she *has* described the darkness. First of all, it is characterized as a "darkness"—and handing out such cognomens to the inchoate is a big step indeed! More exactly, the darkness is "horrible," and it is specifically a darkness "as dark as that between heaven and earth." All these positive descriptions are then both intensified and rendered effectively murky by the subsequent claim to have not described them at all.

This technique is even more succinctly apparent in the fourth vision of part three, where Hildegard explains, "On the very top of the whole column, there was such a bright light that no human tongue can describe it" (215) when, of course, Hildegard has just described it as a "bright light."

A more graphic example of this basic trope is found in this passage from another of Mary Webb's novels, where the protagonist, Deborah Arden, experiences a sudden, expansive revelation:

> Now she saw good and evil mingled, and felt a slumbering terror in the protecting cross, a hidden beneficence in the inimical stronghold across the valley. Beyond both, behind light and shadow, under pain and joy she felt a presence—too intangible for materialization into words, too mighty to be expressed by any name of man's. . . . She had nothing definite to put in their place, only a conception as vague and volatile as light or scent. . . . Instinct told her that the two visions were one. She was content with the balance of life as she found it, being dimly aware that the terror and the beauty intermingled in something that was more wonderful than beauty. (*The Golden Arrow* 279–80)

Despite Webb's protestations and the declared inability to cast such experiences in the medium of words, she has obviously succeeded in doing so, at least up to a point. The fleeting presence that so fills Deborah with awe is here materialized in words, at least to some degree, and the claim to have not done so at all only heightens the effect of this partial materialization. The lingering impression is that the description itself is nullified to some extent after it has already had a chance to evoke in the reader's mind some semblance, a tantalizing foretaste, of the experience.

Another well-known example of such expressions of the inexpressible can be found in Wittgenstein's *Tractatus*. When Wittgenstein observes that "There are, indeed, things that cannot be put into words. *They make themselves manifest.* They are what is mystical," and then goes on to emphasize that "What we cannot speak about we must pass over in silence" (151), one cannot help noticing that Wittgenstein has *not* passed over these perceptions in silence—that he has just put into words a heartfelt impression that specifically announces itself as what cannot be put into words.

Drawing attention to such enigmas is, of course, not to suggest any sort of duplicity, but only to highlight the kinds of contrary motions simultaneously engendered by such perceptions, contrary motions that are inescapably paradoxical and self-annihilating.

We might compare the struggles of Hildegard and Webb to describe the indescribable with what at first might seem to be something entirely different, such as Julia Kristeva's musings on the essence of womanhood: "In 'woman' I see something that cannot be represented, something that is not said, something above and beyond nomenclatures and ideologies. There are certain 'men' who are familiar with this phenomenon; it is what some modern texts never stop signifying: testing the limits of language and sociality" (Marks and de Courtivron 137–38). Though there are worlds of difference between Hildegard, Webb, and Kristeva, one common element is their own assurance that they are aware of things that cannot be captured in words, that they are capable of a level of perception inaccessible to human language systems.

We can also witness the same struggle, the birth pangs of the word, in D. H. Lawrence's efforts to describe the nature of sex in *Fantasia of the Unconscious.* After having repeatedly insisted on the vast difference between "primal, pre-mental knowledge" (32) and conscious cognition, Lawrence continues,

> What is sex, really? We can never say satisfactorily. But we know so much: we know that it is a dynamic polarity between human beings, a circuit of force *always* flowing. . . . To the individual, the act of coition is a great psychic experience, a vital experience of tremendous importance. On this vital individual experience the life and very being of the individual largely depends.
>
> But what is the experience? Untellable. Only we know something. We know that in the act of coition the *blood* of the individual man, acutely surcharged with intense vital electricity— we know no word, so say "electricity," by analogy—rises to a culmination, in a tremendous magnetic urge towards the blood of the female. (106)

Here, as with Webb and Kristeva, Lawrence proclaims the bankruptcy of language when attempting to plumb the depths of so central a mystery; and then, like the others, he proceeds to describe it anyway as best he can. The effect is to highlight the artificial and derivative nature of the discursive rendering as opposed to the essential and primary nature of the experience itself.

Besides such direct appeals to what escapes the weave of words, there are countless ways of creating an implied or tacit sense of inexpressibility, as we saw in the previous chapter's discussion of *St. Mawr*, as well as in the examples from Joyce and Faulkner. The skillful use of "nonsignifying" words, employed at the right moment and with the right touch, can engender a sense of absence, of something vital but missing that ever eludes language, and this felt sense of absence can often become an episode's most vital and lasting effect.

Hildegard, Webb, Kristeva, and Lawrence (along with innumerable others) all share a fundamental assumption that the limits of language do *not* correspond with the limits of human awareness, that the human psyche is capable of overreaching the limits of language, even though it may be ultimately incapable of directly communicating the content of such perceptions or states of mind. They all would concur that, as Rudolph Otto puts it, "Our language has no term that can isolate distinctly and gather into one word the total numinous impression a thing may make on the mind" (39–40). Within this view of language, a basic assumption is that the "total numinous impression"—of sex, the sacred, womanhood, or of anything at all—exists apart from language and remains fundamentally untouched by language.

On a more pedestrian level, this heady lexical dilemma is analogous to the general difficulty we all experience when trying to cast our own fluid and polymorphous experience in the fast-congealing mortar of mere words. There is never an equivalence, never an exact identity, between the experience itself and the words employed to recapture it. In *The Meaning of Culture*, John Cowper Powys returns to this point again and again so that it becomes for him a defining principle of art. For example, remarking that the "most intense and overpowering sensations we receive on earth are bodily ones," Powys notes that

> there are countless sensations and impressions that reach us
> from Nature mounting up sometimes, accumulating and gath-
> ering, till they attain moments of mysterious completeness
> such as could never be caught or expressed by any audible
> sound or by any written word. And yet they are full, in their
> fleeting impact on us, of a revelation that we long to arrest
> and eternalize in some palpable symbol. (60)

This discrepancy between artistic vision and formal execution is felt all the more acutely by poets and writers, who must become accustomed to measuring success according to degrees of failure. This is perhaps the central and perennial paradox of literary art: while our most intense and visionary moments are often perceived as a blankness, as a wordless wilderness beyond the familiar townships of language, this perception often initiates a contrary motion wherein the writer, aspiring to an almost pentecostal gift of tongues, finds that language can at least reach within a finger's breadth of such states—often by importing absence itself into the work via the various "somethings" and "nothings" and other empty phrases stored in the sub-cellars of language. It is in this sense that art in general can be seen as a species of analogy gesturing at something greater than itself.

This view of language and of a knowledge beyond language is, however, fundamentally at odds with a competing perspective that assumes the limits of knowledge and even of consciousness to be *identical* with the limits of language. Broadly speaking, the most salient aspect of recent poststructural literary theory is this tendency to see language as the fundamental stuff of existence, drawing an exact equivalence between what we know and the language that allows us to know. According to such a view, the frontiers of human awareness are synonymous with the boundaries of language.

This practice of identifying language systems with the structure of consciousness has become so ingrained in academic literary culture that today it often goes both unsubstantiated and unchallenged. The uncompromising assumption that all consciousness occurs within the categories of language systems of our own making is often assumed to be self-evident, and the lack of any tangible proof that this is true does not seem to be a hindrance.

The idea that language shapes not only our thoughts and feelings—our rational-logical conceptions as well as our most furtive emotions—has become commonplace in recent times. Indeed, it is taken for granted in certain circles that even our most direct sensory perceptions are made available to us only through the filtering and shaping offices of language. Richard Rorty's confident assertion, for example, that "we have no prelinguistic consciousness to which language needs to be adequate" (21) is not so much proffered as a challenging new idea as a summation of the "linguistic turn" of our century, a turn apparent not only in linguistic philosophy but also generally manifest in the social sciences and, of course, in literary theory.[2]

Contrary to Rorty's position, which echoes similar pronouncements made by Max Müller and Wilhelm von Humboldt in the previous century, I would argue that we always and inescapably do have access to prelinguistic spheres of consciousness, that we are in fact never without wordless modes of cognition, and that consequently language is inevitably called upon to provide analogs to non-discursive modes of perception and "silent" moments of awareness. Such linguistic renderings are always partial and makeshift likenesses, inevitably lacking the dynamic, kinetic, and synesthetic qualities that are fundamentally untranslatable in our most far-seeing moments.

Contrary to Rorty's assumption, I would maintain that there is no purely isolatable "linguistic" consciousness that is not formed upon and intersecting everywhere with nonlinguistic modes of knowledge. We not only feel a direct need to make our words adequate to a prelinguistic consciousness, we do not really have any choice. So much of our knowledge derives from or is influenced by pre- or paralinguistic realms that we are inexorably compelled to try to capture some semblance of them in words, as the previous examples from Hildegard, Webb, Lawrence, and Powys testify.

Moreover, it is precisely because of the dynamic relation between our stores of "tacit knowledge," as Michael Polanyi would call it, and our indispensable facility with language that we are compelled to attempt to render discursively the radically non-discursive. The inevitable discovery that the translation of the wordless into words can be only partial suggests that the studied incorporation of manifest absences in literary works, together with our more overt gestures toward inexpressibility, are often attempts to compensate for this inexorable discrepancy. They are alarms sounded to warn of the looming incapacity of language, and thus point the way back to what cannot be put into words. In this way, failure is transmuted into success. A fissure can be a window; absences can become thresholds, so the question is what we can see beyond the window frame and what such doorways open upon.

More specifically, in terms of our focus on absence and uncertainty, the idea that gaps and manipulated emptiness within language signal states beyond language depends, for its validity, on the assumption that cognition and consciousness exist on a far wider plane than the narrower precincts illuminated by language. If language were identical with consciousness, the significance of manipulated absences and the uncertainty they generate would remain problematic. Appeals to the inadequacy of language could be seen as little more than rhetorical flourishes, and the ultimate significance of fabricated lacunae and blank enigmas could not go beyond the level of stylistic nuance.

But if, as I will argue, language achieves only an imperfect and partial fit with the totality of human experience, then the final significance of manipulated absences and moments of verbal bankruptcy, both overtly declared and tacitly implied, may indeed be seen as among the most vitally significant aspects of literary creation.

4

The Prison-House of Language

When the "what" gestured toward can never be spoken, inexpressibility makes an antistructuralist oath, swearing that language is an escapable system, not man's dwelling.

—Ann Chalmers Watts, "Pearl, Inexpressibility, and
Poems of Human Loss"

Harkening back to Nietzsche's characterization of language as a "prison-house" shackling the forms of philosophic inquiry, Ernst Cassirer contends in his exploration of the origins of language and myth that all our conceptual interactions with the world are mediated by language. "All theoretical cognition," Cassirer posits, "takes its departure from a world already pre-formed by language; the scientist, the historian, even the philosopher, lives with his objects only as language presents them to him" (28).

Though such a focus on the epistemological primacy of language may seem a particularly twentieth-century concern, Cassirer is here openly echoing an observation made by Wilhelm von Humboldt a hundred years earlier. In this regard, we might remind ourselves that we sometimes seem to undervalue our more distant predecessors' profound engagement with these same questions. For example, as Marcia Colish has so forcefully demonstrated, medieval thought stressed the role of the verbal sign as the primary vehicle of cognition. The epistemological centrality of rhetoric for Augustine, grammar for Anselm, or logic made manifest through language for Aquinas represent acute appreciations of the formative power of language over thought—approaches that we too easily dismiss as primitive or archaic, thereby falsely assuming the intense focus on language of our own times to be unprecedented.

In any case, Cassirer stops short of suggesting that we have no access to anything outside of language. Instead, he emphasizes the role of a mythic, wordless apprehension that must accompany language, postulating that beneath both language and myth there is a more primary stratum, an unconscious "grammar" of experience and of "radical metaphor" that proceeds without recourse to conceptual categories.

In a similar vein, Mikhail Bakhtin returns again and again to the idea that language shapes us far more than we can ever hope to shape it. According to Bakhtin, we are born into an "ocean of heteroglossia," a socially and politically determined world whose basis is ultimately linguistic. Bakhtin's heady vision is of a realm of living and metamorphosing languages, of a "polyglossia" of competing discourses always interacting dialogically with each other. According to this view, all our thoughts and actions, all our responses and attentions, are shaped by forces of language larger than ourselves into which we are inevitably thrust and out of which we shape our identity.

To a great extent, language is the very stuff we are made on. We move through it as a fish through the sea, shaping its mercurial mass in small ways according to our will, while being carried along by its larger currents—perhaps unaware of the extent to which we are caught up in them—until we finally expire and bequeath the element to the next generation.

But, like Cassirer, Bakhtin specifically denies the absolute primacy of language or its exact identification with consciousness. Acknowledging the "absolute hegemony of myth over language," Bakhtin stresses that language is both limited and secondary: "language too is under the power of images of the sort that dominate mythological thinking, and these fetter the free movement of its intentions and thus make it more difficult for language categories to achieve a wider application and greater flexibility" (369).

While both Cassirer and Bakhtin exercise a prudent caution in at least acknowledging the role of prelinguistic cognition, others have not been so circumspect. Max Müller, for instance, did not mince words on the subject, and the enormously influential writings of this "untiring prophet of linguistic finalism" (Aarsleff 35) set the tone for many later writers of similar opinion. For Müller, talk of wordless thought is nothing more than idle nonsense. The unit of knowledge is the name, and it is through names that we think, so that there can be little doubt, as he so often insists, that "thought lives in language, and in language only." "Language is the true organ of the mind," he flatly declares. "We think with our words as we see with our eyes" (550). Elsewhere, Müller succinctly sums up his position by declaring that "All I maintain is that, not only to a considerable extent, but always and altogether we think by means of names, and that things are no more to us than what we mean by their names" (35).

Kenneth Bruffee's influential essay on "Collaborative Learning and the 'Conversation of Mankind'" takes a similar stand, confidently affirming that thought is nothing more or less than an internalized and unending conversation within our heads: "because thought is internalized conversation, thought and conversation tend to work largely in the same way" (639). As with many such approaches, Bruffee's wholesale exclusion of prelinguistic cognition and wordless knowledge is achieved summarily by defining the field of inquiry so that only discursively driven, linguistically mediated conceptualization is taken into account. Such a preemptory exclusion becomes even more of a distortion because it remains unacknowledged.

Over the past decades, there has been a continuous stream of similar instances of such a mind-set. Derek Bickerton's *Language and Human Behavior,* to cite one recent example, insists that higher thought is impossible without language and syntax. In laying out his "language-based theory of human behavior," Bickerton takes pains to state his position unequivocally:

> [T]he architecture of cognition, or at least that part of it that is peculiar to our species, *lies within language,* and human cognition has the properties it does have precisely because it came out of language, and not vice versa. . . . I mean, quite simply and straightforwardly, that human cognition came out of language—no more and no less than that. (160, Bickerton's emphasis)

During the heyday of deconstruction, equations positing an exact identity between language and cognition became familiar enough to engender much more extravagant variations on this theme. Earlier pronouncements of language as the sole modality of consciousness gave way to declarations, often curiously rhapsodic, of the apocalyptic effacement of the human in a flood-tide of discourse:

> Since it is true that man is a semiotic structure and since language and man are essentially reified refractions of images endlessly succeeding each other in textuality, one must say that "man" is perplexed, puzzled, by the "tyrannical feedback system" of his knowledge, which hints that he and his actions might be only a set of reflecting and replicating signs drawn off into the infinitude of parallax, "the eternal ongoing rush of discourse." (Spanos, Bové, and O'Hara 3)

Jacques Derrida's familiar refrain that *"there is nothing outside the text"* argues forcefully that we not only exist within impermeable envelopes of discourse—that we are life-termers in the prison-house of language—but also that there is nothing beyond the prison bars, at least nothing that we can directly know. Characteristically, he works his way toward regular crescendos, celebrating the shifting and shadowy linguistic underpinnings that define the nature of all things:

> [T]here has never been anything but writing; there have never been anything but supplements, substitutive significations which could only come forth in a chain of differential refer- ences, the "real" supervening, and being added only while tak- ing on meaning from a trace and from an invocation of the supplement, etc. And thus to infinity, for we have read, in the text, that the absolute present, Nature, that which words like "real mother" name, have always already escaped, have never existed; that which opens meaning and language is writing as the disappearance of natural presence. (*Of Grammatology* 159)

In another essay, Derrida focuses on a hypothetical "rupture" that has "always already begun to proclaim itself" yet is in no way an histori- cal event—a rupture that, as a fall in temperature transforms liquids to solids, has somehow transubstantiated *everything* into "discourse": "This was the moment when language invaded the universal problematic, the moment when, in the absence of a center or origin, everything became discourse" (*Writing* 280).

The general poststructural tendency to equate language with con- sciousness was considerably magnified by deconstructionist methodolo- gies that insisted on the notion of omnipresent, inescapable textuality. As M. H. Abrams has observed:

> French theorists, overlooking their own caveats, have evolved from Heidegger's principle the view, not only that we humans don't speak, but that we don't operationally exist—that "the author is dead" and the human reader liquidated in a sea of linguicity; that man himself is no more than a "simple fold in language" that is fated to disappear. (Lipking 169)[1]

Even in the wake of deconstruction, this view of humanity as nothing more than a nexus of textuality, as a purely "semiotic structure," persists despite some enormous and obvious objections.

Simultaneous with the poststructural elevation of language, how- ever, an undercurrent of dissent always persisted. In his 1961 essay "The Retreat from the Word," George Steiner traces a contemporary move- ment away from the word—a flight from language and discourse into other modes of cognition—by offering numerous examples of extra-lin- guistic or prelinguistic modes of awareness in music, the visual arts, Tao- ism, Buddhism, mathematics, physics, and so on. It is something of a

virtuoso performance, but in its wake it is difficult to conceive how anyone could genuinely hope to subsume all these wonderfully various motions of mind under some overarching conception of language.

More recently in *Real Presences*, Steiner revisits this theme in the
context of a subtle and impassioned argument against the excesses of recent literary theory and of deconstruction in particular. Having asked
earlier on, "What has language, however adroitly used, to *say* in regard
to the phenomenology of painting, of sculpture, of musical structure?"
(16), Steiner goes on to answer the question in a lucid summary of his
decades of reflection on this topic:

> Speech can neither articulate the deeper truths of conscious-
> ness, nor can it convey the sensory, autonomous evidence of
> the flower, of the shaft of light, of the birdcall at dawning (it
> was in this incapacity in which Mallarmé located the autistic
> sovereignty of the word). It is not only that language cannot
> reveal these things: it labours to do so, to draw near to them,
> falsify, corrupt that which silence (the coda to the *Tractatus*),
> that which the unspeakable and unspeaking visitations of the
> freedom and mystery of being—Joyce's term is "epiphany,"
> Walter Benjamin's is "aura"—may communicate to us in privi-
> leged moments. Such transcendental intuitions have sources
> deeper than language, and must, if they are to retain their
> truth claims, remain undeclared. (111–12)

Steiner insists upon the validity of those states of being where words
fail us—those misty and flickering regions where, as Eliot put it, "Words
strain, / Crack and sometimes break." More particularly, by emphasizing that our apprehension of the image or the musical note has nothing
necessarily to do with language at all, Steiner is able to isolate precisely
those phenomena that argue most persuasively against any unqualified
declaration of the absolute hegemony of language.[2]

From a very different perspective, Rudolf Arnheim's cogent arguments
in *Visual Thinking* provide equally compelling reasons to doubt any
claims regarding the supposed dominion of language. Arnheim explores
the "prejudicial discrimination between perception and thinking" (2)
still powerfully active today, tracing its roots back to the theologically
sponsored distrust of the senses and the hostility toward graven images.

In a chapter entitled "Words in Their Place," Arnheim discusses the
pervasive "linguistic determinism" that is particularly widespread among
philosophers, academicians, and linguists. Insisting that "Detached, theoretical thinking can function without words" (230), Arnheim maintains
instead that cognition is founded principally upon perception. Moreover, he maintains that the two varieties of "perceptual thinking," intui-

tive and intellectual, function at a level far deeper than the secondary and derivative operations of language, which is seen largely as a subsidiary though highly organized effect of perception.

Though the relationship between perceptual stimulation and cognitive development in infants provides significant support for Arnheim's views, to those more familiar with recent trends in literary theory such a position may seem both surprising and highly questionable. Nevertheless, recent research in the burgeoning fields of cognitive science and neurophysiology overwhelmingly supports the view that language is just one of many cognitive "modules" or "neural networks" by which we make sense of the world. As J. Allan Hobson puts it in *The Chemistry of Conscious States*: "what we are after here is a more accurate and useful view of the concept of mind than the one afforded by the anthropocentric view that mind entails consciousness, and that consciousness, in turn, entails language" (205).

Regardless of whether they are conceptualized as components of the "modular mind" by cognitive scientists or as complex "neural nets" by neurophysiologists, the many pathways of perception and modes of cognition available to humans bestow specialized knowledge in many forms that simply cannot be fully translated into other modes. This state of affairs is the natural and inescapable consequence of the physiological structure of consciousness. Even though the modules or neural nets function simultaneously in a highly organized, parallel, and interconnected fashion, the modules and nets themselves are still separate and, to some extent, discontinuous; in order to do what they do they are not fully interchangeable.

Coming at the question from a different angle, Ray Jackendoff makes essentially the same point in his closing remarks to *Consciousness and the Computational Mind*:

> Much of what has been said here tends to undermine the often presumed centrality of language to the nature of thought. The processes that we generally call "rational thought" are computations over conceptual structures, which exist independently of language and must in fact be present in non-linguistic organisms. Other kinds of thought, such as spatial thinking and musical thinking, involve structures even more distant from language. (323)

Roger Penrose, author of *The Emperor's New Mind*, a deservedly celebrated exploration of the mechanisms of cognition and intelligence, would certainly agree that we do not necessarily think in words. Penrose also suggests that there is no reason to suppose the mechanisms of thought are identical for us all—that it is quite possible for one person to think in images while another thinks primarily in words and so on. He does, however, categorically refute the idea that human language structures must always and everywhere prevail over human cognition. Quite the contrary, he cites many examples from Mozart to Einstein that suggest this is not the case, and he offers his own testimony as support: "Almost all my mathematical thinking is done visually and in terms of non-verbal concepts. . . . Often the reason is that there simply are not the words available to express the concepts that are required." (424)

Penrose cites a letter from Albert Einstein to Jacques Hadamard[3] that is particularly incisive on this point:

> The words or the language, as they are written or spoken, do not seem to play any role in my mechanism of thought. The physical entities which seem to serve as elements of thought are certain signs and more or less clear images which can be "voluntarily" reproduced and combined. . . . The above mentioned elements are, in my case, of visual and some muscular type. Conventional words or other signs have to be sought for laboriously only at a second stage, when the mentioned associative play is sufficiently established and can be reproduced at will. (424; Hadamard 142–43)

Along these same lines, Danny Steinberg points out a number of seemingly obvious but often ignored problems associated with the equation of language, thought, and consciousness. Though his chapter on "Language and Thought" in *Psycholinguistics* perhaps does not engage the full subtlety of the positions he questions, a number of his objections seem irrefutable. Steinberg points out that thought, consciousness, and the comprehension of language in children all *precede* the speech production stage—that is, children are fully conscious and capable of conceptualizing *before* they acquire language, and moreover they can process language before they can generate it.

A book like Susan Schaller's *A Man Without Words* also quickly reminds us that the possibility of reaching maturity in today's world without acquiring any language whatsoever is very real as well as weirdly instructive. Her intense study of a twenty-seven-year-old deaf Mexican man who has never acquired *any* language, not even sign language, but who plainly possesses a very lively consciousness (though a strikingly bizarre one) provides the kind of test case in which the inadequacies of the extreme theories of language are plainly revealed.

Unfortunately, not enough has been done to explore the implications for literary theory of recent research into the nature of mind, the structure of the brain, and the "problem" of consciousness—a potentially vast field of nearly limitless possibility.[4] But the growing body of evidence concerning the fundamental physiology of the brain amply discredits the literary theorists' too-easily accepted equivalence between language and consciousness, and perhaps even more suspect, between language and the unconscious. Julia Kristeva's critique of Jacques Lacan's influential claim that the structure of the unconscious exactly mirrors the structure of language is especially pertinent in this regard. In her intriguing essay, "Within the Microcosm of 'The Talking Cure,'" Kristeva focuses squarely on Lacan's blindness to "what remains irreducible to language" (39), to the "unsymbolizable" and the "unsignifiable" that Kristeva identifies as the basic feature of what she calls "borderline discourse."[5]

In the collective light of all these remarks—and, it might be hoped, the reader's own intuitive grasp of the issue—the unqualified claims for humankind as little more than a "semiotic structure" or a "simple fold in language" inhabiting a realm where "discourse" is seen as the fundamental stuff of creation seem oddly myopic. Are we to suppose, Arnheim might ask, that when we are confronted with a painting, we do not actually "see" it directly but instead translate each shape, image, and color into some sort of linguistic code, into an ongoing "internalized conversation" with ourselves? And what are we to make of Einstein's perception—shared no doubt by many—that verbalization involves casting extra-linguistic forms of consciousness into words at a secondary stage? And how, Steiner might ask, are we to account for the mysterious workings of music, which certainly are not discursively mediated?

For those who see language as coextensive with consciousness, and who also put great stock in the idea that words undermine themselves in their failure to achieve exact identity with their intended or pretended reference, it becomes a pressing question: To what does a musical note refer or even pretend to refer? What does a chord signify and what does a melody describe? The fact that musical notes, melodies, and harmonies usually carry with them not the slightest pretense of reference to anything other than what they themselves are is an instance of a mode of meaning untroubled by any uncertainty as to its own truth-claims, since it manages to *mean* without recourse to this kind of logic.

Though music does possess a complex "grammar," and the relationship among tones, as with words, is surely a matter of difference, the melodies and harmonies and larger scale structures of music carry with them no necessary expository, discursive, or propositional content. Music is thus completely free from the principal defining characteristic of the literary arts. A B-flat chord is not a sign in any useful sense of the word, nor can the themes from Beethoven's Fourth Symphony (or that of Haydn, Brahms, Sibelius, and so on) be considered "semiotic" in the usual sense of the word. Nevertheless, harmony and melody can move us with a wordless power that perhaps must remain fundamentally inexplicable precisely because music has little or nothing to do with discursive knowledge. As James Winn succinctly puts it, "Meaning in music is a profound mystery, not finally susceptible to verbal accounts" (345).

There is consequently no "crisis of meaning" in music comparable to that which can be conjured up with words, yet meanings in music are replete with an inchoate significance that is all the more powerful because of their absolute resistance to reformulation in any other medium.[6] When we are moved by music, what is it that we are moved by? The failure here and elsewhere to deal adequately with such questions underlines the fact that music is a mode of meaning fundamentally *other* than discursive or verbal modes, while being every bit as real and significant.

Indeed, the intrinsic nature of music is so elusive, yet potentially so overwhelming, that it is often said to be more pure and more fundamental than the other arts. If, as Walter Pater claims, all art aspires to the condition of music, one might tentatively describe this condition as a mode of meaning arising from a source deeper than reflective thought that is able to leap beyond the parameters of discursive knowledge, inspiring a felt response without recourse to conceptual categories.

I should perhaps stress that the point here is not that literary theorists are ignorant of nonverbal meaning in music, non-discursive visual knowledge, or inarticulate perceptual awareness. Plainly, we all experience these things to some degree. The point is, rather, that literary theorists overwhelmingly ignore the significance of these ways of knowing, often because of a mistaken assumption that these planes of consciousness do not have a bearing on literature and language. This is a fundamental mistake. All these faculties are brought into play in literature and are always present to vitalize the language we inevitably enlist when trying to communicate some semblance of their "otherness." Language relates to the whole human being, and literature, though made manifest in words, draws on the full pageant of human experience.

Our response to literature is not just a response to words or a cognitive processing of discursive content. No one can read a novel or poem without calling upon the visual, musical, perceptual, and intuitive faculties we cultivate from birth. The music in words calls upon the musical mind as much as does a symphony. The image in the mind's eye called up by a linguistic description assumes a semblance of visual knowledge no less real for being imaginary. Even the very shapes of words are felt against the retina and processed neurochemically as are other forms and designs. Linguistic descriptions of flavor, of touch, or of smell can never be more than pale reflections of the sensations themselves, yet we easily understand what they are aiming at because we live with such sensations daily, and all of these faculties are engaged by the simplest of bedtime stories or nursery rhymes.

A book is a house made of doors. Turning a page, we open the first to enter in, then turn them, one after the other, until we stumble out. While inside, we live lives as full as any we lead in the world.

Faced with so much evidence to the contrary, one might ask how this contemporary overvaluation of language ever came about. A genealogy of the most recent developments would no doubt focus particularly on the deconstructionist critique of "logocentrism" that, while "problematizing" our illusory fixations on words, often paradoxically insists that our consciousness is not only dependent on language but is identical with it. Thus described, existence comes to resemble a medieval torture device, a rack from which there is no escape; words, themselves ultimately meaningless, are all we are.

Regarding the role of absence in literature, it is important to realize that the familiar deconstructive approach to the wonderful and terrible aporia at the heart of a text is a quest within language, through language, perhaps to the very edges of language. It is a quest made possible by the tools of logic and reason—even though the end result may call into question these same tools—conducted in a rigidly analytic and exhaustively discursive spirit.

In this sense, the deconstructive enterprise itself conceals a displaced and unacknowledged desire for a solid center in language. Perhaps because of this sublimated desire, deconstructive methodologies generally never give credence to the possibility of ways of knowing and of being that are radically non-linguistic in nature. From this perspective, logocentrism is less an affliction of Western civilization than it is of deconstructive theory itself.

The poststructural model of humanity posits the human as an agent of language; we gain knowledge through language and realize our very being through language. Similarly, the deconstructive aporia relates to nothing outside of language. It is completely housed in language, and language is seen as the full extent of our universe. The significance of such aporias become self-fulfilling: We are language. Language is aporia. We are aporia.

Since the deconstructive aporia is reached through a rigidly analytic and conceptual procedure, it seems to be something much more than a simple hole in language exposing a logical impasse. But this is essentially what it is. The deconstructive conception of aporia is not a state of being experienced independently of its own algorithmic, discursive interrogation.

In his essay on "Deconstruction and Sanskrit Poetics," William Haney deftly illuminates the ways in which deconstructive approaches remain blind to the larger implications of their own methods. A basic problem, as Haney sees it, is deconstruction's failure to realize "the distinction between theory and practice, conceptualization and direct experience" because of a "limited rather than a comprehensive view of the full range of consciousness and language" (119–20).

In contrast, Haney offers the example of Sanskrit poetics, which, while fully aware of the enormous role played by language and conceptualization within our consciousness, is also mindful of paralinguistic spheres of experience—higher states of consciousness that "are elusive and cannot be achieved, much less sustained, on the basis of conceptual thought alone" (124). Focusing specifically on Shankara's non-dual Vedanta, Haney explains that

> the unity of language in the Vedic tradition does not constitute a conceptual closure but rather an unbounded experience of pure knowledge as a coexistence of opposites beyond the confines of the rational intellect. This experience, a fairly common one, usually occurs in a flash, as in a revelation or a eureka experience through which we know something instantaneously but cannot put it into words, and later find it difficult to remember clearly. This unity of language does not fit under the "logocentric" conception of the transcendental signified. . . . In terms of Sanskrit poetics, then, the true transcendental signified consists of an unbounded conceptualization subsumed by direct experience. This experience, which is highly intuitive, may be associated more with the feelings than with the intellect, insofar as it touches the heart of our Being and remains elusive to the language of logic. (128)

The radical skepticism of deconstruction and its tendency to characterize aporia as dreadful and uncanny arises from the fact that, though it labors to extricate itself, deconstructive theory essentially remains a captive of what A. R. Ammons calls "fuzzy philosophy's abstruse failed reasonings" (*Garbage* 15).

The absolutist stance adopted by many poststructuralist and deconstructionist critics is brought out sharply by contrasting their claims regarding the hegemony of language, discourse, and textuality with the position of Benjamin Lee Whorf, who is often seen as their forerunner. Completely overturning the "common sense" notion that language only expresses "what is essentially already formulated nonlinguistically" (207), Whorf instead demonstrates how the particular grammar and the conceptual categorizations that go hand in hand with any language system become the very mechanisms governing the formation of our thoughts and concepts. According to this new principle of "linguistic relativity," "we dissect nature along the lines laid down by our native languages" (213) so that "segmentation of nature is an aspect of grammar" (240).

Yet it is imperative to realize throughout all of Whorf's heady revelations that he does not assume rational, linguistically mediated thought to be the full contents of consciousness. This is precisely the point upon which Whorf is often so grossly misrepresented. For Whorf, language is not consciousness itself, but a pervasive "coloring" of consciousness. As Whorf explains in his essay on "Language and Logic,"

> The tremendous importance of language cannot, in my opinion, be taken to mean necessarily that nothing is back of it of the nature of what has traditionally been called "mind." My own studies suggest, to me, that language, for all its kingly role, is in some sense a superficial embroidery upon deeper processes of consciousness, which are necessary before any communication, signaling, or symbolism whatsoever can occur, and which also can, at a pinch, effect communication (though not true AGREEMENT) without language's and without symbolism's aid. (239)

Clearly, Whorf maintains only that our native tongues are pervasive influences over our consciousness. They are not synonymous with consciousness. But seeing language as an "embroidery upon deeper processes" does not devalue language since, as Whorf maintains, language provides us with our most direct access to these deeper processes, which Whorf suspects can never be fully understood.

Though some critics continue to cite Whorf in support of the poststructural trend to equate language with consciousness, this easy overgeneralization is quite misleading. It is only when Whorf's extremely subtle treatment of the relations between language, thought, mind, and reality are boiled down and labeled as "language creates the world" or "different languages create different worlds" that this appears to be so. But this sort of simplification, which reflects the need to reduce delicate complexity to facile slogan, completely distorts the true import of Whorf's thesis.

Whorf's conception of the "noumenal world" and of the "higher mind" that is able to glimpse reality on this plane depends on a level of awareness beyond the shaping parameters of language. Indeed, it is only our innate proclivity to rise toward such a level of awareness that allows us to begin to recognize the constricting and limiting nature of the language we habitually rely upon. One might, of course, strenuously disagree with Whorf's perspective on such matters (developed in his last essays c. 1940–1941 but also foreshadowed in the essays of the 30s), but to ignore this central aspect of his thought and instead focus attention only on his equally brilliant demonstration of the formative and structuring power of language is to fundamentally misrepresent his approach and orientation to language.

Unfortunately, Whorf did not live to organize his radically new ideas into a consistent and fully developed presentation. His last essays are therefore more representative of later stages in his thought. His 1941 piece on "Language, Mind, and Reality," for example, is pervaded by a refreshing combination of scientific rigor and an unabashedly visionary perspective that affirms our inborn ability to achieve a plane of consciousness transcending words: "All that I have to say on the subject that may be new is of the PREMONITION IN LANGUAGE of the unknown, vaster world—that world of which the physical is but the surface or skin, and yet which we ARE IN, and BELONG TO" (248).

Whorf's remarkable marriage of relativist and universalist perspectives becomes strikingly evident by simply comparing the following two passages:

> [E]very language is a vast pattern-system, different from others, in which are culturally ordained forms and categories by which the personality not only communicates, but also analyzes nature, notices or neglects types of relationships and phenomena, channels his reasoning, and builds the house of his consciousness. (252)

> [S]cience, poetry, and love are alike in being "flights" above and away from the slave-world of literal reference and humdrum prosaic details, attempts to widen the petty narrowness of the personal self's outlook, liftings toward *Arūpa*, toward that world of infinite harmony, sympathy and order, of unchanging truths and eternal things. (260)

There is no contradiction in these two passages, and anyone who thinks there is has not fully grasped the subtleties of Whorf's insight. For Whorf, the potentially illusory segmentation of the "noumenal pattern world" effected by a particular language does not prevent us from bypassing the shaping parameters of language to gain a higher and truer perception of reality.

Whorf's entire perspective on language, of its "plane" within consciousness and its relation to a potential "higher consciousness" that is itself not linguistically or discursively driven, is made possible precisely because of his ability to gain access "outside the text," to step through the bars of language and regard the prison-house from the outside looking in. Though Whorf's presentation of these views is obviously textual, and though he is fully conscious that the language facilitating such perceptions inevitably colors them, the vision that engenders them, the spark itself (rather like Hildegard's "shimmering flame") is irreducibly paralinguistic, a motion breaking through the rigidities of language.

Compared to the subtleties of Whorf, Steiner, Penrose, and Arnheim, the strain of poststructuralist thought that draws an exact equivalence between language and consciousness seems hopelessly inadequate and often provokes exasperated responses. For example, speaking of Michel Foucault, Paul de Man, and J. Hillis Miller, Tobin Siebers concludes:

> Language has become their ruler, and they enslave themselves to it, making it their prison keeper and giving it powers in theory that mean their destruction in practice. They resemble the community of frogs in the fairy tale who regret having made the stork their master, after it becomes apparent that the bird is interested in dining on them rather than with them. (39)[7]

There is, of course, no question of the tremendous extent to which our languages shape and organize our habits of thought, but to make such a concession is not to admit that there is nothing else beyond language. Quite the contrary, the most subtle lesson of language is precisely the realization of its own limitations, which are recognizable only because we do have access to what lies beyond these borders. To insist upon the validity of inexpressible knowledge is not to deny the nearly miraculous powers of language, without which we could never realize the full spectrum of human potential. But in our reluctance to fully explore the vital relationship between wordless cognition and linguistically ordered understanding we are in danger of overlooking a central aspect of literary art.

Again, what is at stake here is the status of our claims to inexpressibility and the wider significance of such claims. If we believe, as some would have it, that all our transactions with the world as well as our internal processes of thought are inexorably mediated and shaped by language, then claims to inexpressible knowledge will tend to be viewed as little more than hollow rhetoric or shallow attempts at mystification. But once we acknowledge the authenticity of wordless states and nondiscursive knowledge, a vital awareness of what cannot be captured in words will tend to become a barometer of a writer's own depth of vision. The resulting absences and lacunae in literary works, insofar as they derive from or are representative of the failure of words to approach genuine wordless states, can thus become nodes of the profoundest significance—paradoxically allowing entry into the house of words that which can never be captured in words.

An alternative perspective thoroughly opposed to the poststructuralist equation of language and consciousness was proposed long ago by R. P. Blackmur.[8] Declaring unequivocally that the "mind moves by flashes and jumps, only now and then resting on the web of words," Blackmur's entire orientation to language and literature springs from the conviction that "thought does not take place in words—though it is administered and partly communicated in words, and is by fiction often present in them, and creates further what they do to each other. Surely no one ever seriously thought words were autonomous" (*Outsider* 164–65).

Rejecting the claim for the primacy of language, familiar enough to Blackmur in its prestructuralist incarnations through the works of Wilhelm von Humboldt, Max Müller, and Heidegger, Blackmur proposes an alternative view of "language as gesture" that, while acknowledging the unique role of words in shaping our realities, avoids the more obvious problems associated with an unqualified elevation of language.

5
Language as Gesture

How shall I ponder these in the cold stream,
the wordless and unsummoned sense that springs
indifferent beneath all words?

—R. P. Blackmur, "Of Lucifer"

Have you ever seen an inch worm crawl up a leaf or a twig,
and then clinging to the very end, revolve in the air, feeling for
something to reach something? That's like me. I am trying to
find something out there beyond the place on which I have
a footing.

—Albert Pinkham Ryder

Emerson's deceptively simple question, "Could Shakespeare give a
theory of Shakespeare?" (79) poses a fundamental problem with
which literary critics have always grappled: Given a genius equal to the
artist, can the essence of the work of art be translated into other terms
without seriously distorting the object of one's attention? In the case of
music or art criticism, there seems to be a general acknowledgment that
words must always fail to do full justice to what moves us beyond words.
Consequently, in these fields, commentary is often thought of as a gesture pointing toward a certain level of awareness, though not identical
with it.

Since literary works share the same medium as the commentary upon
them, literary critics are constantly in danger of forgetting the difference
between what the creative word strives toward and what the urge to
explicate leaves us with. It is perhaps worthwhile to insist at this juncture that literary criticism, broadly conceived, need not always be ver-

bal. Though works of art in their own right, there can be few better "readings" of *A Midsummer Night's Dream* than Mendelssohn's wonderful score, few better "explications" of *The Rhyme of the Ancient Mariner* than Gustav Doré's woodcuts, not to mention Blake's own illustrations for his prophetic books or Wagner's unique achievement in marrying music, word, and drama. In all of these cases, each medium mutually illuminates the others.

As the unspoken answer to Emerson's question about Shakespeare implies, the distance between what the literary work does and what we can finally say about it remains ultimately unbridgeable. One reason for this discrepancy is that the full spectrum of effects summoned up by literary works cannot be accounted for solely in the language that comprises them. There seems to be something more in words than their extractable meaning or traces of meanings, some nearly physical residue that constantly reminds the reader that the spoken word is always accompanied by a vast repertoire of gestures that convey at least as much as the ostensible "content" of the words. And it is through this element of gesture, inhabiting not only the spoken but also the written word, that we become aware of far more than we can ever discursively declare.

R. P. Blackmur provides the bedrock statement of this view:

> Language is made of words, and gesture is made of motion. There is one half the puzzle. The other half is equally self-evident if only because it is an equally familiar part of the baggage of our thought. It is the same statement put the other way round. Words are made of motion, made of action or response, at whatever remove, and gesture is made of language— made of the language beneath or beyond or alongside the language of words. When the language of words fails we resort to the language of gesture. If we stop there, we stop with the puzzle. If we go on, and say that when the language of words most succeeds it *becomes* gesture in its words, we shall have solved the verbal puzzle with which we began by discovering one approach to the central or dead-end mystery of meaningful expression in the language of the arts. (*Language* 3)

Blackmur dwells at length on a line from *Othello*, "I understand a fury in your words / But not the words," as a way of emphasizing that what is communicated through words is not necessarily dependent on the words employed—that there is a more ethereal dimension of language where words themselves become superfluous and where gesture and "silence" take over. Far from undervaluing the more obvious attributes of words, Blackmur both celebrates and pushes beyond them, insisting that words are capable of more than we commonly allow— "transformed into gesture," words can "leap beyond the load of meaning":

> [w]ords sound with music, make images which are visual, seem solid like sculpture and spacious like architecture, repeat themselves like the movements in dance, call for a kind of mummery in the voice when read, and turn upon themselves like nothing but the written word. Yet it is the fury in the words we understand, and not the words themselves. (*Language* 12)

In a later and more enigmatic essay entitled "The Language of Silence: A Citation," Blackmur probes even farther into "the reality that drips from live words" via the "throaty linkage of the voice of silence" (*Outsider* 162). Words, Blackmur insists, are only "concentrates and analogues" for the thought-experiences behind them, for the underlying "speechless knowledge" that continually implicates the inadequacies of rational/logical modes of mind.[1]

In this sense, language itself becomes a translation that is never wholly adequate to the original intention. Just as an English rendition of Baudelaire always misses much of what is in the French, language is seen as an imperfect analog of the wordless modes of awareness that give rise to it—the "shimmering flame" that Hildegard of Bingen struggled so mightily and desperately to cast into words. "If we regard speech as translation," Blackmur explains,

> it will, when it does not leave us tongue-tied, find us the right urgency and transpiring rhythm; and thus there is something right about James Joyce's reported remark that though there were plenty of words in English they were not the words he wanted. . . . We live in a world of the *mot injuste* out of which the heart may yet create reasonable forms. (*Outsider* 176–77)

For Blackmur, "gesture" refers to the ineffable ingredient in language whereby a nexus of myriad, untraceable filaments actualizes the vast and unreportable range of the full significance of our utterances. Equally in architecture, sculpture, painting, music, and literature, gesture is the sense of dynamic motion paradoxically residing in the motionless: the arching span of a bridge, the upward-leaping spire of a church, the anxious outstretching of our words straining farther than they can reach.

There are meanings infused in our words that are not themselves linguistically ordered and that draw upon those spheres of mind above, beyond, or beneath the discursively driven domain of consciousness. The fact that "emotion," "feeling," or "pathos" can be registered in certain patternings of words—strongly felt qualities or states of being that themselves cannot live independently within words—suggests that words can and do become vehicles for the wordless. In this way, our mouthed outpourings of breath and inked scratches upon a page can become catalysts for modes of knowing that transcend mechanical conceptualization.

Whatever it is accompanying our words that is not the words but something else, whatever it is stowed away secretly in the cavernous holds between our words, it nevertheless reaches out forcefully to touch us, to move us deeply, and consequently it is felt as a gesture to which we immediately respond. "Meaning is what silence does when it gets into words," writes Blackmur with that gnomically provocative exuberance uniquely his own. By "silence" Blackmur here means all wordless knowledge, all extralinguistic cognition and inarticulate wisdom that, though real, cannot ever be directly or completely expressed: "It is silence that tries to speak, and it is the language of silence which we translate into our words" (*Outsider* 161, 177).

Max Picard's conception of silence is very close to Blackmur's and provides a valuable gloss on Blackmur's use of the term. In that mysteriously beautiful book, *The World of Silence*, Picard notes that "Real speech is in fact nothing but the resonance of silence" (27), and this sentence is intelligible only if we realize that for Picard, as with Blackmur, silence is in no sense a negative quality, but rather is a positive awareness of the overbrimming mystery inhering in all things. In his chapter on "Things and Silence," Picard explains that

> [e]very object has a hidden fund of reality that comes from a deeper source than the word that designates the object. Man can meet this hidden fund of reality only with silence. The first time he sees an object, man is silent of his own accord. With his silence, man comes into relationship with the reality of the object which is there before language gives it a name. Silence is his tribute of honor to the object. . . .
>
> Man does not lose anything because he cannot express this hidden fund of reality in words. Through this literally unspeakable fund of reality man is brought into relationship with the original state of things before the advent of language, and that is important. Furthermore, this hidden fund of reality is a sign that things are not created and not combined by man himself. If things were due to man's creation, he would know them absolutely in language. (78–79)

Just as writers struggle as best they can to cast this overplus and undercurrent of wordless feeling within delicate frameworks of phrases, so too can a reader sense what lies beneath this thin crust of words, reading so that the words themselves crumble and drop away, leaving only those dim and shadowy promptings that hammered and lashed the words together in the first place. And so it is that we can understand the fury in words even when the words themselves signify nothing. The same is also true regarding any other emotion or quality springing up from sources deeper than words can reach—love, faith, evil, desire, bliss—qualities and motions of spirit that words stumble over, stuttering impotently when pressed to describe the vibrant nature of such experiences or explain what they "mean." Yet, of course, we all know what they mean, but in a knowing that is not words alone.

Again, we have come to a crossing where a few concrete examples might better bring home these vaporous ruminations and also serve as vehicles for specifically demonstrating gesture at work in language (or language working as gesture). For instance, this lovely and admirably condensed poem by Bill Kemmett functions precisely in the manner described by Blackmur:

Love Poem

Your foot prints don't bloom
    into roses. Yet
   when you come
next to me the sudden rain
ends with its hint of what
    the hand can never
hold. It's in the eye
  of a fawn
    jumping a chasm
far too wide.

Kemmett succeeds in conveying the ineffable qualities of love—the risks and dangers as well as the miraculous and ecstatic sense of well-being. But this is accomplished more by what is *not* said than what is. The sudden ending of an unexpected cloudburst, by which the approach of the lover is figured, conjures up intimations of "what the hand can never hold," a phrase that not only has no assignable meaning but seems to celebrate its own lexical failure. And it is here, in a phrase like "what the hand can never hold," that we can see clearly the element of gesture at work in language. Such a phrase does not designate anything. In fact, it revels in its own blatant inadequacy—as if it is in the very failure of these words that the poet finds confirmed the reality of the love motivating them. Though this phrase constitutes what seems to be a breakdown in the signifying process, it also functions as a gesture, a pointing toward that which is beyond the reach of words. Paradoxically, it is through this carefully contrived default—this gesture that, though made of words, is yet wordless—that the ineffable state sought for is successfully evoked.

Remarkably, this contentless phrase, "what the hand can never hold," becomes the antecedent for a supplementary and reinforcing verbal gesture, "It's in the eye / of a fawn / jumping a chasm / far too wide." By pointing toward, but not describing, what is in the eye of a fawn during a desperate leap, and by implying that this quality cannot be described, a sense of an image whose totality is beyond words is again evoked through a careful strategy of avoidance.

The accumulating effect of these two "contentless" phrase-gestures, linked in tandem, is to point toward that dim region of the heart wherein love resides. While declaring verbal bankruptcy, these phrase-gestures succeed at least partly in summoning up this wordless region in the artful way they point toward something beyond the reach of the poet's words. To name or directly describe these crucial pressure points could only destroy the effect. More importantly, it is also through this sense of a desperate groping after words, accumulating in these gestures, that this wordless quality takes up residence in the poem. It is through the implied incapacity to say exactly what the rain hints at, or what the hand can never hold, or precisely what is in the eye of that leaping fawn that an aura of transcendence is born.

Such strategies of avoidance, it should be emphasized, can succeed only because we do know dimly what the suddenly ceasing rain hints at, we do have a vague sense of what the hand can never hold, and we can summon up and "see" what is in the eye of that leaping fawn, see it better in our own mind's eye than we can ever describe it.

A similar example can be found in *Nightwood*, where suggestion, avoidance, and gesture are especially marked elements of Djuna Barnes's baroque and craggily prophetic prose. For instance, soon after Felix marries Robin, he finds himself becoming fascinated with the enigmas of her personality:

> He said to himself that possibly she had greatness hidden in the non-committal. He felt that her attention, somehow in spite of him, had already been taken by something not yet in history. Always she seemed to be listening to the echo of some foray in the blood that had no known setting, and when he came to know her this was all he could base his intimacy upon. (44)

We see here devices similar to those used in Kemmett's poem, but they are put to very different use. The notion that Robin's attention is some-how focused on "something not yet in history" is in itself a nearly impossible idea, and the phrase again has no extractable meaning. It is a gesture toward a future unknown and unknowable. Surprisingly, this weightless gesturing toward what is to come is reinforced closely by a subsequent image even more vaporous: While Robin's attention is taken by "something not yet in history," she also seems to be "listening to the echo of some foray in the blood that had no known setting." What exactly this "foray of the blood" might be we cannot say; in fact, it is not even the foray itself, but an *echo* of it, that she seems to hear.

With such "empty" phrases as these, what comes across is not the words but the fury in the words. They gesture gropingly toward what cannot be grasped discursively. Moreover, to heighten this subliminal sense of the beyond, Barnes motions simultaneously in two mutually contradictory directions: While on the one hand Robin is oriented toward vibrations of an impossible future ("something not yet in history"), she also listens to reverberations of an inscrutable past ("the echo of some foray in the blood that had no known setting").

"You have dressed the unknowable in garments of the known," the Doctor remonstrates in *Nightwood*, but these examples of language-as-gesture, these strategies of avoidance, do not domesticate the unknown. Rather, they allow it to keep its distance while setting up observation posts on the unfathomable. A phrase-gesture, such as "the echo of some foray in the blood," constructs a secret arras, curtained in lace through which, in the uncertain light, glimmerings of *something* reside. There is no subsequent unveiling. Uncertainty overflows but does not dissipate.

Looking back over the previous pages, we might recall that we've already encountered many other examples of phrase-gestures and gestures toward the unknowable—passages that capture, almost photographically, those teetering moments when language metamorphoses into gesture. Recall Faulkner's evocation of a smell "like rotting cucumbers and of something else which had no name," Joyce's description of Gabriel's vision of Gretta transformed into a "symbol of something," or Webb's near-desperation in trying to capture Deborah Arden's vision of "something that was more wonderful than beauty," not to mention the ritualistic lapsing into wordlessness so central to *St. Mawr*.

No matter where we look, in fact, we will always and everywhere encounter these kinds of necessary and unavoidable deferrals to blankness. Flip through virtually any short story or novel, and you'll find "blank" passages that gesture beyond meaning, passages containing glimmerings of

something far more deeply interfused,
Whose dwelling is the light of setting suns,
And the round ocean and the living air,
And the blue sky, and in the mind of man:
A motion and a spirit, that impels
All thinking things, all objects of all thought,
And rolls through all things.

(110)

Even here in "Tintern Abbey," we note that Wordsworth installs an absence, a phrase-gesture— "something far more deeply interfused"— at the very hub of the poem. While thus signifying a visionary moment, an arrested spot of time beyond words, Wordsworth also focuses our attention on this obviously mute but gesturing phrase. In this way, he is able to foreground the essential nature of artistic endeavor—that inexorable process of groping toward the unattainable, followed by a falling back into pregnant silence.[2]

It is important, however, to distinguish between ossified and routine conventions, as in pulp romances ("words could never express the urgency of my longing," "a beauty that no words could possibly convey"), and those other marvelously original, arduously wrought constructions exemplified by the passage from "Tintern Abbey" or Kemmett's poem. It is worth remembering, too, that the success and poetically original cast of such genuine phrase-gestures derive as much from the surrounding context that grants them a home as from the language-gesture itself. In Joseph Conrad's *Lord Jim*, for instance, when the anxiety-ridden Jim tries to explain what went through him when he finally became aware of having abandoned ship, Jim finds that he cannot come close to an adequate retelling: "I said nothing. There are no words for the sort of things I wanted to say. If I had opened my lips just then I would have simply howled like an animal" (80). Here, the reason that readers have no trouble accepting Jim's claim of having been propelled far beyond the frontier where words fail is not merely this invocation of semantic inadequacy, but rather the novel as a whole, which has initiated the reader into the inscrutable mysteries of Jim's fall from grace.

A somewhat different state of affairs pertains in the following passage from Thomas Hardy's *The Return of the Native* describing a particularly passionate embrace during one of Clym and Eustacia's early trysts: "They remained long without a single utterance, for no language could reach the level of their condition: words were as rusty implements of a bygone barbarous epoch, and only to be occasionally tolerated" (222). Unlike the example from *Lord Jim*, this passage is shot through with a subtle irony and is not without a tinge of mockery. In the context of the novel as a whole, Hardy has so undercut Eustacia's motivation and so exposed the faultiness of Clym's perception of the situation that the reader cannot help thinking this sentiment of a love beyond words to be nothing more than a defective illusion. Whereas the reader's experience in attempting to cope with the complexities of *Lord Jim* closely parallels Jim's own sense that the ultimate significance of his situation resides on the far side of language and logic, this is decidedly not the case in *The Return of the Native*, where at almost every step of the way the reader is made privy to a level of insight far beyond what is allowed Clym, Eustacia or any other character.

Admittedly, most of the foregoing examples of language-as-gesture have been extreme, which make them particularly useful for the present purpose. Such "empty" phrases function as lexical "null sets," bubbles of silence within the general din, spaces hollowed out in the heart of the word. In a larger sense, though, it is also true that we are always lapsing into gesture and using words as pointing tools extended toward that which we cannot completely grasp. This view of language implicitly acknowledges that ultimate meaning resides as much in the failure of words as in their success, and recognizing the element of gesture in all language also acknowledges that words are not equivalent to what they designate.

Just as we are able to gesture through ourselves without needing any external props, language-as-gesture allows that language is both a part of us (the hand that waves, the finger that points) yet also functions as a tool (the hand that grasps). We ourselves are made out of gestures as much as we use them.

The idea of language-as-gesture, as opposed to language-as-consciousness, does, however, firmly reject the notion of the absolute hegemony of language by insisting that language is but one aspect of consciousness among many others. While denying the traditional idea of language as an entity detachable from the self, Blackmur also avoids the Heideggerian notion that we are mere agents of language.

But these are precarious matters and quicksand abounds. Many critics would perhaps feel vaguely uncomfortable with talk about wordless knowledge or visionary awareness, phrases that might seem more appropriate to Zen Buddhism or Taoism—outlooks that both Blackmur and Steiner find particularly congenial.

6
Patrolling the Misty Frontier

> Now that I have spoken at some length of the ineffable, it is
> easier to see why this is neither impossible nor self-contradic-
> tory. To assert that I have knowledge which is ineffable is not
> to deny that I can speak of it, but only that I can speak of it
> adequately, the assertion itself being an appraisal of this in-
> adequacy.
>
> —Michael Polanyi, *Personal Knowledge*

To some degree, many philosophers, linguists, and literary critics of this century have been caught up, explicitly or not, in the inevitable contradictions and conundrums posed by assuming language to be identical with, or at least necessary for, thought. Indeed, recent theorists do not hesitate to declare that we exist only insofar as we partake of language—that we are more an instrument of language rather than its creator. Others exhibit an anxious and telling inconsistency on the subject.

Richard Poirier's *The Renewal of Literature: Emersonian Reflections* represents what, to my mind, may eventually become one of the most important and influential directions in modern literary criticism. Though nowadays Poirier is seen more as a dissenting voice far from the mainstream, his arguments against the excesses of academic literary theory, the hubbub of anxious cultural studies, and the counterfeit crisis mentality of the "wasteland ethos" of modernism and modernist studies provide a bracing corrective to some of the more dubious trends of the profession. His cogent arguments regarding the largely unacknowledged centrality of our Emersonian inheritance, together with his masterful charting of its dispersion through other "Emersonian pragmatists" like William James, Robert Frost, Wallace Stevens, and Gertrude Stein, suggest many fruitful and productive avenues of inquiry.

In *The Renewal of Literature*, as well as in his other work, Poirier displays a remarkable sensitivity toward the volatile pressures and resistances inhering in words, and yet he also exhibits a striking ambivalence on the question of whether consciousness can ever really reach beyond the web of words. While at one moment Poirier approvingly describes Emerson's notion of "transition" as "catching a glimpse of a thing before it is possible to recognize or name it" (47), in a later discussion of Wallace Stevens he flatly declares that "there can be no escape from naming" and that "to see something without having to name it" is "an impossible possibility" (*Renewal* 209–10).

Regarding the inborn power of human revelation, Poirier aptly observes that "Language is essential to the expression of this power, but it cannot ever fully represent it even in all of its accumulations" (136). But how can such a characterization coexist with the contrary spirit that just as often sees cognition and consciousness as a processes inescapably mediated by language? Poirier no sooner suggests that we do have access to states of mind that our words cannot touch than he turns back on himself and accedes to the notion—so forcefully criticized by Penrose, Arnheim, Steiner, and others—that consciousness comes into being only after (or perhaps during) the filtering and shaping ministrations of language. While on the one hand Poirier describes language "not as a transparency but as an obstruction" (30), as a thing that can exist only "in limitation" (163), he also assumes, on the other hand, that the "influx of divinity into the world," in Emerson's phrase, "does not and cannot reach us except as words" (79).

But is it even possible to conceive of a boundary with nothing beyond it? Can we ever achieve a recognition of language as a limitation or obstruction without having at least a flickering awareness of what lies beyond those limits?

Poirier seems unwilling to admit that non-verbal, non-textual, or non-conceptual modes of awareness can exist except perhaps in the most fleeting "transitions," after which, having somewhat rearranged the more familiar building blocks of consciousness, we fall back again into our habitual discursive habits of mind. Yet, having admitted as much, Poirier seems compelled to withdraw even that scanty admission, hinting that nothing can, after all, really be present for us without first passing through the mediating circuits of language.

Poirier is perhaps not unaware of his own uneasy oscillation between validating and denying what may lie beyond words, as when he declares that "language is both the gift of consciousness and its exacting price" (96), and he is plainly of two minds regarding "the urgency with which literature so often proposes that it uses language only so that we may be taken beyond it" (29). In short, Poirier displays some of the same anxieties and misgivings about language that he ascribes admiringly to

Emerson. This is hardly surprising and, in fact, lends his arguments in favor of Emerson's centrality that much more force.

In any case, the issue here is not simply a matter of right and wrong, but a question of emphasis and orientation. Because he is among the most perceptive of critics, and the least taken in by the more excessive aspects of poststructural and deconstructive theory, Poirier provides a far better opportunity to explore this issue than a lesser critic would afford. Poirier's book is surely one of the most tough-minded and important studies of recent decades, and I am not so much finding fault here as using it as a vehicle to throw light on the intractable difficulties these matters inevitably present to the literary critic, for whom words are a way of life.

Poirier precipitates further difficulties when he declares that a category like "genius" is "useful in direct proportion to its vagueness" when "it conjures up something that cannot be specifically traced out" (68), yet a few pages later he confidently asserts that "Language is the only way to get around the obstruction of language" (72). How else can vagueness be useful if not in that it leaves room for what would otherwise be excluded by more precise words? How else can vagueness be productive if not in that it preserves intact intimations of something not circumscribed or delineated by its own gesture toward meaning? If "genius" is not contained in language and is in fact useful for its vagueness, what is there about it that makes us instantly aware that words are inadequate? How can we confidently label it necessarily and usefully vague unless we have some sense of it that eludes the "obstruction" of language?

To celebrate the salutary effects of vagueness—as when Poirier later declares that ideas regarding the annihilation of the self and of the human are ultimately significant because of their "resistance to formulation in language" (183)—and yet still maintain that "to see something without having to name it" is an "impossible possibility" constitutes a fundamental contradiction. At such an impasse, we witness the inexorable entanglements of language; even as we try to step aside and describe what it is we cannot say, the language we use spins endless filaments that threaten to ensnare us in a web of our own making. It is, however, vitally important to recognize a distinction between the apprehension of the ineffable, of levels of awareness beyond words, and the secondary attempts to describe or recreate those experiences through words that are themselves often radically inimical to the spirit of such experiences in the first place.

More recently, in *Poetry and Pragmatism*, Poirier moves even closer to a celebration of the expressive vagueness that is language's unique capacity:

> We ought to be grateful to language . . . for making life messier than ever, more blurred than we pretend it to be, but also therefore more malleable. Within even a single word, language can create that vagueness that puts us at rest inside contradictions, contradictions which, if more precisely drawn, would prove unendurable. We willingly live with the fact that by its beneficent betrayals language constantly delivers us to ourselves, and makes us known to others within a comforting haze. Like the soul, words can reveal parameters of fate and limitation; just as surely, they open spaces beyond these, horizons of new, barely apprehended possibility. (30)

As true and as startlingly perceptive as this observation is, Poirier even here clings to the notion that our access to these "open spaces" beyond language are made available to us only through language. Though admitting that words, through their saving vagueness and "beneficent betrayals," can open up spaces beyond language, Poirier does not anywhere give credence to the idea that similar openings to the beyond are made available to us through many other avenues apart from language. Instead, Poirier continues to insist that language is constitutive of the human: "The invention of consciousness is simultaneous with the invention of language, which, in turn, measures both the restraint upon and the expression of human freedom. For all practical purposes, human beings are constituted by language; they exist in it, and also by means of it" (133).

The fact that "openings" of the sort Poirier describes can be accessed through visual and musical modes, meditation and mathematics, as well as other avenues that scarcely have a name, does not enter into the scope of Poirier's inquiry. But the fact remains that radically paralinguistic "openings" of this sort are perennially approached by writers and poets who struggle to capture some semblance of these states in a medium that is often inimical to them. Though presented by writers within language, it is a mistake to assume that the states themselves are accessible only or principally through language. As William James stressed in *The Varieties of Religious Experience*,

> our normal waking consciousness, rational consciousness as we call it, is but one special type of consciousness, whilst all about it, parted from it by the filmiest of screens, there lie potential forms of consciousness entirely different. . . . No account of the universe in its totality can be final which leaves these other forms of consciousness quite disregarded. (388)

Contrary to Poirier's embattled position, defending as he does both front and rear, I would suggest, along with Blackmur and Steiner, that achieving states of mind beyond the categories of language or the shackles of textuality is not nearly so rare or problematic as Poirier indicates. When, as happens so often in literature, we attempt to zero in on these "transitional" states, these moments of wordless epiphany, we necessarily and falteringly enlist words in the effort. Their inevitable failure to capture precisely such moments, while muddying the picture considerably, does at least gesture toward such states while acknowledging implicitly that the gesture itself is not coequal with what is gestured at.

In any case, Poirier should not be so begrudging in his allowances for such states of mind, since he himself amply demonstrates them in his own writing. Poirier is one of those rare writers whose eloquence grows in direct proportion to the instability and evanescence of the thought motivating it. The force of his style accumulates according to its apparent fragility and to the load his words are forced to bear compared with their perceived tensile strength. It sometimes seems that the slightest wayward pressure of his pen might shatter his entire enterprise.

Regarding human creativity, for instance, Poirier writes that it "depends for its incentives on the preliminary imagination of something that is simultaneously a support and an obstruction, something that will need eventually to be overcome, some representation of an already existing reality that probably cannot be overcome" (*Renewal* 136). Emerging from all these "somethings" that gesture desperately outward comes not so much a sense of anything tangible as the conviction that the writer himself is embroiled in a campaign, foredoomed to failure, to discover words for a heartfelt perception that categorically resists formulation in words.

A similar situation prevails when Poirier ventures to suggest that we all share a universal feeling that "something was lost, abandoned, betrayed in the process of becoming human," and that we consequently retain a mysterious yearning for "an inarticulateness that once was ours." He, in turn, links these observations to an earlier perception that "Literature from some of its earliest and now classic instances seems *always* to have been nostalgic for something that has been lost. What can be the origin of a loss that was always there?" (124–25)

Such passages, pregnant with unutterable significance, call to mind a blazingly lucid passage from Poirier's earlier study, *A World Elsewhere*. Referring to the verbal touchstones employed by Faulkner, James, and Thoreau, Poirier observes that

> [t]he abstractions to which each of these writers feels subservient—"experience," "things that touch the heart," "nature"— are larger than any to which interpretive criticism can appeal. They refer us not to anything with a settled existence but rather to something of which the style itself is the synecdoche. (84)

Here, in Poirier's blinding phrase, "something of which the style itself is the synecdoche," we witness a heroic effort to cast into words something that can find no adequate expression in words. Plainly, Poirier is almost overwhelmingly aware of this "something of which the style itself is the synecdoche," but it is an awareness that resists direct formulation in language.

When Poirier is forced to fall back on these types of phrases, gestures whose meaning is more an aura of potentiality than anything with traceable contours, he demonstrates forcefully the validity of wordless perceptions despite his own subsequent denials. When we encounter a phrase like "something that is simultaneously a support and obstruction," we may ask of what are such phrases a synecdoche but of those wordless states of awareness about which Poirier exhibits such ambivalence?

As with many others whose lives are linked so closely with words, Poirier exhibits an ingrained tendency to search out such visionary moments in language itself, as embodied in literary style and creative troping. Here such fluid states will never be found directly; rather we can expect only makeshift analogs to them. Poirier sometimes seems to confuse visionary states of mind with their secondary embodiment in language—though elsewhere, and particularly in his own style, it would appear that his sensitivity to what lies beyond language is abundant.

The hard facts are that we will never find these "transitions," epiphanies, or visionary moments directly present in language. What we will find are impressions of something now absent, figurative footprints in the snow, a shape pressing forcefully against the page like a signet stamped into wax that leaves only an impression without substance—which is what phrases like "something of which the style itself is the synecdoche" essentially are. You cannot look for fluid and wordless consciousness living within literary style or troping. What we will find is only an artifact, a skin sloughed off from a writhing awareness that has already angled off elsewhere.

What we will find, in short, are phrase-gestures like Kemmett's "It's in the eye / of a fawn / jumping a chasm / far too wide," or Barnes's "the echo of some foray in the blood that had no known setting." What we will find are empty phrases like Joyce's "There was a grace and mystery in her attitude as if she were a symbol of something," Faulkner's smell of "something else which had no name," or Lawrence's evocation of a "world beyond our world" where "another sort of wisdom" reigns.

A rather different critical perspective is implicit in the following passage from Harold Bloom regarding the work of Samuel Beckett:

> The "beyond" is where Beckett's later fictions and plays reside. Call it the silence, or the abyss, or the reality beyond the pleasure principle, or the metaphysical or spiritual reality of

our existence at last exposed, beyond further illusion. Beckett can not and will not name it, but he has worked through to the art of representing it more persuasively than anyone else. (203–4)

There are at least two levels on which Bloom's basic assumptions come into play here. First, Bloom suggests that Beckett's work points toward a "beyond" (placing the word in quotes to indicate its inadequacy to convey the full import of what is meant), and furthermore that Beckett succeeds, largely by indirection, in representing this "beyond" (or this "silence" or "abyss"). Secondly, whatever this "beyond" is, Bloom maintains that neither he nor Beckett can name it, and yet the thrust of Bloom's analysis suggests a confidence on Bloom's part that his reader will intuitively understand what is meant. In other words, on one level Bloom maintains that Beckett's work gestures toward a "beyond" that Beckett cannot name; then, on a more complex level, we note that Bloom's analysis posits an unnameable "beyond" toward which both Beckett's novels and Bloom's own criticism point. Bloom is thereby able to focus his readers' attention not only on Beckett's work, but also more generally on this unnameable "beyond" at which many other "strong" writers and artists, including Bloom, aim.

While Bloom is fully aware that Beckett everywhere engages in the most tortuous and labyrinthine subversions of meaning imaginable, there is no suggestion on his part that the final thrust of Beckett's work is to subvert all meaning, as is all too common with deconstructive criticism of the last twenty years. Rather, the final sense of what Beckett's work does to a reader is not a plunge into undifferentiated chaos or indeterminate free play, but a quite specific and calculated experience of unresolved uncertainty that Beckett has deftly managed to construct out of carefully selected materials shaped toward this end.

Such analysis, however, is admittedly hampered by the fact that Bloom is aiming to transport readers precisely toward that shadow world beyond the edge of language that Beckett so successfully evokes, and consequently the critic is forced to attempt a discussion of things that cannot be named. In fact, Bloom's predicament is not unlike that of an astrophysicist hypothesizing about the "missing matter" of the universe, compelled by the incontrovertible evidence that 90 percent of the matter in the cosmos is invisible and undetectable—some "stuff" radically different from our familiar conceptions of matter. The astrophysicist of necessity falls back on a term like "dark matter," which does not so much delineate a known entity as to gesture toward a region of inquiry that remains highly tentative and problematic. Though they both do not know exactly what it is they are dealing with, both Bloom and the astrophysicist nevertheless know it is there.

What particularly stands out in Bloom's discussion is the confidence on his part that his readers will be able to follow his argument even when he is forced to use words that stand for things they are really not capable of delineating. Though it may come closer than other terms, "beyond" does not itself convey what Bloom means by "beyond"—which is why the word is placed within quotation marks in the first place. So, in the passage cited above, the motivation for the use of "beyond," "silence," and "abyss" is really to suggest that none of those things is actually meant but rather, as Faulkner put it, "something else which has no name." Yet the tenor of Bloom's encounter with such linguistic quicksand projects his trust that we will be able to follow him through this treacherous terrain, since we all will have had experiences we cannot name and be familiar with states of awareness beyond the confines of discursive reasoning.

In Faulkner's *As I Lay Dying*, Addie Bundren relates an experience of this sort when, in her darkly comic way, she determines that words are "just a shape to fill a lack":

> That was when I learned that words are no good; that words dont ever fit even what they are trying to say at. When he was born I knew that motherhood was invented by someone who had to have a word for it because the ones that had the children didn't care whether there was a word for it or not. I knew that fear was invented by someone that had never had the fear; pride, who never had the pride. (163–64)

When Addie ruminates on how a mere word can become her husband, how "Anse" can simultaneously merge with and repulse that name, she seems to penetrate, momentarily at least, beyond the familiar sea walls of language into an underworld where words are protean features of a haunted terrain:

> I would think about his name until after a while I could see the word as a shape, a vessel, and I would watch him liquefy and flow into it like cold molasses flowing out of the darkness into the vessel, until the jar stood full and motionless: a significant shape profoundly without life like an empty door frame; and then I would find I had forgotten the name of the jar. (165)

In this and other passages, Addie demonstrates her sensitivity to the fact that the moods, meanings, and shivers of the spirit we try to communicate are not themselves language and that they are often violently inimical to it—that what is being communicated through language is often not itself linguistically ordered. Like Meister Eckhart's clay pot, whose usefulness resides in its hollowness, Addie recognizes that a word is only a "significant shape" that, like an "empty door frame," facilitates communication only because the freight we send through such an opening is not itself part of the frame.

7
Malcolm Mooney's Land

> Have I not been trying to use the obstacle
> Of language well? It freezes round us all.
>
> —W. S. Graham, "Malcolm Mooney's Land"

As a way of moving toward a conclusion of this section, or at least a stopping place, a poem by W. S. Graham can help anchor some of the foregoing reflections. Few poets have been so concerned with the problematics of language, with the ways language both facilitates understanding while at the same time threatening to cut us off from the deepest wisdom that lies beyond its grasp. Graham continually tries to bring into focus that which is inaccessible to language, and the poet's situation of being aware of what cannot be described becomes a perennial pressure point in his poems. While focusing on the "caught habits of language" as a way of dramatizing how the poem itself can become "Mainly an obstacle to what I mean," Graham never stoops to dry exercises in self-conscious reflexivity, but offers something startlingly original.

"A Note to the Difficult One" addresses itself most obviously to the poet's muse, but it also retains the flavor of a cryptic note to a lover, not that the two need be distinct:

A Note to the Difficult One

This morning I am ready if you are,
To hear you speaking in your new language.
I think I am beginning to have nearly
A way of writing down what it is I think
You say. You enunciate very clearly
Terrible words always just beyond me.

I stand in my vocabulary looking out
Through my window of fine water ready

To translate natural occurrences
Into something beyond any idea
Of pleasure. Wisps of April fly
With light messages to the lonely.

This morning I am ready if you are
To speak. The early quick rains
Of Spring are drenching the window-glass.
Here in my words looking out
I see your face speaking flying
In a cloud wanting to say something.

(*Selected Poems* 90)

The poet here casts himself as an amanuensis, a devoted, if frustrated, stenographer, uncommonly sensitive to faint vibrations whose significance is felt to be profound but dimly understood. Since this "note" is addressed to "the difficult one," the nameless source that is figured as dictating such notes and jottings, the poem has the flavor of an enigmatic, self-addressed epistle—as if the muse were somehow gently coaxing and admonishing itself.

Significantly, the poet envisions a breakthrough, not yet achieved, of coming upon a "way of writing down" those "Terrible words always beyond" him. But in the present "note," the terrible words themselves remain unrevealed, gestured at in such gnomic and necessarily evasive phrases as "what it is I think / You say."

In the second stanza, the poet is seen "standing" within his own vocabulary, his window on the world that frames and shapes what can be seen through it but also excludes other things that lie beyond such a severely circumscribed vantage point. His task as amanuensis is to translate the underlying significance of "natural occurrences" into words—to cast back into words what the poet's vocabulary has already brought into focus—while also recognizing that the ultimate meaning of such occurrences will continue to elude the reach of words, remaining "something beyond any idea / Of pleasure."

In the final stanza, the "window of fine water" by which the poet's shaping vocabulary was figured is revealed to be a physical window as well. Looking out from his room—again with suggestions of enclosure, limitation, and boundedness—the poet does not, in fact, observe anything outside, but focuses instead on the glass itself. Significantly, the window drenched with spring rain distorts the view beyond it, but in such a way that the obfuscation itself becomes of utmost interest.

The last lines of the poem cut two ways in that the face the poet finally sees can be both the "difficult one," the poet's muse trying to stammer out those hidden, terrible words, but can also refer to the reader mouthing syllables, trying to make sense of this oddly enigmatic poem: "Here in my words looking out / I see your face speaking flying / In a cloud wanting to say something."

As in other of Graham's poems, such as "Untidy Dreadful Table" or "The Constructed Space," the poet literally becomes his words on the page, so that he presents himself as physically looking out from within the poem to watch the faces of anonymous readers scanning the page. If the face is taken to be the reader's, then the "cloud" the face is flying in would be the poem itself, and it therefore becomes ambiguous who or what is wanting to say something in the final line—either the face/reader or the cloud/poem. If the face is taken to be the "difficult one," then the cloud becomes a figurative manifestation of whatever it is that keeps the poet from being able to take down those terrible words.

It is, of course, not a matter of choosing between the two possibilities. Rather, both alternatives work together so that what is highlighted is the naked desire to say something—a desire shared by poet, poem, reader, and muse that seemingly can never be sated but only explored.

In this poem, along with the many others by Graham that share its concerns, we witness such a severe straining to say what can't be said that there can hardly be a better dramatization of Walter Benjamin's notion that "Within all linguistic formation a conflict is waged between what is expressed and expressible and what is inexpressible and unexpressed" (*Reflections* 320). In each stanza, there is a sense of the poet rallying his forces, of approaching nearer and nearer to those terrible words, but each time the poet can manage only a provocatively empty phrase. He has glimmerings of "what it is I think / You say," which would be "something beyond any idea / Of pleasure," so that finally we are left with simply "wanting to say something."

In retreating into such stylistic devices, such carefully chiseled phrase-gestures, Graham *shows* us that there are things he cannot get at but at which he is desperately aiming. Though not direct appeals to inexpressibility, such empty phrases are graphic dramatizations of semantic inadequacy. It is a kind of dumb show spectacle, an anxious pantomime, but most of all it succeeds in what it wants to do: it focuses our full attention on a realm beyond words so that we must all—even the most skeptical of readers—at least tentatively cogitate on what such wordless awareness might be.

Ultimately, these devices, which seem to register only an acquiescence in defeat, actually do succeed in propelling the reader toward those fluid states of mind floating free of words. They become omnibuses for both the weary and the worthy that offer to transport us at least part of the way by requiring that we grapple with what could possibly be meant by such phrases and, on a larger scale, by the enigmatic poem as a whole. We are handed not the end of desire, but only its shifting shadows—terrible words that cannot be enunciated and a "something" beyond all ideas of pleasure.

Though such wordless states will continue to elude the weave of language, they remain of central significance to Graham, as the other poems in *The Nightfishing, Malcolm Mooney's Land,* and *Implements in Their Places* amply demonstrate. Though he will never quite be able to fix them on paper with typing hammers, and what he has learned to aim for is a near miss, the palpable reality of such states of mind is, in an odd way, validated by their refusal to be accommodated within language.

Once we credit the idea that perception involves what Arnheim calls "visual concepts," a mode of thinking unmediated by linguistic structures, once we accede to the notion that music can "mean" without recourse to discursive forms, then we must recognize that there are realms of knowledge above and below the linguistic plane to which language will always strive to be adequate, though always failing to achieve an exact identity with its intentional subject.

Seen in this light, appeals to inexpressibility become irreducibly authentic, and the element of gesture within language becomes as fundamental as R. P. Blackmur long ago proposed. The necessary absences and glaring rifts that inevitably appear in works of literature, often elaborately constructed and plainly premeditated, become artifacts testifying to the real and vital existence of what words cannot express, and yet without which literary art would be impoverished.

To suggest that human language, like our senses, exists in limitation is true enough, but it is barely half the cake—a stale cake if it is also assumed that we can never surpass such limits. But to explore the limitations of language while also acknowledging that we are necessarily attuned and responsive to what lies beyond the reach of words is to recognize a fundamental aspect of aesthetic creation, be it a symphony or a suspension bridge, a sculpture or a ballet, a novel or a jazz improvisation.

Part Three

●

A Mechanics of Uncertainty

The arranger should be seen as something between a persona and a function, somewhere between the narrator and the implied author. . . . Perhaps it would be best to see the arranger as a significant, felt absence in the text, an unstated but inescapable source of control.

—David Hayman, *Ulysses: The Mechanics of Meaning*

I liked carving stone sculpture because it was restrained, restricted and had to synthesize form and shape. But, after a time, I began to realize that it was preventing me from including the full three-dimensional world with air around it, so I began to make holes in sculpture to make the back have a connection to the front. A hole can have as much meaning as a solid mass—there is a mystery in a hole in a cliff or hillside, in its depth and shape.

—Henry Moore, *Henry Moore: My Ideas, Inspiration, and Life as an Artist*

8
"For the Snark *Was* a Boojum, You See"

> [T]he element of the unnamed and untouched became, be-
> tween us, greater than any other, and . . . so much avoidance
> couldn't have been made successful without a great deal of
> tacit arrangement.
>
> —Henry James, *The Turn of the Screw*

When Henry Holiday began his series of illustrations for Lewis Carroll's *The Hunting of the Snark* a curious thing happened. As Holiday later related, "One of the first three I had to do was the disappearance of the Baker, and I not unnaturally invented a Boojum. Mr. Dodgson wrote that it was a delightful monster, but that it was inadmissible. All his descriptions of the Boojum were quite unimaginable, and he wanted the creature to remain so" (129).

Carroll's objection to having his marvelous Boojum pictorially represented is perfectly understandable, since the compelling power of this poem derives almost entirely from absence and the special kind of uncertainty that textual absence generates. The controlling image of the poem is of something *not* present in the text. The "Snark" being pursued by the fantastic shipload of questors is never directly described or encountered in the poem, and, when it begins to be defined somewhat by indirection, the Snark is supplanted by an even more mysterious absence: a Boojum, which is a particular *kind* of Snark. Together, the "absent images" of the Snark and the Boojum exert so much force within the text that they become the central focus despite the fact that they represent little more than glaring gaps in the narrative. Needless to say, any picture of this beast would instantly deflate the whole endeavor. No matter how resourceful, readers cannot fill in or forget these dark and mysterious voids, but are forced to carry them like heavy, if comical, burdens throughout their reading and even beyond.[1]

In Carroll's absurdly funny poem, an empty zone in the narrative assumes a form given shape by the existing contours of the story, and it is this fabricated blankness that usurps all our attention—just as with Swiss cheese, it is the absence of cheese, or the characteristic holes, that has become its chief distinguishing feature. But Carroll's poem is also unaccountably disturbing because the very heart of the story remains absent throughout, and this absence, paradoxically, takes up residence in the reader's mind as a hauntingly ineffable presence that becomes all the more powerful for remaining maximally vague.

In the *Snark*, the use of absence as a device could not be more obvious, but what we might call the "Swiss cheese" aspect of narrative—the ever-changing quotient of presence and absence necessary to produce the substance and suspense of narrative—is usually more subtly manipulated than in Carroll's poem. In the first paragraph of Faulkner's *Light in August*, for example, the adroit balancing of what is said with what is not is immediately apparent:

> Sitting beside the road, watching the wagon mount the hill toward her, Lena thinks, 'I have come from Alabama: a fur piece. All the way from Alabama a-walking. A fur piece.' Thinking *although I have not been quite a month on the road I am already in Mississippi further from home than I have ever been before. I am now further from Doane's Mill than I have been since I was twelve years old.* (1, Faulkner's emphasis)

With this opening, Faulkner engages his readers at once. By seeming to presuppose a familiarity with the character and situation that, of course, does not exist, Faulkner throws his readers into immediate uncertainty. Everything we are told immediately illuminates what we are not told: Who is Lena? Where is she going? Why is she on foot? What does she look like? Why has she left Alabama? Why is she sitting on a hill? Who is in the wagon?, and so on.

Though the effect of this beginning may seem to depend wholly on Faulkner's technique, it more likely derives from the implicit difference between itself and the deeply ingrained conventions and expectations that experienced readers bring to any novel. The difference between Faulkner's opening and more traditional novelistic procedures is dramatically revealed by comparing it with the first paragraph of Theodore Dreiser's *Sister Carrie*, published thirty-two years earlier, which also describes a woman setting out on a quest and bears several interesting parallels to Faulkner's opening:

When Caroline Meeber boarded the afternoon train for Chicago her total outfit consisted of a small trunk, which was checked in the baggage car, a cheap imitation alligator skin satchel holding some minor details of the toilet, a small lunch in a paper box and a yellow leather snap purse, containing her ticket, a scrap of paper with her sister's address in Van Buren Street, and four dollars in money. It was August, 1889. She was eighteen years of age, bright, timid and full of the illusions and ignorance of youth. Whatever touch of regret at parting characterized her thoughts it was certainly not for advantages now being given up. A gush of tears at her mother's farewell kiss, a touch in the throat when the cars clacked by the flour mill where her father worked by day, a pathetic sigh as the familiar green environs of the village passed in review, and the threads which bound her so lightly to girlhood and home were irretrievably broken. (3)

Dreiser goes to great lengths to orient the reader in terms of character, time, and place. We are told the heroine's last name and her exact age, and we are treated to lengthy descriptions of her person, mood, and temperament. We are informed of the time ("afternoon," "August, 1889"), and of her destination ("Chicago," "her sister's address in Van Buren Street"). When Caroline passes a local landmark ("the flour mill"), we are immediately informed of its significance ("where her father worked by day").

Faulkner, on the other hand, leaves precisely these same orienting factors blank in his first paragraph. We are not told Lena's last name, and there is no description of her character save what is implied by her own inner thoughts. Lena's age remains problematic—she is older than twelve, but how much older? We are not informed of the actual time, only the relative time that Lena has been traveling (almost a month). Remembering that the title is *Light in August*, however, a reader might tentatively suppose that this opening scene, as with *Sister Carrie*, occurs in August. We are given no hint of Lena's destination, and when she remembers a landmark, which, curiously, is also a mill ("Doanes Mill"), we are given no clue as to its significance.

The tantalizing uncertainty and suspense generated by the opening of *Light in August* derive largely from Faulkner's deliberate strategy of leaving things out that traditionally would be included in a novel's exposition. A gap, however, can be perceived as an absence only if a reader has a previous bias toward having such information supplied. In this case, *Sister Carrie* represents a more traditional narrative, which can be used as a template to neatly expose the gaps in *Light in August* when the two are superimposed. These textual absences, in turn, result in a pervasive, but hard to define, sense of uncertainty that makes Faulkner's saga so compelling.

Between the obvious absences in the *Snark*, which are somehow comic and dreadful at the same time, and the subtly evanescent "avoidances" in Faulkner, we can get a rough idea of the enormous range and potential that absence and uncertainty have when used as strategic devices in literature. Though fully aware of the usual strictures against discussing authorial intention, I would suggest that such effects are received, as the preceding epigraphs suggest, as the work of some arranger who is a felt presence behind and within the words—perhaps a now-absent arranger who, rather like the god of the Deists, has since withdrawn beyond the surface of creation. For it is the encounter with conspicuous omission and motivated reticence that, more than any positive quality of the narrative, indicates most directly the hand of such an arranger. Sometimes, this implied personality behind the words seems to willfully infuse uncertainty and fabricate puddles of darkness with what seems a faintly puckish exuberance for the task of orchestrating stylistic techniques intended to further entangle those already caught within the web of words.

A quite different type of manufactured absence—one that shows the hand of such an arranger who, in an obvious and comical way, literally rearranges what you read almost under your eye—can be found in *Tristram Shandy*, Laurence Sterne's maddeningly wonderful improvisation. Though extended analysis of Sterne's literary antics sometimes places the critic in the uncomfortable position of explaining jokes, two of his more memorable gaps are well worth extended consideration.

The most notorious absence in *Tristram Shandy* is not merely a lacuna in the narrative but is, Sterne insists, a material absence as well. The famous "missing" chapter (chapter 24 of Volume 4), supposedly torn out because it was so much better than the other chapters that it would have destroyed the balance of the whole work, serves to highlight the issue of what inevitably goes missing in stories in general and thereby illuminates the more subtle gaps that occur on every page of the novel.

Naturally, the chapter following the "missing" ten pages of chapter 24 comments at great length on the preceding gap—in fact, chapter 25 is so entirely devoted to the circumstances and subject matter of the missing chapter it is safe to say that if chapter 24 were present, chapter 25 would not and could not exist. In other words, even if chapter 24 were somehow "restored" to its rightful position, there would still be as glaring a gap as when it was missing.

Textual gaps, as Sterne so comically demonstrates here, can never be done away with. To fill one gap inevitably leads to the creation of another somewhere else. Narrative gaps are a vital part of the literary game—just as empty squares are indispensable in chess: whenever a piece is moved to fill an empty square, it simultaneously empties a full one. With chess, as in literature, you can't fill all the spaces because there would then be no game to play, no story to tell.

Having said this, it should also be pointed out that, in another sense, chapter 24 isn't missing at all. In chapter 25 the reader is told

> the chapter I was obliged to tear out, was the description of this cavalcade, in which Corporal Trim and Obediah, upon two coach horses a-breast, led the way as slow as a patrole— whilst my uncle Toby, in his laced regimentals and tie-wig, kept his rank with my father, in deep roads and dissertations alternately upon the advantage of learning and arms, as each could get the start. (312)

Here we have the "missing" chapter 24, reduced from its supposed ten pages to a single paragraph, but arguably as present as any of the other chapters. The reader is given only the barest scaffolding for what happens in the missing chapter and must flesh out this framework imaginatively, but—and this seems a primary point of all this looniness—a bare scaffolding is all the reader ever gets, and the reader always does flesh out this bareness while reading.

Elsewhere, Sterne leaves an entire page blank, explaining that he cannot possibly describe the erotic allure of the widow Wadman. Instead, he instructs his readers to paint their own conception of her according to their fancy. But this blank page is really less blank than it appears. Elsewhere in the novel, there are abundant instructions that sharply delineate the range of possible portraits of the widow. As Tristram remarks, "never did thy eyes behold, or thy concupiscence covet anything in the world, more concupiscible than widow Wadman." (450) The widow, we are told, appeals to our most basic sensual urges, and she in turn feels these same impulses. She is the stuff of an erotic dream. From this and many other remarks concerning her sprinkled throughout the novel it is obvious that, despite the blank page, the widow is as fully described as any of the other characters. The flip side of this, of course, is that we have been given a figurative "blank" page for each and every one of the characters to fill in as we see fit, guided by the limiting parameters of Sterne's descriptions.

Throughout this novel, Sterne's manipulation of absence is a prime example of what we now commonly refer to as "reflexive" or "metafictional" techniques. Invariably, the abundant gaps and lacunae in the narrative serve simultaneously as structural devices integral to the plot and also as a way to comment on the nature of the device itself—a technique more commonly associated with postmodern works, but also a favorite of Cervantes.

Readers of *Tristram Shandy* are always half-writing what they read. This is probably true of all literature, but it is a source of endless delight in reading Sterne because of his indefatigable efforts to baldly expose his narrative techniques in order to confront the reader with them in as provocative a way as possible. When, for instance, Tristram confesses that he wrote the "chapter upon sash-windows" in order to complete his father's *Tristra-paedia*—the book outlining how Tristram himself is to be brought up—he is holding up a mirror in which his readers are invited to see themselves engaged in a partnership to compose that which they are destined to receive.

All these delicious uncertainties result from the reader running hard up against conspicuous absences. Such sudden nothings can range from Faulkner's dimly pulsing aura of nescience casting subtle pockets of shadow across the page, and Carroll's Snarks and Boojums that raise a banner, so to speak, and shout about their nothingness, to Sterne's dislocated three-ring circus of a novel. However, the still-prevailing school of thought these days—a holdover from the era of deconstruction—tends almost systematically to disregard or minimize the significance of these varieties of provocative absence, preferring to focus instead upon what many theorists would characterize as a pervasive and fundamental indeterminacy that supposedly is the basis of all language, words, and meanings, as well as all interpretations. As I shall try to show, there are some excellent reasons for viewing such an approach with skepticism.

9
Uncertainty vs. Indeterminacy

"All philosophy," I told her, "is based on two things only: curiosity and poor eyesight. . . . The trouble is, we want to know more than we can see. Again, if we could really see things as they are, we would really know something, but we see things other than as they are. So true philosophers spend a lifetime not believing what they do see, and theorizing on what they don't see, and it's not, to my way of thinking, a very enviable situation."

—Bernard le Bovier de Fontenelle, *Conversations on the Plurality of Worlds*

In "Concerning the Unpredictable," an essay on Loren Eisely, W. H. Auden touches on a matter that, while some might brush it aside as semantic hairsplitting, is really of the utmost consequence. Auden sharply contrasts the diverging senses of "random" and "unpredictable," castigating those who casually label things "random" without sufficient justification. The problem, as Auden explains it, is that while "unpredictable" is a valid description of so much of what we observe or experience, "random" pushes forward another unjustified step and tacitly concludes that the operative principle behind such phenomena is chance and chance alone. Concluding that something is "unpredictable"—which preserves the possibility of some hidden, perhaps undiscoverable, governing principle—is usually as far as we can justifiably go. Furthermore, while "unpredictable" implies that the uncertainty is due to the limitations of the perceiver, "random" implies some definite knowledge that no higher or hidden order exists.

A similar observation might be made of the related use of "indeterminacy," as opposed to the more even-handed "uncertainty," in contemporary literary theory. The current sense of "indeterminacy," a lasting legacy of deconstruction, is unavoidably troubled by a faint hint of duplicity (no doubt unintentional). Briefly put, the dilemma is this: To suggest that a certain word or string of sentences or series of signs is "indeterminate" is to declare unequivocally that no intrinsic meaning or single valid interpretation is possible—and yet such a declaration is plainly determinate, in fact tyrannically so. To insist upon the impossibility of meaning is just as myopic and closed-minded as to insist upon a single, univocal meaning.

"There can be no certainty!" someone proclaims, slamming a fist down on a table, and, lo, a quasi-certainty has whelped its way into existence unrecognized by the one who engendered it. "Uncertainty," on the other hand, does not convey the sense of finality and conclusive designation that infects "indeterminacy" with unforeseen irony. Just as "unpredictable" avoids the unjustified, discussion-ending nature of designating things "random," "uncertainty" remains open to future adjustment and reconsideration in a way that "indeterminacy" does not.

In this sense, the current conception of "indeterminacy" subtly siphons off a portion of the dynamic multivalence it purports to celebrate by tacitly removing from the picture the ever-present, though perhaps unrealizable, possibility of achieving a more complete understanding. For it is precisely this unsatisfied and seemingly unquenchable desire for some ultimate understanding that constantly sifts through the shards and fragments of our sense-making proclivities, providing the sharpest edge to any resulting sense of unresolvable, competing meanings: The fact that we never seem to find our grails does not prove that they do not exist.

A similar sense of this issue informs Phillip Herring's *Joyce's Uncertainty Principle*, where Herring carefully avoids "indeterminacy" in favor of "uncertainty." Unlike the deconstructionist notion of indeterminacy, which is characterized as a necessary attribute of all language, Joyce's use of uncertainty results from "a devious authorial strategy the Irish have always associated with Joyce" (xi)—a masterful control over language to produce certain effects, most especially when the sought-for effect is precisely one of unresolved uncertainty.

To be sure, some critics occasionally use "indeterminacy" in a looser sense, with connotations roughly equivalent to those implied by the above characterization of "uncertainty." But in much contemporary literary theory this is decidedly not the case. Overwhelmingly, "indeterminacy" has been invoked and reified as an unquestioned condition of discourse, "textuality," and language.

This current sense of "indeterminacy" derives largely from Jacques Derrida's now-familiar postulate that in the absence of a "transcendental signified" the "play of signification" is extended infinitely. Though it is, no doubt, Derrida's less original imitators who have so woodenly taken up this theme and applied it as if it were a formula, these secondary applications have probably been more influential in defining the deconstructive enterprise as it is now popularly conceived. In a survey of recent developments in literary theory, for instance, we are told that

> it is Derridean free play which has given us the notion of textual indeterminacy and that free play stands in opposition to representation, to language representing a world and the world representing itself in language. . . . In other words, the openness and disruption which leads to indeterminacy is a feature not only of the text but of the theory body as a whole, of discourse in its heterogeneous guise. (Natoli 119)

The *a priori* assumption that not only language but interpretation and theory must always be shot through with indeterminacy became a cardinal rule for many, an inaugural proposition that dictated from the outset a particular set of assumptions governing the approach to and characterization of language and meaning. The fact that rules are more usually thought of as sense-making does not make the tenet of linguistic indeterminacy any less of a rule, especially since the insistence upon indeterminacy is not compromised by any uncertainty as to its own validity.

Some of the most eloquent explorations of indeterminacy warn against this tendency, as when Geoffrey Hartman declares that "Indeterminacy as a 'speculative instrument' should influence the way literature is read, but by modifying the reader's awareness rather than imposing a method. To methodize indeterminacy would be to forget the reason for the concept" (269). A similar prudent hesitancy informs the work of a few notable others on the same subject, such as Barbara Johnson and J. Hillis Miller; yet clearly in other quarters indeterminacy has become a method, both as a starting point and as a procedure.

The following passage from an essay on "Free Play in Samuel Richardson's *Pamela*," for example, demonstrates the often absurdly reductive notion of linguistic indeterminacy as it has filtered down to critics eager to emulate new literary fashions:

> [W]riting does not merely signify the referent or "reality" but also precedes "reality". . . . This is the epitome of the Derridean endless proliferation of the signifier and the signified that itself is a signifier, a dissemination where writing (the signifier) produces "reality" (the signified) which requires more writing to represent, another signifier which in turn produces another domain of "reality" (the signified). There is no natural bond between the logocentric primary signified and the secondary signifier. The free play of signs for significa-

tion and the secondariness of both signifier and signified are
obvious here. (Zhang 314–15)

The patently false presumptions hidden in such jargon-ridden opacities
have become so common that one imagines Derrida himself grimacing
at such easy and shallow-minded effusions. If one assumes at the outset
that all discourse is really only "a free play of differences for signification" (Zhang 318), then any and all texts examined will seem to bear
this out.

While the now-routine championing of indeterminacy purports to
be maximally open and fluid, the fact is that such an attitude quickly
ossifies into stale convention once it is assumed that indeterminacy must
"always already" be present. Mystery is a thing to be discovered, to
astonish and bewilder; a familiar armchair holds little mystery even if it
is uncomfortable. But to suggest that this general "problematizing" of
language is both inaccurate as well as reductive is not to assume that
single, untroubled, and determinate meanings must necessarily exist.
Contrary to the rhetorical strategies of some theorists, these are not the
only two options, and to disprove one does not validate the other.

If by calling language, interpretation, and meaning "indeterminate"
we simply intend to emphasize the fleeting and inchoate nature of all
understanding, and affirm the age-old wisdom that Truth knows no voice
but the wind's, then there can be no quarrel. Such a frame of mind is, of
course, nothing new. But if we claim to have uncovered the absolute
nexus of indeterminacy and to have become familiar with its darkest
secrets, then there is ample justification for skepticism.

Such claims have been commonplace over the last twenty years or
so, primarily under the guise of an alleged final decipherment of the
problem of language and referentiality. They still linger on in the veiled
assumptions of critics brought up on deconstructive methodologies.
Typically, the work of Ferdinand de Saussure is invoked for purportedly
sundering our last illusions regarding the bonds between word and world,
showing instead that words and signs are invested with meaning only
through their relations with other words and signs. These in turn play
off still others in an infinite regress that can have no final stopping point.

But such a perspective on the problem of language derives from a
misunderstanding of Saussure so fundamental that any supposed "free
play" of signs bearing his imprimatur must be regarded as fatally flawed.
The crux of the matter is that, while Saussure does explore the arbitrary
relationship between signifier and signified, this does not imply that language is entirely self-enclosed and self-referential, or that there is no
connection whatsoever between language and the physical world—all
of which have become, curiously, the commonly accepted consequences
of Saussure's conception of the sign.

On the contrary, Saussure's conception of the arbitrary nature of the *sign*, which is not to be confused with the arbitrary relationship between signifier and signified, hinges on the perception that our conceptual division of experience and the physical world does not depend on distinctions intrinsic in the world, but rather on distinctions at least partly imposed upon that world through language. For example, despite our inevitable preconceptions in such matters, the distinction between trees and shrubs is not an inherent feature of reality, but an imposed, useful, distinction created by the English language. While not in any way being a necessary distinction intrinsic to reality, the concepts and sound-images for "tree" and "shrub" are not thereby rendered "indeterminate," but are, quite the contrary, relatively determinate and circumscribed within the larger system of the language.

Saussure's crucial observation about the necessary and arbitrary segmentation of reality that language imposes may not seem in need of lengthy demonstration or justification, especially in the wake of further developments along this line by others like Benjamin Lee Whorf and George Lakoff. But it is precisely on this point that the notion of linguistic indeterminacy in current literary theory goes awry. In his 1983 study, *A New Mimesis*, A. D. Nuttall took note of this erroneous reading of Saussure, and more recently John Ellis has explored the effects of the resulting widespread misconception. As Ellis points out in *Against Deconstruction*, the root of this "wholesale garbling of Saussurean terminology" (68) seems to arise from a disabling confusion of Saussure's three-term conception of the sign for the cruder, dualistic view that divides language into words and the things to which words refer. In Saussure's system, using the example of an apple, the 1) *signifier* (or "sound-image") of "apple" is inexorably bound to its 2) *signified* (the concept of "apple" or "applehood"), and these twin aspects together make up the *sign*, which in turn relates to a particular 3) *referent*—in this case, the "roundish thing out there hanging from the branch." The endemic misconception of the Saussurean sign is that the "thing hanging from the branch" is itself the signified, which completely misses his most important contribution. The signified is the *concept* of apple, not the thing itself.

What Saussure puts forward as a new perception regarding the nature of language is not that words are different from things and not that signifiers bear an arbitrary relation to signifieds, but rather that the system of signs—that is, of signifiers bound to specific signifieds—necessarily divides reality into certain circumscribed conceptual categories, even though the full range of possible systems for such division is potentially infinite.

George Lakoff's discussion of Dyirbal, an Australian aboriginal language, provides a valuable "strange" perspective on the inner workings of linguistic categorization. Dyirbal, for example, makes use of a word, *balan*, which is a kind of adjective or "classifier" preceding a noun. Its meaning includes "women, fire, and dangerous things," as well as dogs, the stars, scorpions, and fireflies. Lakoff's lucid consideration of the full significance of language categories and cognitive models cannot be quickly summarized, but it suffices to note for our purposes that even such a seemingly bizarre range of meanings does not render *balan* "indeterminate," nor does it initiate a "free play of signification." On the contrary, the range of meaning *balan* provides is quite definite. The conceptual division of reality mapped by Dyirbal is worlds apart from more familiar languages, but such huge differences do not imply that particular languages in general are therefore "indeterminate."

As Nuttall puts it, after having discussed how, for example, the Greek language constructs a model of reality quite different from that allowed by the distinctions inherent in English or French, "The AA road map of England employs not only different colours but also different conceptions from those used in the *Times Atlas* physical map of England. But no sane person concludes from that that England does not exist" (32).

For Saussure, the signifier or "sound-image" represented by "apple" is inexorably linked to a signified or concept of "apple" or "applehood," and together this sign, the inviolable union of signifier and signified, delimits a particular referent— "that certain edible thing hanging from the branch." That this distinction is true of the model of reality constructed by English does not suggest that such a distinction is inherent in reality (or, as Whorf calls it, the "noumenal pattern world"), nor does it imply that a similar distinction will be evident in all languages. Precisely the reverse is true. It is not difficult, for instance, to imagine a language that would not distinguish between apples and pears or even between apples and walnuts, but would instead have a single word for, say, "all edible things hanging from trees." But rather than rendering "apple" indeterminate, "apple" is almost rigidly determinate within the system of signs out of which it arises.

Though the larger "noumenal pattern world" supports and sanctions any number of sign systems whereby concepts compartmentalize fluid flux into fact, the resultant signs themselves are anything but indeterminate. This is exactly the point where many unwary literary theorists seem to go awry. For Saussure, it is the relationship of a particular sign system *as a whole* to the larger reality it seeks to categorize that is arbitrary—not the individual signs themselves, which, within particular sign systems, are relatively, even rigidly determinate. As Saussure puts it

> The linguistic sign unites not a thing and a name, but a concept and a sound-image. . . . The two elements are intimately united, and each recalls the other. Whether we try to find the mean-

ing of the Latin word *arbor* or the word that Latin uses to designate the concept "tree," it is clear that only the associations sanctioned by that language appear to us to conform to reality, and we disregard whatever others might be imagined. (66–67)

As Ellis has shown, Saussure explores two different ways in which signs are arbitrary, but with two very different senses of "arbitrary." The first connotes randomness and the second connotes agreement based solely on convention. The first aspect is the very old recognition that the connections between particular signifiers and signifieds are essentially arbitrary or random (as Nuttall succinctly puts it, "A rose might have been called a blug"). The second aspect implies that the conceptual division of reality carried out by a certain system of signs is arbitrary; that is, it is based solely on agreed upon conventions that have evolved through the ages. As Ellis puts it,

Arbitrariness in this sense, then, refers not to randomness but to the reverse, to the fact that there is a definite agreement on the particular system of terms to be used and on how they are to be used. It does not mean that the meaning of a given word is arbitrary, for unless that word has a place in a system of terms, there is no system, no agreement, no meaning, and thus no language and no communication. (50)

One could, of course, argue with Saussure's characterization of the sign, as Roman Jakobson does in his essay on "The Quest for the Essence of Language," but the point here is simply that the familiar deconstructionist tenet of indeterminacy, insofar as it invokes Saussure's conception of the sign, makes no sense at all.

That a great many respected literary theorists and critics have completely misunderstood the true import of Saussurean categories is admirably demonstrated by Ellis in his chapter on "Deconstruction and Language." As Ellis makes clear, many of the most celebrated spokesmen for cutting-edge trends in theory have, in various ways and in various contexts, demonstrated fundamental misunderstandings regarding the nature and consequences of Saussure's notion of the sign. Commonly, literary critics erroneously collapse Saussure's three-term construct into the more "intuitive" and primitive two-term opposition between words and things, mistaking "signified" for the "thing" to which a word refers.

For Saussure, the linguistic sign is an inviolable union of signifier and signified, of sound-image and concept. A "signifier" cannot exist alone as a separate element divorced from any conceptual content, since it necessarily exists only by merit of a concomitant signified. As Saussure insists: "The linguistic entity exists only through the associating of a signifier and signified. When one element is retained, the entity vanishes" (102–3).

In mistaking Saussure's characterization of signifier and signified for the difference between words and things, and further mistaking his notion of arbitrariness as solely a description of the relation between words and things, many critics and theorists are completely off-track in their rationale for identifying such ideas as the basis for a fundamental indeterminacy or "undecidability" of meaning in language.

No one has ever yet demonstrated how a radical indeterminacy of signs might work. It has only been talked about, and this at great length. Such discussions inevitably focus on a limited number of particularly multivalent words, demonstrating that their range of meaning subsumes several competing or contradictory meanings. This is not free play; nor is it indeterminacy. Indeed, the identification of *specific* competing meanings, even when they are contradictory, is an argument for determinacy. The idea that all words and language in general could be shown to mean everything and anything, and therefore nothing, is plainly an impossible and self-contradictory idea—an idea "always already" disproved by the simple fact of language and its continued employment.

Even Blackmur's notion of language as gesture, which insists on the limitation of language and the authenticity of paralinguistic knowledge, does not imply that words themselves are unanchored or free-floating. The recognition of ways of knowing beyond words does not suggest that language is indeterminate but simply that it is often inadequate.

In a discussion of Saussure's conception of language, using the example of the temperature of water and "warmth" in particular, Ellis cogently summarizes the issue:

> [T]he word *warm* gives us information about our language only given our recognizing temperature variations. And the word *warm* gives us information about the world only given our ability to understand and use English. *It is just as wrong to say that warmth is simply a fact of nature as it is to say that warmth is simply a fact about language*; and the greatest error of all would be to assume that the falsity of the first of these alternatives required us to turn to the second. (49, Ellis's emphasis)

The epistemological implications of Saussure's theories are indeed profound.[1] By showing that language systems, conceived as a whole, segment reality according to arbitrary schematics upheld by convention, Saussure indicates how language gives rise to value systems that are formed to a great extent according to the conceptual structure of that particular language. As Saussure puts it,

> A linguistic system is a series of differences of sound combined with a series of differences of ideas; but the pairing of a certain number of acoustical signs with as many cuts made from the mass of thought engenders a system of values; and this system serves as the effective link between the phonic and psychological elements within each sign. Although both the signified and signifier are purely differential and negative when considered separately, their combination is a positive fact. (120)

By shedding light on the ineluctable tendency of language to partition reality in ways that do not bear any essential relation to pre-existing features of reality, Saussure provides the groundwork for a more probing examination of the limits of language. And in this respect, some of the larger questions engaged by deconstructionists do remain both valid and pressing. The train of thought, however, that leads to the familiar poststructural notion of a radical indeterminacy infecting all language makes no sense at all and in no way derives from these larger epistemological concerns.

Indeed, the widespread notion of linguistic indeterminacy seems to derive, at least partly, from a rapidly disseminating misreading of Saussure that oftentimes has had the effect of catapulting the level of linguistic sophistication back to a pre-Saussurean framework. For it is precisely Saussure's point that within a particular system of signs, individual signs are bound rigidly to their motivating concepts, though such concepts need not be univocal. Works of literature, which exist through the medium of a particular language, are born of the very capacity of words to mean, to signify, to convey concepts within that linguistic framework. To speak of words or signs without concomitant conceptual content is to speak of something that is not and cannot be language. That words also function as gesture, conveying intimations beyond any definite discursive content, does not annul their signifying role. That there is an ever-present residuum of "silence" in words does not prevent them from conveying less problematic messages.

There are therefore two pressing reasons for opting to speak of "uncertainty" rather than "indeterminacy" when discussing instabilities made manifest in language. There is, first of all, the inevitable sense of final and unimpeachable judgment that "indeterminacy" has come to imply. Secondly, insofar as the current notion of indeterminacy derives from a flawed understanding of the Saussurean linguistics that is its purported foundation, the specific theoretical model for an inherent intra-linguistic indeterminacy is grievously flawed.

Obviously, to reject the notion of a fundamental indeterminacy infecting all language is not to imply that words and meanings are pure, univocal, and transparent. Quite the contrary, as many of my own examples in previous chapters show, an inherent and valuable property of languages is exactly this capacity to manufacture uncertainty by forcing certain nodal areas into shadow and suggestive obscurity. Such uncertainty, however, arises not from the failure of words to mean, but precisely from their success. Carroll's Snarks and Boojums, for example, are created not by merit of some inherent indeterminacy of the words used in association with them, but rather by the intrinsic property of words to suggest a certain limited range of meanings well enough so that constructing paradoxical forms and "characters"—even conspicuously "empty" ones—is made possible.

To return to our example from *Nightwood*, when Robin is described as "listening to the echo of some foray in the blood that had no known setting," our puzzlement derives not from any confusion over what the words mean, but rather because we know only too well what they mean. The words themselves are simple and untroubled, the imagery evocative and direct. Yet working together, brick upon brick, these words frame an uncertainty that does not derive from any intrinsic fracture in the individual words or their mortar. The word-structure is solid enough here, but the structure houses a paradox. Similarly, when W. S. Graham writes of translating "natural occurrences / Into something beyond any idea / Of pleasure," the calculated movement from relative clarity to relative darkness is palpably felt—the word "something" functioning rather as a cave-mouth through which the sentence descends into darkness and uncertainty.

In these brief examples, there are nodes of uncertainty that stand out sharply only because the surrounding terrain that provides their context is relatively more stable. The simple fact that uncertainty is felt more strongly in some passages rather than others, in certain phrases and words as opposed to all phrases and words, is evidence enough that characterizing linguistic indeterminacy as a kind of background radiation infused equally through all discourse is to completely miss the more significant ways that words can be purposely manipulated to produce uncertainty. Such uncertainties do not simply arise unbidden from the use of any and all language, which is the unavoidable implication of the deconstructionist sense of indeterminacy. Rather they are arduously wrought by skilled artists who depend on words to convey a certain limited range of meanings.

Within artistic works in general, the mechanics of uncertainty is not so much a question of chance as an issue of design and conscious technique. In the literary arts, the manufacturing of uncertainty inevitably depends on the reader's perception of some *absence* that, insofar as it is constructed out of a careful patterning within a finite verbal structure, can be described as a "structured absence."

10
Absence and "Structured Absence"

I shall . . . proceed to shew, First, what Nothing is; Secondly, I shall disclose the various kinds of Nothing; and lastly, shall prove its great Diversity, and that it is the End of everything.

—Henry Fielding, "An Essay on Nothing"

While absence may indeed make the heart grow fonder, it also makes the mind grow more focused and attentive. Whenever the mind is confronted with a perceived absence, it becomes more highly sensitized, more aware, observant, and expectant. The perception that something that could or should be present is not there becomes vaguely threatening, requiring some sort of resolution or closure. In context, silence, not sound, can make one's hearing more acute. Similarly, whenever we are plunged into uncertainty, we become more speculative, more given to hypothetical and creative reasoning, as we attempt to compensate for the disquieting multivalence that makes rational analysis infinitely more complex and difficult.

Paradoxically, absence can be perceived only if the expectation of something is not satisfied, and this expectation always arises because of something present. E. D. Hirsch, in his sometimes quixotic attempt to rescue literary texts from what he sees as a morass of conflicting interpretations, makes precisely this point: "The unknown must somehow (even if gropingly and wrongly) be assimilated to the known, otherwise there would be no rational access at all to the unknown—not even of a tentative nature" (175).

It is out of this relationship of the known and the unknown, this seesaw balancing presence and absence, that uncertainty is generated, and the expectation of resolution that accompanies uncertainty can be prolonged or suspended for five seconds, ten pages, or indefinitely, depending on how this relationship is manipulated. Any discussion of uncertainty in texts must therefore address the question of how it is manufactured, of the secret mechanics that can generate uncertainty as a force seemingly impelled by some hidden internal combustion. Before turning to individual works, though, a slight detour can provide a valuable analogy.

Anyone who has ever been out driving at night and approached a busy intersection without any visible traffic signal will understand how absence can make one instantly more cautious, expectant, and observant. In fact, the lack of a signal may even trigger more caution than the flashing yellow light designed to provoke this reaction. And how often are we prompted to apply the brakes precisely because there is no stop sign on a street corner?

Anyone new to driving in the Boston area, on the other hand, who comes upon one of its flashing *green* traffic signals will very likely experience a jolt of adrenaline, a transitory confusion, or perhaps even panic. To a person familiar with the code of traffic signals, but not with this particular flashing green signal, the uncertainty concerning the light's meaning will probably result in a lightning-quick chain of speculation that may or may not lead to some action. The local driver, however, who is aware that the signal designates a trolley car crosswalk, will probably watch to make sure the light doesn't turn red, but will experience none of the disorientation of the out-of-town driver. Because of its unknown significance, such a signal calls far greater attention to itself than any determinate sign, no matter how bright or obtrusive.

The uncertainties arising from these two situations are directly tied to their particular contexts: intersections and street corners generate expectations for traffic signals or stop signs so that the lack of a signal or sign in these locations is perceived as an absence. On the other hand, there is no general expectation of stop signs along a street, so the lack of them down the length of an avenue is never perceived as an absence. Similarly, whenever a traffic signal is encountered, it generates a very limited range of expectations, and if the actual signal does not lie within this range, as in the case of a flashing green light, uncertainty results.

Since they involve the interpretation of signs (or lack of signs), these examples are especially well-suited to a discussion of absence and uncertainty in texts. Though unsubtle, the above situations closely parallel the kinds of impasses we oftentimes experience in literary works. Language, by its nature, is thoroughly and unavoidably peppered with absences (in the sense that language is *schematic*, not indeterminate), so that the process of reading is, in a way, a continual negotiation with what is *not* there on the page.

This principle, so vividly demonstrated in *Tristram Shandy*, has often been explored by contemporary critics, especially those associated with a "reader response" approach. In *The Literary Work of Art*, for instance, Roman Ingarden emphasizes the necessarily schematic structure of anything described in language, insisting that no textually represented object can ever be exhaustively described, since there will always be "spots of indeterminacy" that are not fleshed out. For instance, when in a story a "table" is mentioned, we know well enough what is meant even though we often do not know of what material the table is made, its shape or height, its design or color, and so on. Even if some of these spots of indeterminacy are filled in, the new information supplied will also create new spots of indeterminacy so that the essentially schematic nature of linguistically represented objects cannot ever be removed. Rather as a seat cushion seems solid enough but actually houses innumerable pockets of air, or as with the structure of matter at the atomic level, language is likewise riddled with lacunae and is therefore always fundamentally incomplete.

In a similar vein, Samuel Hayakawa's famous discussion of "Bessie the cow" demonstrates that linguistic representation can never subsume the full range of information associated with any given thing:

> Bessie is a living organism, constantly changing, constantly ingesting food and air, transforming it, getting rid of it again. Her blood is circulating, her nerves are sending messages. Viewed microscopically, she is a mass of variegated corpuscles, cells, and bacterial organisms; viewed from the point of view of modern physics, she is a perpetual dance of electrons. What she is in her entirety, we can never know. . . . It is impossible to say completely what Bessie or anything else really *is*. (166)

As the compliant Bessie illustrates, language can never exhaust the potential information a thing has to offer, so the actual description of anything will necessarily be limited and inadequate. Consequently, the inevitable campaign of language to account for reality can potentially obscure what it seeks to elucidate by seeming to be adequate and complete in itself.

Ingarden's discussion of "spots of indeterminacy" focuses, for the most part, on the inherent gaps always present in language. But Wolfgang Iser's related concept of "blanks" in texts treats absence more in terms of conscious technique and the dynamic that these blanks set in motion between text and reader. In *The Implied Reader*, Iser posits that such blanks are necessary to the novel. There must be, and always are, vacancies in our stories that call on the reader to supply whatever is missing. These vacancies engage the reader's imagination and activate the sense of discovery and suspense fundamental to literature. According to Iser, all novels "shade off, through allusions and suggestions into a text that is unformulated though nonetheless intended" (31). The reader must provide this unwritten part of the story, and, by doing so, "formulates something that is unformulated in the text and yet represents its 'intention'" (287). Iser sees this process as the central dynamic between book and reader:

> [T]he written text imposes certain limits on its unwritten implications in order to prevent these from becoming too blurred or hazy, but at the same time these implications, worked out by the reader's imagination, set the given situation against a background which endows it with far greater significance than it might have seemed to possess on its own. (276)

While both Iser's and Ingarden's discussions of absence are valid, both fail to make a crucial distinction. Neither Ingarden's "spots of indeterminacy" nor Iser's "blanks" distinguish between the absences that inevitably result from the schematic nature of language and the conventions of literary form, and what I will refer to as "structured absences," the very different sort of vacancy that is specifically and intentionally implicated. To revert to our previous example, they do not distinguish between the lack of traffic signals along an avenue and the lack of one at an intersection. Two simple sentences will serve to illustrate this point:

1) Her hair made me wistful.
2) The color of her hair made me wistful.

Assuming, of course, that these sentences were encountered in some real narrative context, we notice that in both of them the hair color is not named and could therefore constitute a "spot of indeterminacy" or a "blank" according to Ingarden's or Iser's terminology. But the failure to discriminate between what is happening in these two sentences exposes a shortcoming in these approaches to absence.

In both of these sentences, hair color is absent and, according to Iser and Ingarden, the reader may "formulate" or "actualize" such details in imagining the scene described. The reader will compensate for the lack and, in so doing, may add a vividness to the reading experience not wholly derived from the text.

However, while this may be true for the first sentence, it is certainly not so with the second. In the first sentence, hair color is not a "structured absence"—that is, hair color is not specifically implicated in the statement. Here, hair color could be the cause of the wistfulness, but it could also be any other attribute of the hair, such as texture, style, or length, or just the hair itself.

In the second sentence, however, the color of the hair is a "structured absence." The color is still not named, but it is specifically implicated as the cause of the wistfulness. Because of this, something rather strange occurs: while in the first sentence it is possible that a reader may supply the missing color in imagining the scene, in the second sentence this is precisely what the reader will not do. Because the color of the hair has been spotlighted, and the vacancy in this regard has been singled out as being of special importance, a reader will be more likely to suspend any inclination to supply this missing attribute—at least until further pertinent information is forthcoming. In a way, the reaction of the reader to this sentence is similar to the reaction of the driver approaching an intersection without any visible traffic signal. The driver, along with the reader of the second sentence, experiences disorientation and will proceed with caution and a heightened sensitivity.

The difference between a structured absence and the general sort of textual absence that results from the schematic nature of language may not, at first, seem especially profound. But these two types of absence are of wholly different orders and call into play completely different responses. It is the difference between a specific absence *made present* within a text and the general undifferentiated emptiness, the background flux, out of which a text emerges—between a "structured absence" to which the text specifically calls attention and the inevitable schematic incompletedness that is always a part of language.

A structured absence has nothing to do with the inherently schematic nature of language, but rather with the intentional use of language to call attention to something missing in a specific and recognizable way. There are innumerable things not said in a particular text, but only a limited number of these are directly implicated by the text itself. The blankness of a sheet of paper, for example, can be seen either as a single undifferentiated absence, or as containing an infinity of absences that can be segmented in an endless number of ways. But not one of these potential absences is apparent or differentiated from the larger absence of the page. A zero, we might say, is a graphic emblem of a structured absence. It is a line circumscribing an emptiness that structures and thereby calls attention to the void it encompasses. A zero, the universal sign for nothing, represents an absence made present. A structured absence is the literary equivalent of this graphic sign.

By analogy, we might also note that the *Venus de Milo* presents us with a structured absence. As soon as we look at this statue, we instantly notice the missing arms only because the surviving bulk of the statue "structures" this particular absence. But even though we know precisely that the arms are missing, we still cannot actually "formulate" or "concretize" the missing arms because of the potentially infinite variety of possible positions. This is what Gaston Bachelard has in mind when he discusses the special nature of a "precise unknown." Such an unknown is "precise" insofar as it is both implicated and structured.

The sentences about hair and wistfulness are, of course, only a simple demonstration. Since they lack any wider context, they might seem more indeterminate and less problematic than they would in a novel, a poem, or a story. While the kinds of structured absences encountered in literary works are usually more subtle, they are not necessarily any less obvious or disorienting. The first sentence of Henry James's "The Beast in the Jungle," for example, reads:

> What determined the speech that startled him in the course of their encounter scarcely matters, being probably but some words spoken by himself quite without intention—spoken as they lingered and slowly moved together after their renewal of acquaintance. (*Portable* 327)

There are several structured absences interacting in this passage, most obviously the identity of "him" and that of the person he encounters. These implicated gaps, however, are subsequently filled in when we learn the names and the backgrounds of these characters. Far more important is the larger structured absence that this sentence as a whole delineates, which can roughly be paraphrased as, "What was it that he said to her that made her say what she did to him?" Obviously, readers cannot hope to answer this question, and they will probably store this unresolved issue in a suspended state throughout their reading, expecting that the story may eventually provide more information on this point. Throughout the bizarre chronicle of John Marcher and May Bartram's relationship, however, this point is never resolved, and, despite the narrator's assertion that it "scarcely matters," this "absent cause" becomes all the more haunting as the reader wonders what initiated their liaison. In the end, May's death and Marcher's bone-chilling rationalizations are intensified by the lingering uncertainty set in motion by this germinal structured absence.

As the example of "The Beast in the Jungle" suggests, the practice of employing an inaugural structured absence as a way of generating curiosity and suspense is particularly common. This device instantly creates a sense of motion and direction, as in the James short story or the opening lines from Frost's "Mending Wall":

> Something there is that doesn't love a wall,
> That sends the frozen-ground-swell under it
> And spills the upper boulders in the sun,
> And makes gaps even two can pass abreast.

(33)

The first line of this poem contains a structured absence in the phrase "something there is," which in itself is almost entirely devoid of meaning, and yet is the focus and center of the poem. Unlike the common riddles that Frost's opening mimics, the observations that follow are insufficient to resolve the enigma expressed in the first line. Instead, they magnify the initial uncertainty by applying it to an ever-widening range of circumstances.

These examples of structured absences also raise another important point of contention with Iser's treatment of blanks. "Balance," writes Iser, "can only be attained if the gaps are filled, and so the constitutive blank is continually bombarded with projections" (*Act* 167). By definition, Iser's blanks must always be filled and, though the reader's projections may be modified, the blank is never really empty at all. But this assumption is surely an easy overgeneralization, as the above examples demonstrate. We have absolutely no way of knowing what it was that Marcher said to May to initiate the renewal of their acquaintance, and so we are forced to store this unresolved question, whether consciously or not, during our reading. It is very doubtful that any competent reader would "bombard" such a gap with any projection at all. Similarly, the "something there is that doesn't love a wall" of Frost's poem is never named, and it is doubtful that any reader's projection can adequately fill this vacancy. Moreover, the effect of these works depends precisely on these absences not being filled and the resulting uncertainty experienced by the reader.

It is Iser's contention, however, that a reader must always "concretize" the series of "cues" that makes up a text in such a way that the work is rendered internally consistent. A work's blanks must be "normalized," or systematically reduced to a kind of negotiated stability. Once again, this flaw in Iser's approach can be traced to his failure to make the crucial distinction between those absences that are an inherent feature of language and those that are specifically implicated and must therefore remain open.

A reader almost surely does compensate when faced with certain types of narrative vagueness. When confronted with a structured absence, however, even if we can imagine ways to resolve it, such possibilities are never actually installed in the implicated vacancy, since to do so would amount to a conscious disregard for the design of the story as well as its implicit intention. Attempts to resolve the uncertainty generated by structured absences must be suspended until new information, which may or may not be forthcoming, allows us to rule out alternatives.

In Kafka's *The Trial*, for instance, the opening sentence announces "Someone must have been telling lies about Joseph K., for without having done anything wrong he was arrested one fine morning" (1). To project hypotheses into the gap concerning who may have been telling such lies would be to seriously misconstrue the text, and it is doubtful that any reader would do so since it is so conspicuously and repeatedly implicated as the story unfolds. Moreover, there is at first absolutely no background material available to formulate such hypotheses. Soon we suspect that we will never learn the identity of the supposed informant and, because the longer this structured absence remains unresolved the more corrosive it becomes, we also begin to doubt seriously if there really is a specific person responsible for K.'s arrest.

Far from having to be filled in, structured absences must remain open, suspending a field of simultaneous potentialities that often cannot be resolved. This kind of absence calls into play what Keats long ago referred to as "negative capability," the capability "of being in uncertainties, Mysteries, doubts, without any irritable reaching after fact and reason" (261). As in the case of a sentence like "The color of her hair made me wistful," where the reader will resist filling in the absence because it is implicated, textual vacancies often obligate the reader to defer indefinitely all attempts at resolution.

Of course, we have already encountered many examples of structured absences in previous chapters. When in Joyce's "The Dead," Gabriel at last can see Gretta in terms of "a grace and mystery in her attitude as if she were a symbol of something," when Faulkner refers to a "smell of rotting cucumbers and something else which had no name," or when Lawrence serves us up a feast of resonant and veiled "somethings" that so obsess Lou Witt in *St. Mawr*, we are dealing, in all these instances with essentially the same thing—structured absences carefully crafted within their own unique contexts that defy any resolution or "filling in."

Similarly, when we encounter those groping efforts to reach out beyond the limits of language, as with Kemmett's sudden rain ending with "its hint of what the hand can never hold" or the unnameable *whatever* that is in the eye of a fawn jumping a chasm, we are also dealing with structured absences. They are a certain recognizable class of utterances that, while unique in themselves and in their particular context, nevertheless share a common motive and nature. As with Djuna Barnes's "impossible" image of "the echo of some foray in the blood that had no known setting," or W. S. Graham's vision of "flying in a cloud wanting to say something," such "phrase-gestures" function as provocative and tantalizing structured absences to which the drift and inflection of the text unmistakably calls our attention. In all of these cases, we witness language gesturing toward something that must remain undisclosed and unresolved—some structured absence whose "content" is ethereal and elusive, but that is made manifest in words as "solid" as words can be.

Structured absences are also a primary means of conveying a sense of the purposely incomplete or pregnantly "unfinished" state of a work that can potentially amplify readerly dynamics a hundredfold. Often, though certainly not always, either direct or tacit appeals to inexpressibility accompany the use of structured absences so that the art of leaving things out is subtly tied to an awareness of what cannot be said.

Potentially, a structured absence might be any aspect of a work implicated in such a way that a reader is made aware of its irresolvable "openness." Invariably, structured absences engender uncertainty, and the characteristic response to them is a consciousness of deferral, noncommitment, and studied indecision. The use of structured absences both engages and places burdens on readers, forcing them to carry questions forward or project them back in an unresolved state.

Perhaps the most familiar use of structured absences is to be found in the genre of the riddle. Here, the production of uncertainty, albeit transitory, is the unconcealed intention of the text, as well as the expectation of the reader or listener. Needless to say, most riddles are created precisely in order to be solved, so we can consider them to be structured absences only for as long as they remain a puzzle. It should be emphasized, however, that the uncertainty generated by a riddle, no matter how ephemeral, lingers on long after its resolution in much the same way that the experience of confusion preceding enlightenment may be etched as deeply in our memory as the new understanding eventually achieved.

In the following mother goose rhyme, the strategic "avoidance" characteristic of riddles is immediately apparent:

> Two Brothers we are,
> Great Burdens we bear,
> All day we are bitterly pressed,
> Yet this I must say—
> We are full all day,
> And empty when we go to rest.
>
> (Baring-Gould 268)

As with most riddles, we sense here that every word is charged with ambiguity. We detect a calculated duplicity and are unsure which terms to take literally and which metaphorically. From the very beginning, we are aware of a fundamental uncertainty and focus immediately on the words and tropes that generate this effect. Unlike the situation in previous examples, most people will eventually settle on "a pair of shoes" to plug the fissure opened up by this riddle, since this particular absence is structured to the point where plausible hypotheses can be formulated and the enigma can eventually be solved.

Once a riddle's solution is found, the structured absence collapses into sense and the void it brought to light is filled. The initial uncertainty it generated, however, does not simply evaporate, but lives on in our memory. This is a point made convincingly by Andrew Welsh in his study of lyric poetry: "The riddle is more than simply substituting one name for another. . . . the sense of paradox is present even in the initial act of seeing and is never completely resolved. . . . the process of resolving the paradoxes implicit in the imagery becomes a way of knowing" (32). It is the experience of a riddle, not its solution, that is the heart and soul of this ancient form. The predicament of coping with mystery, of plunging headlong into uncertainty, is vastly more significant than the moment when the enigma is resolved. It is the uncertainty, not the answer, that is the riddle's gift.

The lasting resonance of uncertainty is much more apparent in the following riddle from the tenth-century *Exeter Book*:

> I'm a strange creature, for I satisfy women,
> a service to the neighbors! No one suffers
> at my hands except for my slayer.
> I grow very tall, erect in a bed,
> I'm hairy underneath. From time to time
> a beautiful girl, the brave daughter
> of some churl dares to hold me,
> grips my russet skin, robs me of my head
> and puts me in the pantry. At once that girl
> with plaited hair who has confined me
> remembers our meeting. Her eye moistens.
>
> (Bryant 127)

As with many of the Old English riddle poems, each phrase in this amusing bit of ribaldry adds a parameter, but the sum of the parameters is incomplete in some fundamental way. A riddle, paradoxically, gestures at something not within itself, but out of which it is formed. If enough parameters have accumulated to allow for the ruling out of alternatives, then the riddle can be "solved." If not, the riddle remains unresolved and all the more frustrating. Once again, we can consider this poem as a whole to consist of a single structured absence. The riddle's solution is the absolute center of the pattern formed by the various statements that structure the riddle, and yet this center is not present in the text at all. In a sense, each phrase of the riddle draws tangents almost touching upon this center without ever penetrating the magic circle. A riddle constructs a zero around something. It frames an absence.

Even after this riddle is solved, and we realize that the answer is simply "an onion," we continue to focus on our initial uncertainty when we wondered if these lines might really be referring to something less presentable. Rather than the solution displacing our uncertainty, it is the uncertainty itself—our humorous hesitancy to name what we first suspect the answer to be—that lives on as the riddle's lasting effect.

In general, though, a riddle can be considered a structured absence only for as long as it remains unsolved. Once solved, the absence that the riddle uncovered is filled and the uncertainty it generated is to some degree dispersed. This temporal constraint is fundamental to any consideration of uncertainty in texts more complex than riddles, and must be balanced against the more obvious spatial considerations. From a spatial perspective, a structured absence is located within the text at a certain position in relation to other textual features. From a temporal perspective this absence becomes implicated at a specific point in the reader's experience, and the uncertainty that results can be either magnified or diminished by what follows.

Even in riddles, structured absences are not always resolved as easily as in the last two examples. There are many riddles that cannot be solved and that leave their reader in a state of indefinite suspension. For instance, a zen koan like "What is the sound of one hand clapping?" depends on the unresolvable uncertainty it generates for its effect. Or, to take a somewhat different case, there is the tantalizing unsolved riddle of William Whewell:

> A handless man had a letter to write,
> And he who read it had lost his sight;
> The dumb repeated it word for word,
> And deaf was the man who listened and heard.
>
> (Bryant 193)

This structured absence has remained "unfilled" for over a hundred years, and it may well remain that way forever. A primary difference between Whewell's riddle and the zen koan, however, is that with the zen saying uncertainty *is* the meaning—exposing the limits of human rationality is the whole point—whereas Whewell presumably had a real answer for his puzzle.

The riddle paradigm has often been used as a way of channeling uncertainty into higher realms of inquiry. Emily Dickinson's poem "This World is not Conclusion," for example, exploits the formulas and techniques of the riddle, but adds a new twist in the way it turns back on itself (and its reader):

> This World is not Conclusion.
> A Species stands beyond—
> Invisible, as Music—
> But positive, as Sound—
> It beckons, and it baffles—

> Philosophy—dont know—
> And through a Riddle, at the last—
> Sagacity, must go—
> To guess it, puzzles scholars—
> To gain it, Men have borne
> Contempt of Generations
> And Crucifixion, shown—
> Faith slips—and laughs, and rallies—
> Blushes, if any see—
> Plucks at a twig of Evidence—
> And asks a Vane, the way—
> Much Gesture, from the Pulpit—
> Strong Hallelujahs roll—
> Narcotics cannot still the Tooth
> That nibbles at the soul—[1]

(384–85)

Dickinson's opening lines invoke the familiar riddle formula, challenging the reader and calling for an answer. The statement "This World is not Conclusion. / A Species stands beyond" seems to refer to the afterlife, to whatever lies on the other side of death, but it can also refer more generally to all those aspects of *this* world that are hidden from human perception and thought. This thing beyond death or human comprehension is represented lexically as a glaring absence. The word "species" appears as a mere mask that screens the mysterious something that would be the poem's "solution." This indefinite subject then becomes the antecedent of the indefinite pronoun "it," which assumes the role of subject for all that follows. We are then confronted with a series of parameters that seems to delineate this absent subject ("To guess it, puzzles scholars— / To gain it, Men have borne / Contempt" etc.), but these clues, these "twigs of evidence," are wholly inadequate to a final solution precisely because any answer is beyond the reach of human rationality.

Just as important as the thematic content of this poem, however, is the fact that the reader is actually made to experience what the poem describes, since the form of the poem replicates the situation that is its subject. Because of the initial riddle formula, readers cannot avoid reading with an eye toward solving this puzzle and will proceed with the expectation that the following lines will provide enough information to achieve this end. Even readers familiar with Dickinson who are aware that this might not be the case must still experience the poem on these terms, since its formal aspects demand that it be read in this way. And so the reader proceeds line by line, assessing each in turn, trying to assemble something that will at last unmask what the word "species" hides.

It is in this sense that the final ironic couplet cuts two ways. Thematically, it announces that we cannot ever know the answer to the question posed, but these lines also function as a reflexive commentary on the reader's hopes and expectations while reading the poem. The tooth that "nibbles at the soul" refers simultaneously to the universal wondering at what lies beyond and to the conventional expectation of resolution that readers bring to any poem or story. Just as this world is not conclusion, Dickinson's poem is not "concluded," but remains a structured absence indefinitely suspending resolution.

These kinds of structured absences that are suspended indefinitely can also become central to many longer and more complex works. From *Tristram Shandy* to *Waiting for Godot*, from *Moby Dick* to Thomas Pynchon's *V.*, uncertainty can be placed at center stage, as in the Dickinson poem, and our confrontation with it somehow becomes the most important thing we take away from these works. The structured absences employed in such works are of special interest since they often go to incredible extremes to thwart the expectation of resolution, and they thereby assume a more and more prominent place in the reader's experience.

The example of riddles also demonstrates that textual absences can vary in degree, as paradoxical as this may sound. Solving riddles can be easy, challenging, or impossible according to their solution's relative degree of absence, as a comparison of Whewell's riddle with the first two riddle poems illustrates. An implicated void can be more or less empty in that the spectrum of parameters circumscribing the absence can vary, either limiting or expanding the range of possible alternatives. Adding another word to a sentence like "The color of her hair made me wistful" so that it reads "The *dark* color of her hair made me wistful" injects an added parameter and thus narrows the range of alternatives. In both sentences the exact color is still absent (is it brown or black or perhaps red?), but it was "more" absent before the word "dark" was added, that is, when blonde and white and so on were also still possibilities.

This point may seem fairly self-evident, but it needs to be made. Most discussions of textual blanks tend to suggest that all narrative gaps are similar, that they are merely a lack, an empty space. A blank is a blank—it is nothing—and we tend to see nothing as equal to itself. Such a way of thinking, however, ignores the point that textual absence can only be perceived in terms of something present—that is, the parameters circumscribing the absence that combine to give any particular absence a characteristic "structure."

In Thomas Pynchon's *The Crying of Lot 49*, for example, the central enigma, the hollow core around which the plot revolves, concerns the existence of a vast underground conspiracy involving a secret communications network. But neither Oedipa Maas nor the reader can ever be sure if she is uncovering an actual organization, if she is the victim of some absurd practical joke, or if she is, in fact, possibly insane or hallucinating.

In one epiphanic moment—or perhaps it is a parody of epiphany—Oedipa realizes her plight in a climactic interior monologue:

> Either you have stumbled indeed, without the aid of LSD or other indole alkaloids, onto a secret richness and concealed density of a dream; onto a network by which X number of Americans are truly communicating. . . . or you are hallucinating it. Or a plot has been mounted against you so expensive and elaborate, involving items like forging stamps and ancient books, constant surveillance of your movements, planting of post horn images all over San Francisco, bribing of librarians, hiring of professional actors. . . . Or you are fantasizing some such plot, in which case you are a nut, Oedipa, out of your skull. (128)

These "symmetrical four" are Oedipa's alternatives as well as the reader's, and at the novel's conclusion this central uncertainty remains unresolved with each and every possibility in a state of suspension.

This issue is the central structured absence of Pynchon's novel, but it is an absence fairly well defined in terms of recognizable parameters. Quite a different situation prevails in Henry James's *The Sacred Fount*, an equally enigmatic narrative. Whereas in *The Crying of Lot 49* we knew about the conspiracy Oedipa thought she was uncovering in great detail, in James's novel we don't really know what it is that the unnamed narrator thinks he is discovering—though, once again, it is very possible that there is actually nothing to uncover. Beyond the fact that the narrator suspects two of the characters at a house party to be drawing the "life force" from their mates in some sort of vampirish relation, we have absolutely no idea what this life force is nor how someone could drain it from another. Characteristically, the structured absences that describe the situation are much more radically "open" than in Pynchon's novel. For instance, the narrator tells us early on:

> I felt from the first that if I was on the scent of something ultimate I had better waste neither my wonder nor my wisdom. I was on the scent—that I was sure of; and yet even after I was sure I should still have been at a loss to put my enigma itself into words. (22–23)

Here, contrary to Oedipa's confrontation with four distinct possibilities, James's narrator finds himself in pursuit of an almost unquantifiable openness. "Something ultimate" is a phrase with little or no assignable content, and yet this is the object of the narrator's quest and the center of the plot. Furthermore, whereas Oedipa can imagine and verbalize all the various facets of her predicament, James's narrator is forced to declare a kind of bankruptcy when it comes to depicting what it is he's after; though his declaration of being at a loss for words is not without irony since, after all, he is moved to write a rather lengthy narrative devoted to this ineffable something.

As these examples show, uncertainty can potentially result from either a surfeit or scarcity of meaning, from a bewildering overplus or a puzzling bareness of assignable significance. Used in combinations and in more elaborate patternings that might, for example, intermix surfeit and scarcity, the manipulation of structured absences of both species can so vary in effect and in the distinctive flavors of uncertainty they conjure up that we may rightly speak of a *spectrum* of structured absences.

11
The Spectrum of Structured Absences

The sublimity connected with vastness is familiar to every eye. The most abstruse, the most far-reaching, perhaps the most chastened of poet's thoughts, crowd on the imagination as he gazes into the depths of the illimitable void. The expanse of the ocean is seldom seen by the novice with indifference; and the mind, even in the obscurity of night, finds a parallel to the grandeur, which seems inseparable from images that the senses cannot compass.

—James Fenimore Cooper, *The Pathfinder*

Uncertainty is primarily an affair of too much or too little. Structured absences are born of either a plethora or a dearth of interpretive possibilities. We can therefore distinguish between "rarefied" and "impacted" structured absences, to borrow the terms used by Martin Nystrand in his work in composition theory.[1] Whether it is the bewildering abstruseness of an impacted structured absence or the equally bewildering vagueness of a rarefied structured absence, the same basic reaction is evoked in the reader—an awareness of multiple possibilities, a suspension of interpretive commitment, in short, a purposeful uncertainty.

In the opening paragraph of *Light in August* discussed at the beginning of this section, readers cannot presume to draw conclusions about the reasons for and object of Lena's journey because there is almost nothing from which to draw conclusions. So, as in the case of the narrator of *The Sacred Fount* pursuing an ineffable "something ultimate" or Carroll's Snarks and Boojums, we can speak of these textual features as "rarefied" structured absences. In each instance, it is the purposeful vagueness concerning crucial issues that is so arresting.

Conversely, in *The Crying of Lot 49*, readers cannot determine the true nature of Oedipa's investigation because there are at least four distinct possibilities, none of which can be ruled out. Though the production of uncertainty remains a common denominator, we can distinguish this instance from the preceding ones by referring to it as an "impacted" structured absence.

Obviously, the anatomy of uncertainty in almost any work will be rooted in the use of both rarefied and impacted structured absences, often used in combination, which accumulate and intersect, tracing labyrinthine patterns of absence structured by relatively more solid textual features. In this way, the element of *what we do not know*, or *what is not there*, in our stories often assumes a characteristic "fingerprint" that is palpably before us as we read.

In Faulkner's *Light in August*, for example, the signature pattern, the distinctive textual "whorl" of the novel's many enigmas, is generated by the simple word "perhaps" and its sibling "possibly," which together construct numerous impacted structured absences that, rather like a river flowing toward a waterfall, signal the onset of turbulence in the unfolding story. When, for instance, Joe McEachern goes off for a squalid sexual encounter, we are purposely left in the dark about his perceptions and motivations leading up to the sinister violence that ensues:

> Perhaps he did not yet know himself that he was not going to commit the sin. . . . Perhaps he did not even think of it as a sin until he thought of the man who would be waiting for him at home. . . . Then it seemed to him that he could see her— something, prone, abject; her eyes perhaps. . . . He kicked her hard . . . hitting at her with wide, wild blows, striking at the voice perhaps. (146–47)

This periodic return of "perhaps" effectively suggests various possible reasons or explanations while also instilling an equal portion of doubt as to their adequacy.

The situation is mirrored and intensified through recursion a few paragraphs later when Joe returns home to face the expected punishment from his stepfather:

> Perhaps he was thinking then how he and the man could always count upon one another. . . . Perhaps he saw no incongruity at all in the fact that he was about to be punished, who had refrained from what McEachern would consider the cardinal sin. . . . Perhaps the boy knew that he already held the strap in his hand. (149–50)

The effect of all these "perhaps" clauses piling up one upon the other is to suggest a number of possible explanations, each one put forward so tentatively that it cannot be wholly embraced, so that we are left wondering whether some or all, or perhaps none, of the conjectures might actually be true. Each suggestion is plausible but not necessarily probable, so the reader is left with a sense of partial or veiled revelation, a disclosure so tenuous that the true state of affairs, we half suspect, may well have completely escaped apprehension.

Louis Bromfield's sadly neglected novel, *The Strange Case of Miss Annie Spragg*, makes similar use of impacted structured absences to simultaneously suggest and discount at precisely those junctures where a more complex sense of mystery can generate a productive uncertainty. After Annie and her brother Uriah are run out of town, suspected of witchcraft and the black arts, we do not know clearly the reasons why they must then wander the world as outcasts. This is not because this issue is avoided, but rather because we are offered too many competing possibilities:

> It may have been that the consciousness of their own queerness set them apart, or it may have been as Signora Bardelli, the janitress, believed afterward—that Miss Annie Spragg sold her soul to the Devil, a bargain made perhaps on the day Uriah found the body of Leander Potts lying in her bower by the bend in the river. Perhaps she preferred the Devil to such a God as Uriah worshipped. (132)

The effect here is not so much to supply additional information as to amplify our sense of what we do not know. Primarily, we are left only with a sense of reverberant mystery, whereas without such a passage it might never have occurred to a reader that this question was of any necessary importance.

This is also a characteristic technique of Thomas Pynchon. For instance, when in *V.* the enigmatic Mélanie is impaled during a ballet, we are purposely left unsure as to the reaction of her lover, the even more mysterious "lady V.," and various conflicting opinions are offered without apparent prejudice:

> Of the woman, her lover, nothing further was seen. Some versions tell of her gone hysterical backstage, having to be detached forcibly from Mélanie's corpse; of her screaming vendetta at Satin and Itague for plotting to kill the girl. The coroner's verdict, charitably, was death by accident. Perhaps Mélanie, exhausted by love, excited as at any premier, had forgotten. . . . Itague thought it was suicide, Satin refused to

talk about it, Porcépic suspended judgment. But they lived with
it for many years.

Rumor had it that a week or so later the lady V. ran off... (389)

After so much detailed exposition, the most lasting effect of such an impacted structured absence is to *magnify* our nascent uncertainty, to focus on the small perturbations of incipient doubt and stir them into a
gathering whirlwind. The detailed and incremental impaction of such
issues creates the illusion of assembling information, of conflating hypotheses, while in fact what accumulates is only an exponentially expanding volume of uncertainty.

For a final example of an impacted structured absence, we can turn
to Nathaniel Hawthorne, that master of simultaneous conflicting possibilities. "Ethan Brand" is the story of one man's search for the Unpardonable Sin, a sin that Ethan believes he has finally found and intentionally committed. At one point Ethan explains that:

> It is a sin that grew in my own breast. . . . A sin that grew
> nowhere else! The sin of the intellect that triumphed over the
> sense of brotherhood with man and reverence for God, and
> sacrificed everything to its own mighty claims! The only sin
> that deserves a recompense of immortal agony! (277)

Despite all these partial disclosures, which are individually and cumula-
tively inadequate as answers, we never really discover what the Unpardonable Sin is, even to the point of doubting that Ethan truly knows
what it is or that he actually committed it. Ethan, too, has recurrent doubts.

Later in the story, a brief and tantalizing allusion to a "psychological experiment" that Ethan performed on someone named Esther, and
the arrival of an old German Jew who claims to be carrying the Unpardonable Sin in a diorama, only add to the reader's puzzlement, further
impacting this central structured absence.[2] What Hawthorne has done
here, through a marvelous sleight of hand, is to invite us to read a story
about a man who searches for the Unpardonable Sin, then subtly coax
the reader into an active search for the sin itself. We readers *become*
Ethan searching for the Unpardonable Sin, not in the world but in the
text, unwittingly reenacting Ethan's diabolical search, realizing sooner
or later that the same dark potential exists in our hearts as in Ethan's.
This central impacted structured absence surrounding the Unpardonable Sin leads us on a puzzling chase that ends, not with an ultimate unveiling, but with our suspicions being turned back on ourselves and on
our own motivation.

The same is true of Hawthorne's "The Minister's Black Veil," a story
about a minister who inexplicably dons a black veil one day without

explaining its significance to his befuddled congregation. The manifold uncertainties clustering around the black veil (another impacted symbol) have the effect of placing the reader in the minister's congregation, trying to decide what the veil stands for and thus pass judgment on the minister. The reader is thereby implicated along with the congregation as well as the minister himself, who alone recognizes his guilt and (perhaps) dons a black veil as its emblem. As with the Unpardonable Sin, we cannot finally say with confidence what the black veil signifies because there are too many partially disclosed possibilities, too many warring hypotheses that cannot be reconciled.

In both cases, an impacted structured absence breeds a pervasive uncertainty that seeps through every line and every page of the story. In the end, we are left keenly aware that, while they seem to promise revelation, the stories are actually hollow vehicles for something forever missing—the secret and elusive unveilings that never come.

Rarefied structured absences intrude more softly upon a reader's attention, probably because they often seem to offer very little substance for analysis. Whereas impacted structured absences can provoke endless streams of speculation, rarefied structured absences seem emphatically mute and gnomic, often intimating that just beyond their blank surface there might lurk undisclosed depths of unspeakable significance.

In Kate Chopin's *The Awakening*, for instance, the vague unrest and turmoil that so troubles the soul of Edna Pontellier is never definitely articulated, which is what makes her plight so vivid and authentic. Typically, rarefied structured absences are employed whenever this absent cause is approached:

> An indescribable oppression, which seemed to generate in some unfamiliar part of her consciousness, filled her whole being with a vague anguish. It was like a shadow, like a mist passing across her soul's summer day. (8)

Since the whole action of the novel turns on Edna's sense of something vital but missing in her life, a pointedly empty phrase like "an indescribable oppression," vague and shadow-like, is paradoxically forced to bear a great weight, narratively speaking. Simultaneously a declaration of inexpressibility as well as a rarefied structured absence, this crisply mute passage conveys more of Edna's sense of uneasiness and dissatisfaction than any finely detailed description. By using structured absences, a space is created for such central but inarticulate promptings, while preserving intact the novel's aura of mystery. What lures Edna from the straight-and-narrow remains a richly suggestive but blank "something unattainable" (42), and Chopin marshals rarefied structured absences whenever the enigma is broached. As Edna explains, "it's something which I am beginning to comprehend, which is revealing itself to me" (62), but this something remains always on the brink of revelation.

Rarefied structured absences often harbor at least an implied declaration of inexpressibility, but sometimes a rarefied structured absence is closely reinforced with a direct appeal, as in the opening lines of W. S. Merwin's "The Bones":

> It takes a long time to hear what the sands
> Seem to be saying, with the wind nudging them,
> And then you cannot put it in words nor tell
> Why these things should have a voice.
>
> (14)

The initial deferral to a rarefied structured absence, "what the sands / Seem to be saying," presents us with a phrase without content, a mutely gesturing motion, an arrestingly "empty" observation. Following close on its heels, a direct appeal to inexpressibility, "you cannot put it in words," underlines in bold caps, so to speak, the previously implied verbal inadequacy. Perhaps most importantly, however, the legacy of this "failure," this richly expressed incapacity, is the insistence that the sands *do* speak to us, though in ways that are not verbal and consequently cannot be verbalized. The voice and message of the wind-driven sands are thus paradoxically validated by these carefully shaped lines, which lucidly convey only their inability to translate exactly what is being communicated. The poem speaks the sands' wordless message by carefully framing the unspeakable.

The dynamics set in motion by rarefied structured absences derive from the suggestive power of obscurity, from the latent positive energy of darkness artfully manipulated to act as a catalyst of wonder, as a verbal gateway opening on the imponderable. Such narrative strategies call to mind Edmund Burke's contention that the mysterious power of words actually resides in their indistinctness, an insight that both William James and Richard Poirier have also, in turn, embraced and elucidated. Burke's focus on "the sublime"—that touchstone of the eighteenth century—on that which transports the mind beyond its usual or habitual capacities, led him to the seemingly extreme position that the vagaries of reference and hazy associations summoned up by words are actually their supreme advantage, exalting the verbal above pictorial representation: "the most lively and spirited verbal description I can give, raises a very obscure and imperfect *idea* . . . but then it is in my power to raise a stronger *emotion* by the description than I could do by the best painting" (60).[3]

For Burke, it is the capacity of words to directly convey the obscure and unleash the suggestively mysterious within a reader's mind that is language's greatest and unrivalled quality:

> [H]ardly any thing can strike the mind with its greatness, which does not make some sort of approach towards infinity; which nothing can do whilst we are able to perceive its bounds; but to see an object distinctly, and to perceive its bounds, is one and the same thing. A clear idea is therefore another name for a little idea. (63)

We would obviously be on extremely dangerous ground to assert the complement to Burke's formula—that a vague or unclear idea is the hallmark of profundity—but, from the perspective of narrative technique and readerly dynamics, this is often quite true. Rarefied structured absences, as in the examples from *The Awakening* or Merwin's poem, can quickly generate a resonant and shadowed darkness that assumes quite palpable features in a reader's mind, effectively conjuring up the sought-for aura of mystery in a way that seems experientially authentic.

O. E. Rölvaag's *Giants in the Earth*, for example, tells the story of a pioneer family traveling into an expansive, unsettled prairie, a "bluish-green infinity" that seems only a "nameless, abandoned region." The mother, Beret, grows obsessed with the disturbing and inexorable emptiness, with the "vast, wind-swept void" that becomes their home. The gradual unhinging of Beret's mind occurs in direct relation to this "nameless, blue-green solitude, flat, endless, still with nothing to hide behind" (97).

Surrounded paradoxically by immensity within void, infinity abiding in emptiness, the specter that so haunts Beret is likewise a dark and nameless thing without attributes, and Rölvaag turns to rarefied structured absences whenever the inchoate evil enters the picture: "something vague and intangible hovering in the air would not allow her to be wholly at ease" (36). In another example, a magnificent sunset metamorphoses into a slouching, threatening "presence": "In the eastern sky the evening haze was gathering; it merged slowly into the purple dusk, out of which an intangible, mysterious presence seemed to be creeping closer and closer upon them" (56).

Such rarefied structured absences bring sharply home to readers that neither we nor Beret can adequately verbalize or analyze this inescapable presence that seems to pursue her so relentlessly. It is something real enough to precipitate Beret's madness, and as readers watch her gradually lose touch with reality, the presence becomes all the more real to us as well. Save that it is associated with the vast prairie's nameless and homogeneous expanse, simultaneously void and infinite, we can say little else about it. It is in such instances that we clearly grasp how the vagaries and uncertainties unleashed by language can become a major strength. As Will Ladislaw says in Eliot's *Middlemarch*, "Language gives a fuller image, which is all the better for being vague" (222).

Rarefied structured absences are particularly common at those moments when an author attempts to portray a character's perception operating at the uttermost limits of human awareness. For instance, in Willa Cather's *My Antonia*, Jim Burden describes his grandmother:

> She was a spare, tall woman, a little stooped, and she was apt to carry her head thrust forward in an attitude of attention, as if she were looking at *something*, or listening to *something, far away*. As I grew older, I came to believe that it was only because she was so often thinking of *things that were far away*. (10, my emphasis)

Here, in order to communicate the sense of mystery beyond human perception to which the grandmother is so well attuned, simple indefinite pronouns without clear antecedents are employed. Syntactically and semantically they may appear to be little more than place holders used to refer to whatever we cannot better name, but, in context, they are the most crucial feature of the passage. While conveying an implied claim of inexpressibility, the uncertainty these somethings generate in the novel mirrors the essential uncertainty, the quality beyond words, that characterizes such liminal moments in life.

The use of structured absence to mark a deferral to a realm beyond human comprehension is especially prominent in the work of John Cowper Powys. In *Wolf Solent*, for example, night scenes animated by wind and trees whisper half-heard secrets that declare themselves in print only through a recurrent refrain of verbal inadequacy. We are thus brought into a living empathy with Wolf's own lucid awareness that "Behind the pulse-beat of his body stirred the unutterable" (603):

> Something unutterable, some clue, some signal, had touched the dark bulkheads of this night-voyager; so that hereafter all might be different. What was this clue? All he knew about it now was that it meant the *acceptance* of something monstrously comic in his inmost being, something comic and stupid, together with something as grotesquely non-human as the sensations of an ichthyosaurus! (277)

> There, below this girl's figure, below the darkened roses, was there not hidden some deep, spiritual transaction? The feeling passed away quickly enough; but as it passed, it left behind

it a stabbing, quivering *suspicion*, a suspicion as to the solid reality of what his senses were thus representing, compared with something else, something of far greater moment, both for himself and for her. (580)

In these passages, and in others of similar cast, we travel with the protagonist to the limits of what words can say, then press on just a bit further to gaze out beyond the margin of the page. Momentarily escaping the confines of the book, we are cast loose in a world beyond human shaping, beyond words and beyond the body. Such, at least, is the effect of Powys' formidable style, as ominous and beautiful as a thunderstorm.

Once again, rarefied structured absences, words and phrases almost entirely devoid of content, are used to suggest mysteries beyond the capacity of language or rational understanding. But, as Dickinson's poem on "the tooth that nibbles at the soul" demonstrates, to suggest such things without naming them, to gesture at them without delineating, is probably the most effective way to incorporate such matters into texts.

Rarefied structured absences do not, of course, always convey overtones of inexpressibility, and they are not always concerned with such transcendent and philosophically weighty material. More commonly, rarefied structured absences deal with plainer matters, but in such a way that the implicated absence is elevated to a position of importance simply by refusing to unveil it.

The kinds of gaps and provocative veils used in detective fiction, for instance, typically fabricate pools of uncertainty through the use of structured absences, though in this genre they are usually resolved sooner or later. In E. C. Bentley's classic *Trent's Last Case*, for example, we find passages that typically call attention to *what we do not know* but presumably need to discover, such as this description of Trent's activities:

> In the afternoon, he had walked from the inn into town, accompanied by Mr. Cupples, and had there made certain purchases at a chemist's shop, conferred privately for some time with a photographer, sent a reply-paid telegram, and made inquiry at the telephone exchange. (89)

Though we have no clue what Trent buys at the chemist's or says to the photographer, and though we cannot know the contents of the telegram or the specifics of the telephone inquiry, we are nevertheless made to feel that these actions are of vital significance. The fact that the narrator so obviously withholds this specific information while divulging much else seems to assure us that it is the most important information. The effect is to convince the reader that the most significant aspect of the description is whatever is pointedly left in darkness.

In most detective stories these little mysteries and enigmas are soon resolved or displaced, and similar techniques are ubiquitously used to generate suspense and uncertainty in any narrative. But even in this simple description of Trent's activities, we have what amounts to a series of rarefied structured absences that in this case will be resolved, but provocative gaps nevertheless that generate for the moment the intended uncertainty.

Almost any literary work will make use of both rarefied and impacted structured absences. Sometimes, however, both types interact to produce a kind of hybrid construction that blends surfeit with vacancy to produce an especially baffling effect. For example, in *Light in August*, which contains a wealth of such moments, Mr. McEachern shadows his adopted son Joe, who is stealing away to a late-night dance:

> Hidden in the shadows of the lane halfway between the house and the road, he could see Joe at the mouth of the lane. He too heard the car and saw it come up and stop and Joe get into it. Possibly he did not care who else was in it. Perhaps he already knew, and his purpose had been merely to see in which direction it went. Perhaps he believed that he knew that too, since the car could have gone almost anywhere in a country full of possible destinations with roads that led to them. Because he turned now back toward the house, walking fast, in that same pure and impersonal outrage, as if he believed so that he would be guided by some greater and purer outrage that he would not even need to doubt personal faculties. (189)

The focus of this passage concerns how Mr. McEachern is able to follow Joe, with seemingly clairvoyant knowledge, straight to the site of a dance miles away. The reader is initially given a number of possible reasons, each one preceded by a "possibly" or a "perhaps" so that it is simultaneously suggested and placed in doubt: "Possibly" he does not need to know who else is in the car, "perhaps" he somehow already knows this, "perhaps" he only needs to see the direction the car will take, or "perhaps" he somehow already knows this.

Here, as in the example from Pynchon regarding Oedipa's "symmetrical four" alternatives, we have an impacted structured absence taking shape, but in this case there is a sudden deferral to a rarefied structured absence when we are finally told it is "as if" McEachern is guided by "some greater and purer outrage." Exactly what this pure outrage might be, or how it could guide a person telepathically, is left an open question. The cumulative effect of this hybrid construction is to suggest a number of unremarkable possible explanatory factors for McEachern's behavior without providing enough evidence for the reader to accept any of them with conviction, then to cast doubt on all these everyday possibilities by implying that some all-embracing occult faculty might ultimately be responsible.

The common denominator at work in both rarefied and impacted structured absences is the production of uncertainty. Both cause the reader to hold some issue in a state of suspension, unresolved and problematic, so, from the point of view of intention and effect, they belong to the same family. Of these two kinds of "vastnesses," the impacted presents glimmerings of many competing possibilities so embedded and entangled that they cannot be reduced to unitary meaning. The rarefied ostensibly presents a sheer blankness, an unfathomable emptiness, often with a tacit or direct appeal to inexpressibility. In both cases the mind is thwarted by something too vast to accommodate or comprehend, but this process of thwarting, when carefully constructed, becomes productive and vitally important when accounting for a work's lasting effect on the mind.

It is also worth noting in this regard that impaction, at some deeper level, is usually a function of rarefaction. In the passage quoted from *The Crying of Lot 49*, for example, each of the "symmetrical four" alternatives contains an element of vagueness or incompleteness. Put another way, we can say that an impacted structured absence is composed of rarefied alternatives. In this sense, all structured absences are cut from the same cloth.

In *Wolf Solent*, for instance, when Wolf puzzles over the unnatural expression in Mr. Otter's eyes, this puzzlement is dwelt upon at some length. But rather than clearing up the matter, the uncertainty regarding this issue is magnified through the use of structured absence: "His expression seemed to protest against something that had been inflicted on him, something unexpected, something that struck his natural acceptance of life as both monstrous and inexplicable" (23).

These three something-phrases form a series of rarefied structured absences, none of which offers anything particularly substantive. But since they cluster tightly around this single enigma of Mr. Otter's odd expression, they form a larger *impacted* structured absence; or perhaps it would be more accurate to say that here there is a sense of rarefaction and impaction folded into each other. Together, the rarefied phrases form something resembling a riddle, but a riddle not intended to be solved in the usual sense.

When dealing with structured absences, rarefaction is therefore the fundamental quality and impaction is usually a secondary operation brought to bear at a later stage. With impacted structured absences, however, it is this sense of clustering, of a knotted jumble of many tangled filaments, that eclipses exclusive interest in any individual strand, so it seems best to treat them at this level with a special designation.

The myriad ways in which structured absences can accumulate and organize into larger patterns brings up another necessary distinction briefly addressed in the previous discussion of riddles, namely the "order" of a structured absence and the "sphere of influence" in which the resulting uncertainty operates. Structured absences are by no means limited to sentence-level concerns. Such things as genre, setting, point of view, and character can become uncertain or problematic through the patterned use of lower-level structured absences that, taken together, can sometimes construct a single global structured absence. The most famous, or infamous, example of this is probably the endlessly discussed issue of the governess's state of mind in James's *The Turn of the Screw*, where a staggering number of local uncertainties feed into this larger issue that, though never explicitly formulated in the text, nevertheless becomes the central focus.

It will be useful, therefore, to distinguish between *local* structured absences, functioning within individual sentences and paragraphs, and *global* structured absences that come to light when considering the narrative or plot as a whole. Caution is necessary when applying such labels, however, since many structured absences function at both levels simultaneously. The "something ultimate" in the passage from *The Sacred Fount*, for instance, is a local structured absence that generates uncertainty in an individual sentence. As the reader becomes gradually aware through additional encounters with similar constructions, however, this same nebulous "something ultimate" soon establishes itself as the heart of the entire narrative.

A similar situation pertains when a structured absence is used as a title, as in, for instance, Joseph Heller's *Something Happened* or Henry James's *What Maisie Knew*. Since each title is the "name" of all that follows and is, in a sense, made equivalent to it, these single phrases function immediately on a global level. Even before the first sentence of these novels, uncertainty has been unleashed, an uncertainty far in excess of what any title inevitably generates, because these particular titles gesture so provocatively at something central but undisclosed. The reader must focus at once on a glaring absence and is sensitized to look for the "thing," whatever it is, that will happen in Heller's novel, or the knowledge, whatever it could be, that Maisie has acquired.

Just as important as the wide spectrum of structured absences and the resulting spheres of influence of such implicated impasses is a third consideration, namely, the manner of interaction between individual structured absences. Generally, structured absences can relate to each other according to two basic modes, which might be characterized as the difference between a "cipher" and a "halo."

12
Ciphers and Halos

Our feeling for beauty is inspired by the harmonious arrangement of order and disorder as it occurs in natural objects—in
clouds, trees, mountain ranges, or snow crystals. The shapes
of all these are dynamical processes jelled into physical forms,
and particular combinations of order and disorder are typical for them.

—Gert Eilenberger

Though of interest in themselves, the isolated examples of structured
absence examined so far assume much greater importance when we
begin to investigate how they can be woven into patterns whose cumulative effect is far greater than the sum of the parts. Though in one sense
the possible patterns of absence and the uncertainties they generate exhibit an infinite variety, it is also possible to distinguish two fundamental ways in which structured absences interact. In the first mode, one
structured absence is logically linked, embedded in, or subordinated to
another structured absence. In the second mode, a number of structured
absences are related only by exhibiting a family resemblance to one another without any overt links to knit them logically together.

In many works, it is not uncommon to encounter a smaller textual
absence situated within a larger controlling absence, and to find oneself
forced to contemplate uncertainty within uncertainty. Such a pattern is
typically governed by a strict cause-and-effect logic that establishes specific hierarchical layers of uncertainty. Structured absences deployed in
this way are related "hypotactically," so that one absence is made subordinate to or dependent upon another.

At other times, a work's repeated deferrals to absence can have the
very different effect of delineating a separate region of uncertainty—a
"sphere" of absence that sometimes seems to encompass the work itself.

The relationship between structured absences in this mode is bereft of any logical or hierarchical implications. Such absences often seem to accumulate, almost at random, and steadily intensify by merit of their proliferation. Structured absences deployed in this mode are related "paratactically," that is, they manifest themselves without any overt elements of coordination or subordination.[1]

To demonstrate the first mode characterized by cause-and-effect logic, hypotaxis, and hierarchical layering, we can return to the example from an earlier chapter concerning hair color. Even without any wider context, these sentences demonstrate clearly how structured absences can be embedded one within another:

1) The color of her hair made me wistful.
2) The color of her hair made me wistful because of her age.

In both of these sentences, hair color is a structured absence, but in the second sentence this structured absence is in a hierarchical relationship with an additional, "controlling" structured absence. Here, age is specifically implicated but absent, and this absence governs or subsumes in some way the color of the hair, which is also implicated but absent. Even in such a simple example, the cause-and-effect logic and hypotactic nature of this mode is clearly visible.

The effect of this strategy is, in a sense, to situate readers within a series of concentric zeroes, to place them within a labyrinth and tacitly challenge them to solve the puzzle. With this in mind, the term "cipher mode" seems appropriate. A "cipher" is a zero, a cryptogram, or the key to a cryptogram. The notion of a "cipher mode" simultaneously suggests all three. First and foremost, the cipher mode situates absences in a text according to a logical pattern so that it seems to build an elaborately constructed puzzle. It often proceeds by uncovering enigmas and investigating mysteries through logic and analysis in the tradition of the detective story, though it is sometimes most significant when it fails to achieve resolution. Finally, the cipher mode presents itself as a key to the enigmas it delineates, tempting readers into an often futile effort to discover the Rosetta Stone that will reveal all the hidden meanings and relationships between the provocatively structured absences interwoven throughout the story.

In the cipher mode, structured absences form chains, each absence nested within others in a controlling hierarchy.[2] Out of this larger pattern, a central uncertainty sometimes arises, such as Carroll's Boojum, Melville's white whale, Hawthorne's letter A, or Pynchon's V., and whatever it is that is at the center—or, more precisely, what is *not* at the center—is, paradoxically, what holds the work together.

As before, our initial example does not adequately suggest the evanescent interplay of uncertainty possible in longer works, such as, for example, in Henry James's "The Beast in the Jungle." Perhaps the finest achievement of this story is that the "sounded void" of John Marcher's life is fully replicated in the sounded voids of the narrative itself. The story's construction—its architecture and anatomy—is modeled on the psyche and world view of its protagonist, which is founded solely on nullity, negation, and absence without a shred of positive vision. As a result, the story is an incredible network of dozens of interlacing structured absences, which often shimmer on the frontiers of resolution only to fall back into obscurity. To trace all these absences and chart their relationships would take a book in itself, but examining just a few of these nested structured absences will illustrate the underlying mechanics.

As Marcher and May Bartram are walking together, after having accidentally crossed paths for the first time in ten years, Marcher cannot remember what it is that was so special about their past friendship. May does remember, but before she reveals this thing, the narrator describes Marcher's reaction to her revelation:

> He felt as soon as she spoke that she had been consciously keeping back *what she said* and hoping to get on without it; a scruple in her that immensely touched him when, by the end of three or four minutes more, he was able to measure it. *What she brought out*, at any rate, quite cleared the air and supplied the link—the link it was so odd he should frivolously have managed to lose.
>
> "You know you told me *something* I've never forgotten and that again and again has made me think of you since; it was that tremendously hot day when we went to Sorrento, across the bay, for the breeze. *What I allude to* was *what you said to me*, on the way back, as we sat under the awning of the boat enjoying the cool. Have you forgotten?"
> (*Portable* 333, my emphasis)

In this passage, the initial structured absence concerning what she said is "resolved" by nesting it within another "wider" structured absence so that the resolution of the original gap is no resolution at all: May's revelation turns out to be that the foundation of their special relationship was something Marcher told her, though we still haven't the slightest idea what this might be.

For several pages after this passage, the suspense over the question of what Marcher had said to May is extended to an almost absurd degree. When we finally learn what it was that Marcher said to May so long ago, May's explanation is yet another "false resolution":

> You said you had from your earliest time, as *the deepest thing within you*, the sense of being kept for *something rare and strange*, possibly prodigious and terrible, that was sooner or later to happen to you, that you had in your bones the foreboding and conviction of, and that would perhaps overwhelm you. (336, my emphasis)

Here again the structured absence concerning what he said, which was embedded in the previous gap concerning what she said, turns out to be yet another structured absence. The "something rare and strange" that Marcher tells May he is being kept for is nebulous to the point of meaninglessness, and yet the weight of the whole story rests on this phrase. The fact that the operative word in this statement is itself a word without substance—our shy but omnipresent friend "something"—only exacerbates the situation.

This pattern continues to spread through the tissue of this story, forming a network of astonishing and exasperating complexity, until a final negation, the death of May, is revealed (possibly) as the "great vagueness," the "Beast in the Jungle," that Marcher, and the reader, have been "kept for." Death, both May's physical death and Marcher's spiritual one, intervenes as the ultimate structured absence.

The other basic mode for sowing structured absences, characterized by parataxis and a principle of equivalence, is more difficult to demonstrate in a simplified example. For the sake of continuity, we can approximate its effect by contrasting a sentence in the cipher mode like "The color of her hair made me wistful because of her age" with something like "The color of her hair made me wistful; a church bell in the distance tolled the hour."

In both of these sentences there are two structured absences that, examined individually, are quite similar. The relationships between the two absences, however, are radically different. The first sentence operates according to the cipher mode, subordinating one absence to another so that an explicit hierarchy is established and a kind of puzzle delineated. In the second sentence, however, there is no logical cause-and-effect relationship between the absences. The color of the hair is implicated but absent; the hour being tolled is also implicated but absent, but there is absolutely no subordination or embedding established between the absences. There is no sense of a puzzle, rather only a sense of uncertainty heightened by repetition. In the second sentence, the structured absences are equivalent to each other, related analogically by an implied parallelism.

Often, the effect of this second mode is not to situate the reader amid a series on concentric zeroes but to delineate a separate realm or "sphere" of uncertainty enveloping the characters and events of the narrative. For this reason, the term "halo mode" seems appropriate as a fitting contrast to the very different cipher pattern, a "halo" being an apt analogy for the effect of outward dispersion characteristic of this mode.

In a famous passage from her essay, "Modern Fiction," Virginia Woolf declared:

> Life is not a series of gig lamps symmetrically arranged; life is a luminous halo, a semi-transparent envelope surrounding us from the beginning of consciousness to the end. Is it not the task of the novelist to convey this varying, this unknown and uncircumscribed spirit, whatever aberration or complexity it may display, with as little mixture of the alien and external as possible? (*The Common Reader* 150)

Using structured absences in the halo mode is a primary technique for rendering this "unknown and uncircumscribed spirit," which, if it is to be successfully evoked, must of necessity proceed by indirection and strategically placed absences.

This technique is especially evident in D.H. Lawrence's *The Rainbow*, where the repeated deferrals to the unknown occur without warning, cropping up everywhere and anywhere so that an aura of uncertainty seems suspended over the landscape, the characters, and their actions. The second paragraph of the novel serves almost as a keynote, establishing the tonal relationships and harmonies of the story that follows:

> There was a look in the eyes of the Brangwens as if they were expecting *something unknown*, about which they were eager. They had that air of readiness for *what would come to them*, a kind of surety, an expectancy, the look of an inheritor. (1, my emphasis)

At the very outset of this family chronicle, the Brangwens are collectively placed in a special relationship with the ineffable, which continually reasserts itself. A few examples follow, drawn from the many that spring up on almost every page.

The Brangwen women, Lawrence writes, "were set to discover what was beyond" and their "deepest desire hung on the battle that she heard, far off, being waged on the edge of the unknown" (3). This deferral to a kind of ultimate uncertainty hovering just beyond the limits of human perception is characteristically accomplished through rarefied structured absences with phrases like "what was beyond" or "the edge of the unknown," which are little more than gestures toward something inchoate but vitally real.

During the episode when Tom Brangwen takes his stepdaughter Anna to feed the cows in the barn, a blood-intimacy is forged between them that will last a lifetime:

> The two sat very quiet. His mind, in a sort of trance, seemed to become more and more vague. He held the child close to him. A quivering little shudder, re-echoing from her sobbing, went down her limbs. He held her closer. Gradually she relaxed, the eyelids began to sink over her dark, watchful eyes. As she sank to sleep, his mind became blank.
>
> When he came to, as if from sleep, he seemed to be sitting in a timeless stillness. What was he listening for? He seemed to be listening for some sound a long way off, from beyond life. (75)

Once again, this evocation of "some sound a long way off, from beyond life" is accomplished through a rarefied structured absence that signals the mystic depth of the communion between father and daughter.

A final example again concerns Anna, now married and a mother, as she experiences an epiphanic moment:

> But she felt as if she were not in Cossethay at all. She was straining her eyes to something beyond. And from her Pisgah mount, which she had attained, what could she see? A faint, gleaming horizon, a long way off, and a rainbow like an archway, a shadow-door with faintly coloured coping above it. Must she be moving thither?
>
> Something she had not, something she did not grasp, could not arrive at. There was something beyond her. But why must she start on the journey? She stood so safely on the Pisgah mountain. (192)

Again, as a character strains toward her limit, the narrative must defer to rarefied structured absences, to "something beyond" that remains an ungraspable something, like the symbolic rainbow Anna sees in her instant of lucidity.

The effect of the narrative regularly giving way to these kinds of structured absences is to delineate an aura of uncertainty that, like the rainbow of the title, arches across the heavens, forever unattainable and yet the root of human desire. Employing structured absences in the halo mode produces a categorically different effect than the cipher mode, but this difference has nothing to do with the individual structured absences themselves. Both modes make use of the same basic devices. There is no intrinsic difference between "something rare and strange" in "The Beast in the Jungle" and "something beyond" in *The Rainbow*, and so it is the *relationships* between the absences in each work that account for this vast difference.

The structured absences in "The Beast in the Jungle" are logically and causally related to each other. By subordinating one to another, James is able to establish a hierarchy of uncertainty that, like a riddle, has the effect of tacitly challenging the reader to "solve" the puzzle. In *The Rainbow*, on the other hand, the interaction of structured absences contains no hierarchical or hypotactic overtones. There is no causal or logical principle relating the absences, and the effect is to invoke by indirection a pervasive atmosphere of uncertainty enveloping the characters and happenings of the narrative. By continually foregrounding this aura of uncertainty, Lawrence forces his readers to focus on it, though we realize full well that there is no question of resolving it, but only of experiencing it.

With the cipher mode, the process of logically embedding absence within absence creates a sense of an inward spiraling, a progressive descent into tighter and tighter turns. With the halo mode, the spirals seem to open outward, tracing ever-wider arcs of dispersion. The logical hierarchy established by the cipher mode lends it a heavily algorithmic cast, establishing a sense of enigmas chained together in an ordered, step-by-step, progressive network. The paratactic play of the halo mode is not only non-algorithmic, but seems to actively thwart such linear and progressive operations. As opposed to the cipher mode's sequential and infolded demeanor, the hallmark of the halo mode is simultaneity and parallelism.

While both modes usually coexist, in some proportion, within most literary texts, some works are more heavily oriented to one at the expense of the other. For example, James's *The Turn of the Screw* is constructed upon a marvelously self-similar cipher pattern where, rather like Benoit Mandelbrot's fractal images, the characteristic structured hollows are repeated across ever-finer scales. In Brontë's *Wuthering Heights*, the halo mode prevails. Textual enigmas proliferate without self-embedding so that the mysterious and unknowable aspects of the action and the characters are suspended intact, stark, and inviolate. In *Jane Eyre*, the modes are perhaps balanced, the cipher mode uppermost when dealing with the densely embedded mysteries surrounding Rochester's secrets, while the halo mode predominates when the focus is on Jane's "growth of the soul," including her eventual reunion with Rochester.

Very broadly speaking, we might even risk the suggestion that two of the major movements in postmodern literature can be characterized by their respective orientations to these poles. The magical realism of the South American "boom," as in Gabriel Garcia Marquez or Isabel Allende, gravitates strongly toward the outward dispersion of the halo mode while the French New Novel of Alain Robbe-Grillet or Michel Butor is largely built on inward-turning ciphers.

13
The Jamesian Cipher

> It was as though a trail had been laid for me, at each stage of
> which I was allowed to see the end of the next stage, a trail
> which was to lead me hopelessly astray.
>
> —Michel Butor, *Passing Time*

As a paradigm of the cipher mode, there are few finer examples than
Henry James's masterful short story "The Figure in the Carpet." In
this detective's detective story, the reader is handed a deerstalker and a
lens, so to speak, and drawn into the Holmesian intricacies of an irre-
sistible "case." Often bypassing the somewhat oafish and obtuse narrator, the reader-as-detective meets the writer-as-criminal-mastermind, an
unseen arranger who, Moriarty-like, always anticipates, always lays traps,
and foresees all contingencies.

The premise of the story concerns the "figure in the carpet," the hidden "general intention" running through the works of the famous novelist
Hugh Vereker—an "exquisite scheme" that no one has ever suspected.
During a serendipitous meeting with Vereker himself, the unnamed narrator is informed of the figure's existence, but, despite all his efforts, he
is not able to discover what the figure is. He begins to suspect Vereker of
a practical joke, but passes on the information to George Corvick and
Gwendolyn Erme, who in turn take up the pursuit of the figure.

This process of transference, from the narrator to Corvick and Gwendolyn, is repeated when readers find themselves drawn in, searching in
this short story for the elusive figure. Logically, there is no reason to think
that the figure is a feature of James's own work, yet invariably readers assume that, whatever the figure is, it must be present in this story if it is
anywhere at all. This odd twist is so deftly managed that we do not particularly feel the fact that we have no access whatsoever to the enigmatic writ-

ings of Hugh Vereker. Though they form the axis of the story, Vereker's works are nowhere present, not even a single quoted line. In a sense, the text of James's story becomes a surrogate for Vereker's, and we scrutinize every word with a sharp eye, searching for evidence of the figure.

Even before the existence of the figure is revealed, the pattern of James's story is established with the first structured absence—a provocatively hollow receptacle that becomes a kind of matrix for the dozens upon dozens that follow. When the narrator agrees to take on Corvick's obligation to supply a magazine with a review of Vereker's latest work, Corvick tries to convey what it is he would like the narrator to get at:

> Corvick almost groaned. "Oh you know. . . . he gives me a pleasure so rare; the sense of"—he mused a little— "something or other."
> I wondered again. "The sense, pray, of what?"
> "My dear man, that's just what I want *you* to say!" (359)

This simple rarefied structured absence, the sense of "something or other," provides the keynote for a teeming mass of similar structured absences that hover around the central orbit of the omnipresent, but absent, "figure" for which everyone searches.

Corvick's passionately felt but seemingly inexpressible "something or other" is quickly reinforced by another rarefied structured absence, "what I want *you* to say," that sounds the octave of this first chord. These inaugural structured absences quickly transform into the narrator's equally substanceless but somewhat skeptical "what Vereker gave him the sense of," and the long and twisting chains of logically related lacunae are set in motion—a perpetual motion, as it turns out.

This scene is soon mirrored when Lady Jane, having read the narrator's review, tries to explain to Vereker himself the nature of her response: "'The man has actually got at you, at what I always feel, you know.' Lady Jane threw into her eyes a look evidently intended to give an idea of what she always felt; but she added that she couldn't have expressed it" (361). Then, just as Vereker is revealing to the narrator the existence of the figure, the narrator repeats Corvick's very words, now inversely applied to what Vereker's own explanation seems to lack: "his account of his silver lining was poor in *something or other* that a plain man knows things by" (366, my emphasis).

The key phrases in all these passages function rather as empty basins, hollow bowls ready and waiting for whatever this essential *thing* might be. This proliferating circumlocution is accomplished through rarefied structured absences, through indefinite pronouns, something-phrases, and other indefinite noun phrases, such as the omnipresent what-phrases. These devices, while substanceless in themselves, nevertheless bind the story together through the densely intertwined relations among the absences.

For instance, after the narrator relates to Corvick what Vereker has told him of the figure, this elusive "general intention" is directly linked with the "sense of something or other" that Corvick had previously sensed in Vereker: "The thing Vereker had mentioned to me was exactly the thing he, Corvick, had wanted me to speak of in my review" (371). Though he is not quite able to verbalize his nebulous awareness more clearly, Corvick goes on to explain that, had *he* reviewed Vereker's new book as originally planned, "*What he would have said* . . . was that there was evidently in the writer's inmost art *something to be understood*" (371, my emphasis).

So Vereker's ungraspable "figure" becomes the larger, central absence in which Corvick's already disclosed but mute "something" is embedded, which is also tied to Lady Jane's "what I always feel," and so on throughout the tissue of the story. Through all the narrative's "deft dregs of delay," readers are drawn onward by the increasing allure of the hidden figure and the promise that "the final knowledge of it was an experience quite apart" (385). But the story concludes with no unveiling, and we must instead remain content with the "golden glory in which the mystery was wrapped" (397).

To discuss all the many individual absences and chart their relationships would take volumes, but it is instructive to merely list a few of the rarefied structured absences employed when referring to the unnameable figure:

> "he had caught whiffs and hints of he didn't know what" (371)
> "something to be understood" (371)
> "what we so desired to hear" (389)
> "what Vereker gave him the sense of" (359)
> "something that can't be got into a letter" (382)
> "what I thought you knew" "what would come"
> "what you allude to"

All these various rarefied structured absences, each one in its particular context and with its particular shades of significance, are connected to their siblings by shadowy filaments that radiate from a central knot— the tangled nexus that is the forever hidden figure itself.

Intersecting everywhere with this network of rarefied structured absences are the equally numerous impacted structured absences, and both varieties continually play off each other. Vereker's own guarded revelation of the existence of the figure becomes the fundamental impacted absence, throwing out hint after hint, each one vague and inadequate but together forming an increasingly clotted mystery:

> By my little point I mean—what shall I call it?—the particular thing I've written my books most *for*. Isn't there for every writer a particular thing of that sort . . . the thing without the effort to achieve which he wouldn't write at all, the very passion of his passion, the part of the business in which, for him, the flame of art burns most intensely? Well, it's *that*! . . . It stretches, this little trick of mine, from book to book, and everything else, comparatively, plays over the surface of *it*. The order, the form, the texture of my books will perhaps some day constitute for the initiated a complete representation of it. (365–66)

Though this riddling description creates a sense of information incrementally accumulating, hint after hint, facet upon facet, none of this turns out to be of much practical value in solving the puzzle. Since Vereker wants to avoid a direct explanation of what the figure is, he turns to metaphor to both mask and mark what he gestures toward, and the partial hints and prompts steadily increase:

> The thing's as concrete there as a bird in a cage, a bait on a hook, a piece of cheese in a mousetrap. It's stuck into every volume as your foot is stuck into your shoe. It governs every line, it chooses every word, it dots every i, it places every comma. (368)

These metaphoric masks are scattered tantalizingly throughout the story, seemingly suggestive but bewilderingly diverse: Vereker's hidden "general intention" is "like a complex figure in a Persian carpet," or it is "the very string. . . that my pearls are strung on" (374), and so on. As these broad analogies and blankly suggestive metaphors accumulate, their seemingly unstoppable propagation steadily impacts the issue rather than resolving it.

Again, a partial sample, even without commentary, demonstrates the tendency of such surrogates and stand-ins to perplex rather than to clarify. The figure is variously referred to as:

a little trick	a beauty so rare and great
the unimagined truth	the element in question
a buried treasure	my great affair
my little point	my little secret
the great thing	an exquisite scheme
a special substance	the organ of life
his silver lining	the very mouth of the cave

the particular thing   the finest full intention
a hidden music   the idol unveiled

As with Humpty Dumpty, no mere process of assembly can ever gather together all these hollow hints to reconstruct the figure itself. The more there are, the more difficult it becomes. This seeming-wealth of resources leads only to an ever-murkier and clotted impaction.

When viewed in its entirety, the labyrinthine hierarchy of both rarefied and impacted structured absences, microscopically interwoven and knotted, produces an extremely baffling and deliciously provocative effect. The hidden figure in Vereker's works (and, it seems, also in *this* story) seems simultaneously fully impacted *and* fully rarefied, lending it the flavor of an "impossible object," a paradoxical construct rather like an M. C. Escher waterfall. All the myriad structured absences are so elaborately interrelated, logically linked, and intricately embedded that together they form as dense an example of the cipher mode as can probably be found.

This self-perpetuating process of finely crafted evasion and grandly orchestrated lacunae is so much the main engine of the story that this pivotal dependence upon absence is perhaps the most deserving candidate for the hidden figure, for the enigmatic "exquisite scheme" that so obsesses the story's characters as well as its readers. The figure—at least in the James short story if not necessarily in Hugh Vereker's unavailable works—may be precisely this dependence on structured absence—these myriad, gaudily painted and loudly implicated gaps and vacancies enlisted to tell the story of another ever-absent and veiled figure hidden away in books we will never see. Yet to suggest that the use of absence can become a way of covertly demonstrating the central role of absence is really not to "solve" this riddle, but rather to gain a wider perspective on it.

With this in mind, it is interesting to note that it makes sense in an odd way to read *literally* the numerous "somethings" and "nothings" that mask the figure, setting them mentally between quotation marks. We are informed, for instance, that

> the thing we were all so blank about was vividly there. It was something, I guessed, in the primal plan; something like a complex figure in a Persian carpet. He [Vereker] highly approved of this image when I used it. (374)

If instead of reading "something" as the usual indefinite pronoun we read the passage as if it refers to the actual and specific word "something," it almost seems to make a great deal more sense. The same holds true in many other places, as when we read "Corvick's possession of the tip may, on his part, really lead to something," or "the two together would puzzle something out" (373).

If we take all this as referring directly to this central use of non-signifying words—this crucial dependence on hollow shells and strategic indirection—these passages begin to seem like self-reflexive references to the very techniques they themselves embody. Read in this way, we feel a kind of recursive feedback loop in operation—a "strange loop," as Douglas Hofstadter would call it—that uses structured absence to demonstrate covertly the necessity of structured absence within the web of words.

A series of delightfully melodramatic twists propel the later pages of the story. Corvick discovers the secret, at least he says he does, but stubbornly withholds what he knows. He marries Gwendolyn, and apparently reveals it to her. Then Corvick dies in a freak accident, followed soon by Vereker himself, and finally Gwendolyn, too, passes away, never having breathed a word of the secret to the narrator or her second husband, Drayton Deane.

Along with the reader, the narrator and Drayton Deane are left not without a clue but with far too many, each one as insubstantial as air or a mute "something." Through the deft manipulation of structured absence in an intricately embedded cipher mode, James invites the reader to peer into zeros within zeros within zeros in a seemingly infinite regress. We are left to marvel equally over the power of Nothing to fascinate and the artful framing of emptiness that so curiously arrests our full attention.

14
The Woolfian Halo

The meaning of an episode was not inside like a kernel but out-side, enveloping the tale which brought it out only as a glow brings out a haze, in the likeness of one of those misty halos that sometimes are made visible by the spectral illumination of moonshine.

—Joseph Conrad, *Heart of Darkness*

Virginia Woolf's *To the Lighthouse* is without a doubt one of the best examples of the way great art conceals itself. The strikingly origi-nal innovations in style, technique, and narrative structure do not in-trude unduly upon the reader (as they do sometimes in Joyce), but are so subtly and unostentatiously enlisted in the effort to create a world that we often feel their effect while remaining largely unaware of the means. Precisely because they succeed so well in their purpose, the enormous technical innovations do not call particular attention to themselves. With Woolf, we tunnel far into the secret recesses of consciousness—deep into the depths of identity, fate, and existence—and the startling views at-tained tend to eclipse the reader's attention from the approaches em-ployed. The critic, of course, naturally resists.

In an essay on Thomas Hardy, Woolf notes that, though his works are uneven, "there is always about them a little blur of unconsciousness, that halo of freshness and margin of the unexpressed which often pro-duce the most profound sense of satisfaction" (*Second* 269). This is an astute observation regarding Hardy, but it is even more so regarding Woolf. Such approval implies certain aesthetic assumptions that perhaps reveal more about Woolf than her subject. For it is just this "halo of freshness," this hovering "margin of the unexpressed," that we feel so palpably in her own works. "Life is a luminous halo," Woolf notes else-where, and it is just this quality that she recaptures so supremely in her own stories.

A primary resource toward this end involves the manipulation of structured absences, a device so common in Woolf that it is sometimes nearly invisible. The most characteristic pattern is to present impressions, illuminate emotions, and excavate our inmost moods, while yet preserving their inherent mystery by emphasizing their ultimately inexplicable and fathomless source. Typically, a timely deferral to a rarefied structured absence intercedes to reestablish the essential mystery at the heart of such matters just when we seemed about to gain some final access.

In *To the Lighthouse*, for instance, when Lily braces herself for the "awful trial" of having someone look at her painting, we are granted a glimpse of what she feels is at stake, though the core of the matter remains completely in shadow:

> [I]f it must be seen, Mr. Bankes was less alarming than another. But that any other eyes should see the residue of her thirty-three years, the deposit of each day's living mixed *with something more secret than she had ever spoken or shown* in the course of all those days was an agony. (80–81, my emphasis)

The rarefied structured absence intrudes on the very brink of revelation, functioning as an experiential analog to what Lily herself can never verbalize but of which she feels an overwhelming sensibility. Lily's painting, that scrap of canvas and pigment so central to the novel, draws on sources deeper than words, deeper perhaps than her self or the sea that ceaselessly surges around all the characters in this novel.

Similarly, Lily's vexing difficulty with the painting at the end of the novel is mutely characterized as having to do with something she can distinctly feel but cannot name:

> [T]here was something displeasing about the placing of the ships.
> The disproportion there seemed to upset some harmony in her mind. She felt an obscure distress. . . . She must try to get hold of something that evaded her. (286–87)

Always, characters treading the frontiers of consciousness reach out beyond the perimeter of words. The narrative, in order to give shape to such impulses, lapses into inarticulate and overbrimming gesture with structured absence at its center.

Such techniques are not just associated with important issues like Lily's painting. Rather, they crop up unpredictably when least expected in all areas of human affairs. For instance, a simple walk into town with Mrs. Ramsay so excites and disturbs Charles Tansley that we are made to feel it is somehow the most important action that Tansley undertakes in the course of the novel. The sources of his heightened passion, however, remain in darkness: "He felt many things, something in particular that excited him and disturbed him for reasons which he could not give" (20). Or, when young James's attention shifts from a storybook to the blinking lighthouse, Mrs. Ramsay "saw in his eyes, as the interest of the story died away in them, something else take its place, something wondering, pale, like the reflection of a light" (94).

Or, when Minta is driven to tears over the loss of her brooch, the true source of her sadness is not simply the lost memento: "It was her grandmother's brooch; she would rather have lost anything but that, and yet Nancy felt, it might be true that she minded losing her brooch, but she wasn't crying only for that. She was crying for something else. We might all sit down and cry, she felt. But she did not know what for" (117). Or, when at dinner Mrs. Ramsay senses the serenity and contentment in the "profound stillness" of this shared moment, the narrative lapses into a kind of necessary incoherence to convey the evanescent impression:

> It partook, she felt, carefully helping Mr. Bankes to a specially tender piece, of eternity; as she had already felt about something different once before that afternoon; there is a coherence in things, a stability; something, she meant, is immune from change, and shines out. . . . Of such moments, she thought, the thing is made that endures. (158)

At other times, the reader is handed unanswerable questions that set off what we do not know in sharp relief, as when Lily wonders about Mrs. Ramsay's inmost perceptions: "What did the hedge mean to her, what did the garden mean to her, what did it mean to her when a wave broke?" (294), or when Cam wonders about her father in the novel's closing scene: "What could he see? . . . What was he thinking now? she wondered. What was it he sought, so fixedly, so intently, so silently?" (307).

Even the most pedestrian matters take on an alluring patina of mystery, as when the children laugh at some private joke that neither we nor Mrs. Ramsay are privy to: "It was something quite apart from everything else, something they were hoarding up to laugh over in their own room. It was not about their father, she hoped. No, she thought not. What was it, she wondered" (164).

This is but a very small sampling of the dozens upon dozens of similar structured absences Woolf employs so regularly that they form a kind of internal, subliminal rhythm. In all these passages, we find the same types of rarefied structured absences that James put to use in "The Figure in the Carpet," but the effect is entirely different. In *To the Lighthouse*, there is no hierarchical embedding of the absences, no syllogistic relations linking them together, no sense of a carefully plotted puzzle binding them logically together. On the contrary, the absences in Woolf's novel pop up as so many soap bubbles in bath water, iridescent and fragile, each one entire in itself without any sense that the bubbles taken together construct a larger riddle challenging the reader's rational faculties.

In *To the Lighthouse*, all things potentially shade off into the unknown. All human action, all perceived objects, all conscious moments of attention seem enveloped in a luminous mystery equally dispersed in all directions, ultimately inexpressible. Whereas in "The Figure in the Carpet" a central enigma governs a hierarchy of more local absences that are densely embedded and logically linked, there is in Woolf's novel no purely isolatable pivotal enigma controlling and ordering all the others. There is also no sense that Woolf's unknowns can be "solved" or rendered more intelligible, or that pursuing one might lead to a general revelation touching on all the others.

In James's short story, a fundamental "figure" becomes a kind of grail or Rosetta Stone that, if discovered, would work as a key to unlock all the other more local mysteries. Though the elusive figure escapes and consequently cannot be directly named, there is a lingering sense that this inexpressibility might be overcome in the future if only we keep at it a little longer or study the patterns with greater concentration.

In *To the Lighthouse*, however, the reason why we accept the structured absences as they come and are not particularly driven to "solve" or unmask them is *because* they are not embedded, *because* they are not logically linked and algorithmically arranged. They emerge paratactically and are not made dependent on or subordinate to each other. Since they stand alone, we leave them alone. They accumulate in number, page by page, but we allow them their self-identity, each standing alone, and the effect is a parallel outward dispersion—a simultaneous sense of myriad mysteries emanating from myriad sources. If there is a sense of a "greater mystery," it is simply that all things are mysterious. Whereas in "The Figure in the Carpet" the Great Mystery is felt to be a single, potentially recoverable entity, in *To the Lighthouse* the Great Mystery simply envelops all things in a luminous haze.

This, then, is the basic difference between a cipher pattern and the halo mode. Both works employ structured absences of similar cast, but their manner of deployment creates completely different effects. As a result, these two stories conjure up entirely dissimilar universes, presenting us with versions of existence as different as night from day. Here, it is perhaps worth mentioning that both James and Woolf in other works adopt the opposite mode, or, more commonly, use both patterns together, as in *The Wings of the Dove* or *Mrs. Dalloway*.

There are, to be sure, a few instances in *To the Lighthouse* where the structured absences are embedded, but these moments are fairly isolated, and the "chains" they form do not extend far. For instance, when Lily is trying to pinpoint the "something that evaded her" in her painting, we are informed that "*what she wished to get hold of* was that very jar on the nerves, *the thing itself* before it has been made *anything*" (287, my emphasis). Or, in the "Time Passes" section, we are told that "*whatever else may perish* and disappear, *what lies here is steadfast*" (191, my emphasis). In both passages, structured absences are placed in logical relationships, one depending upon the other, as in "The Figure in the Carpet." But these hypotactic patterns do not link up with the many other absences strewn across Woolf's pages, so the overall paratactic arrangement eclipses these transient and comparatively weak hierarchies.

In the cipher mode, our reaction to individual structured absences is typically hesitant and tentative. Because these absences are made dependent on other unknowns, our perplexity holds our response in check. When numerous absences are linked, we rapidly approach the point of "cognitive overload," since we cannot keep so many open variables simultaneously in mind. The elaborate structured absences clustering round the "figure" in the James story focus our attention on *what we have not grasped*, initiating a search for a nameless but seemingly isolatable something so that we are kept ever-expectant, ever-alert, holding back in our response because we are forever trapped in the provisional.

In the halo mode, individual structured absences often initiate a more complete reaction, potentially radiating a good deal more positive energy than in the cipher mode. The more open and unfettered structured absences in *To the Lighthouse*, for example, encourage a free and expansive response unchecked by any suspicion of a larger conspiracy binding the story's silences together. For instance, when Mrs. Ramsay muses over Lily's special qualities, they come across vibrantly because they remain partly veiled:

> With Lily it was different. . . . in her little grey dress with her little puckered face and her little Chinese eyes. Everything about her was so small. . . . There was in Lily a thread of something; a flare of something; something of her own which Mrs. Ramsay liked very much indeed, but no man would, she feared. (157)

All these mute somethings force the reader to accommodate qualities that can't be named, ineffable and fleeting feelings that must remain unspecified. But we do have a sense of this something-quality of Lily's from the book as a whole, especially when the narrative perspective periodically occupies Lily's own consciousness. So Woolf's retreat into structured absence in the above passage is not so much perceived as a failure or short circuit, but rather as a positive assertion that Lily's special quality will remain inchoate and inexpressible though deeply felt. The reader is warned away from words and encouraged to recognize and cultivate other avenues of response.

In themselves, structured absences and inexpressibility tropes are not difficult to manufacture, and in lesser hands they can quickly scuttle an entire novel. As noted in the previous chapter, gestures of inexpressibility and declarations of wordless feeling can easily lapse into cliché and maudlin sentimentality. The structured absences and gesturing phrases bent to such ends are not always or necessarily profound, or even effective, as many a Harlequin romance testifies. So it is the larger context in which these elements live that determines whether they generate a dynamic and vital energy or completely misfire. "A light here required a shadow there" (82), notes Lily, but it is the quality of the light that determines the success of the shadows.

As the previous examples from Djuna Barnes and Bill Kemmett demonstrate, along with the many others we have examined since, inexpressibility tropes do not absolve the writer of the burden to "make it new," and there is no end to constructing new approaches to the domain of the wordless. In *To the Lighthouse*, it is in a sense Mrs. Ramsay herself who becomes the living incarnation of wordless awareness and silent wisdom. Through Woolf's seemingly effortless shifts in perspective and voice, we share in Mrs. Ramsay's lucid perceptions, her flashes of insight, as well as her deep and wordless sorrow in the face of death, change, and the passage of time. In short, we come to think of her in much the same way as Lily does, and we long for some closer union, some more direct and complete access to her way of seeing and her ways of knowing.

There is a memorable passage where Lily senses all this that stands as one of Woolf's most striking evocations of inexpressibility, emphasizing the failure of words while yet using words to affirm the vital reality of that which words fail to approach:

> [S]he imagined how in the chambers of the mind and heart of the woman who was, physically, touching her, were stood, like the treasures in the tombs of kings, tablets bearing sacred inscriptions, which if one could spell them out, would teach one everything, but they would never be offered openly, never made public. What art was there, known to love or cunning, by which one pressed through into those secret cham-

bers? What device for becoming, like waters poured into one
jar, inextricably the same, one with the object one adored? (79)

Such inaccessible tablets spirited away in hidden chambers are made
at least partially available through just such devices, through just such
deftly embroidered absences woven into the fabric of art.

15
Unnaming the World

> She wanted to say not one thing, but everything. Little words
> that broke up the thought and dismembered it said nothing.
> . . . one could say nothing to nobody. . . . Words fluttered
> sideways and struck the object inches too low. . . . For how
> could one express in words these emotions of the body? ex-
> press that emptiness there? . . . It was one's body feeling, not
> one's mind.
>
> —Virginia Woolf, *To the Lighthouse*

Something" is a word we pass over lightly. It is everywhere we look,
and yet we do not see it. When we do stumble up against it, we shrug
it off as meaningless "filler," a "place-holder," or an innocuous "indefinite pronoun." It is simply not important, certainly not as important as
the Big Ideas like God or the Life-Force or Eternity, hardly worthy of
consideration by minds engaged in far weightier topics like metaphysics
or deep structure or Derridean "différance." "Something" is slighter than
slight. It doesn't matter much. It's nothing at all.

Such an attitude, though virtually universal, is sadly benighted. It completely misses the enormous importance of a word we habitually impress into the service of our most profound thoughts, yet a word that, by
definition, does not mean anything at all. The fact is that when we do try
to talk about God or the Life-Force or Eternity, whenever we attempt to
articulate thoughts on metaphysics or deep-structure or différance, we
find that we cannot get anywhere at all without using "something" at the
most crucial junctures.

In a passage about the essence of religion, for instance, Alfred North
Whitehead grapples with *what cannot be said*, and wordless feeling is
able to break through into sense only because the ministrations of "something" allow the fleeting, the inchoate, and the undefined to take up temporary lodging in words:

> Religion is the vision of something which stands beyond, be-
> hind, and within, the passing flux of immediate things; some-
> thing which is real, and yet waiting to be realized; something
> which is remote in possibility, and yet the greatest of present
> facts; something that gives meaning to all that passes, and yet
> eludes apprehension; something whose possession is the final
> good, and yet is beyond reach, something which is the ulti-
> mate ideal, and the hopeless quest. (*Science* 275)

If we could unmask the antecedents of these somethings, the mystery of
existence would be solved. But we know we cannot unmask them, so
they stand as emblems of veiled revelation, totems signifying the end
of desire.

It might be argued that these same intimations could be expressed
without using "something," but this is really not so, for then the effect
would be categorically different. Whitehead's repeated deferral to "something," to an inchoate touchstone, continually reaffirms the actual existence of this unnameable entity. "Something"—not so much an empty
word but rather one of ever-virtual potential—grants transcendence a semantic and grammatical home, thus implicitly legitimizing such visionary
awareness without incurring any obligation to explain it. Indeed, the
complete reliance on such a weightless and untethered word tacitly suggests that such flickering intimations will always remain beyond final
discursive embodiment.

In constructing his castle in the air, Whitehead deftly employs a series of rarefied structured absences ("something which stands beyond . . .
something which is real . . . something which is remote . . ." etc.), yet
interestingly the cumulative effect of so many rarefied structured absences is to fabricate a larger *impacted* structured absence. So we are left
with a complex sense of reverberating uncertainty that is simultaneously
rarefied and impacted—an absence built up out of a series of inscrutable
somethings cemented together like so many hollow bricks.

Ostensibly a "definition" of religion, Whitehead's repeated retreat
into blankness becomes a tacit rejection of the word "religion" (or any
words for that matter) to fully convey the essence of the actual experience or quality that the words seek to encompass. By virtually replacing
"religion" with the more richly inchoate "something," the paradoxical
and self-contradictory attributes that Whitehead goes on to describe seem
to incrementally annihilate all linguistic intrusions into this realm.

In his influential *Lectures on Art and Poems* of 1850, Washington
Allston uses a stylistic strategy similar to Whitehead's in discussing the
essential nature, not of religion, but of art. For Allston, our response to
art testifies to the mysterious "unknown Power" at its source:

> [T]he several characteristics, Originality, Poetic Truth, Invention, each imply a something not inherent in the objects imitated, but which must emanate alone from the mind of the artist. (106)

As he draws near to the essence of great art, Allston gives way to a mute "something," emphasizing the unknowable and indescribable nature of this central mystery. By declaring that a "something" emanates from the artist's mind to imbue the canvas with life, Allston not only leaves this ungraspable something-entity undisclosed, but he draws particular attention to the fact that he cannot better describe it. In this way, Allston emphasizes the poverty of language when venturing into these precincts, while also using language to illuminate them as best he can. In fact, Allston's continual dependence on "something" at just such moments is one of the most characteristic aspects of his work. In other places, he even further emphasizes this elusive "something" by italicizing it (as in "a certain *exclusive something*" or "a *peculiar something*"). Though Allston was a respected poet, his perspective is that of a painter for whom the limitations of language in these matters are always graphically apparent.

Allston's outlook is plainly indebted to Coleridge and the German idealists, but the most distinctive aspect of this first American art treatise is the emphasis on the subjective nature of art. For Allston, art is expression, not imitation; communication, not representation. Art is a projection of an internal awareness that must find suitable forms. And yet the power within us that struggles toward expression must remain suggestively vague when rendered in language: "May it not be something *from ourselves*, which is reflected back by the object,—something with which, as it were, we imbue the object, making it correspond to the reality within us?" (86). These crucial somethings function to preserve and celebrate the inscrutable inner workings of the artistic process.

In this sense, "something," the supremely empty word, does actually accomplish its intended purpose by marking the exact spot where language gives out. Throughout this discourse on art, "something" maps the coordinates of deepest mystery. In Allston's elaborate and elegantly evasive style, "something" becomes a pivot point to signal a difficulty and acknowledge mystery. In fact, without such rarefied structured absences, Allston could not adequately convey this complex sense of positive assertion intermixed with vibrant uncertainty.

The same general situation obtains in Sir Thomas Browne's musings on the soul in *Religio Medici*:

> Thus are we men, and we know not how; there is something in us, that can be without us, and will be after us, though it is

strange that it has no history, what it was before us, nor can tell how it entered us. (43)

Here, as in the previous examples, the word that bears the full weight of Browne's searching speculation is "something," a word that gestures toward something it itself is not, toward something, it is hinted, that cannot now or ever be adequately named. On the level of readerly dynamics, we can also note that the vaporous sense Browne is trying to convey regarding the unnameable essence within us is replicated lexically by this "something," the unnameable essence of this sentence. By analogy, our inmost self is figured as a cryptic sentence that makes a motion toward meaning, but which comes to a full stop before achieving its desired goal.

We might refer to this special type of something as an "ontological something," since it insists upon the being and irreducible actuality of an ineffable entity. Classifying such ontological somethings as nothing more than "indefinite pronouns" or "indefinite noun phrases" simply packages them in such a way that we completely miss their true centrality. By lumping them together with other more casual and untroubled uses of "something," we allow ourselves to ignore the yawning breach in our signifying systems that these central somethings genuinely represent.

Such somethings are not just "place-holders," because in these instances there is nothing definable for them to be holding the place of. These somethings are not just temporary stand-ins or surrogates for weightier cognomens with more specific meanings. These somethings are completely on their own, simultaneously signifying nothing and everything, providing habitation for the ineffable in their hollow hallways. At our most far-seeing moments, what must remain wordless signifies its inevitable attendance by this, its most common calling card—"something."

In these three passages, we witness a calculated effort to "unname" religion, to unname art and unname the soul, to strip away our too-comfortable acquaintance with these seemingly unproblematic words in order to liberate the vital mysteries at their root. If, as Ernst Cassirer posits, "all theoretical cognition takes its departure from a world already preformed by language" (28), we might counter by insisting that there is always an accompanying residuum of doubt, a lingering awareness of the limitations and falsifications of language. For this reason, our fullest experiential perceptions often become, at least in part, a process of unnaming and bringing into conscious awareness all those aspects of existence that language misses and that words cannot convey. "Language is incomplete and fragmentary," Whitehead notes elsewhere, "and merely registers a stage in the average advance beyond ape-mentality. But all men enjoy flashes of insight beyond meanings already stabilized in etymology and grammar" (*Adventures* 291).

Even if it is primarily through language that we can analyze, conceptualize, and categorize experience, language can also become a formidable obstruction, cutting us off from as much as it bestows by forcing everything into preformed cubbyholes. In this sense, our most completely realized experiences often reject the very language that may have already functioned as that experience's most important catalyst.

This strategy of unnaming does not assume that language is indeterminate or undecidable, but rather springs from the perception that language is simply inadequate. In spirit, the use of such ontological somethings flies in the face of the poststructural notion of omnipresent, inescapable textuality, since they implicitly trust in and insist upon the verifiable reality of other ways of knowing. Like Chaucer's retraction or Kafka's instructions to burn his manuscripts, these passages make a gesture toward self-erasure and unnaming, but it is the gesture itself that is the mainspring of the writer's hoped-for effect. With any true erasure or ultimate unnaming, we would be left with nothing at all and could not even detect a gap or an absence since there would be no text left to house them.

Though words fail, the use of ontological somethings and structured absences dramatize this failure in such a way that meanings beyond words, or at least their shadows, are ushered into the theater of the printed page and seated in its white space.

Insofar as these pressurized somethings gesture toward an inaccessible realm, a felt something beyond the reach of words, we might relate them, at least tentatively, to the linguistic notion of *deixis*, but a deixis of a very special and extreme mode that we might designate as "default deixis." Linguists generally define deictic words as those that point to things indexically within a certain contextual setting. Words like "this" and "that," "here" and "there," shift in meaning and referent from instance to instance as the frame of reference shifts. Linguists typically further distinguish between *person deixis* (I/you, we/they), *place deixis* (this/that, here/there), and *time deixis* (now/later, before/after). All such manifestations of verbal deixis taken together simultaneously reflect and establish the spatial, temporal, and directional axes of a contextually bound utterance (Rommetveit *Words* 51–54). Time deixis also employs verb tense, and there are intrinsically deictic verbs as well, such as "come" and "go," "bring" and "take." In context, a sentence like "I brought this here for you" consists almost entirely of deictic terms, as does "You came to take that there for me?"

Since ontological somethings function primarily as a way of *pointing-toward* from within a discursively specific frame of reference, they are at least partly deictic in nature. But the enigmatic fact that what is pointed toward is singled out as being beyond the limits of language and is, in fact, rather loudly advertised as a "thing" that cannot be named, suggests that these somethings represent a deixis in default—a mute but vigorous gesturing toward an inchoate blankness.

In this regard, it is important to distinguish between "something" in its more mundane usage as an untroubled indefinite pronoun ("There's something in my eye." "Bring something to read.") and the special somethings employed by Whitehead, Allston, and Browne. These ontological somethings are neither anaphoric nor cataphoric—that is, they are not bound to any previously disclosed antecedent or to an "antecedent" yet to be revealed. They are simply what they are, and what they are is precisely what we cannot discursively grasp.

The common factor running through all such somethings is an inarticulate gesturing beyond the parameters of their particular discursive framework. Whether the topic be religion, art, or the soul, it is as if each of these authors is saying "With regard to what we are focusing upon, something exists that cannot be put into words but of which I am nevertheless aware." This insistence upon the actuality and the ontological validity of such nameless somethings is the most subtly significant aspect of these constructions.

We have, of course, already come upon quite a few of these somethings, and it might be well to enlarge our pool of specimens by recalling several for further inspection. When in Joyce's "The Dead," Gabriel, during his climactic vision of Gretta at the stairhead, fleetingly recognizes that "There was a grace and mystery in her attitude as if she were a symbol of something," the vibrant yet inchoate nature of Gabriel's recognition is effectively brought home by depending so utterly on "something". Wordlessness or, more exactly, a word devoid of content, becomes the only suitable analogue to the vision itself. In Lawrence's *St. Mawr*, when Lou attempts to explain why she has chosen to remain alone on the secluded ranch, her impassioned outpouring bears certain similarities, rhetorically and stylistically, to Whitehead's musings on religion:

> There's something else for me, mother. There's something else even that loves me and wants me. I can't tell you what it is. It's a spirit. And it's here, on this ranch. It's here, in this landscape. It's something more real to me than men are, and it soothes me, and it holds me up. I don't know what it is, definitely. It's something wild. . . . (158)

These somethings are not temporarily undesignated entities with recoverable antecedents but rather are indexical signs pointing toward a dimly perceived but unformalizable presence. As in the previous examples, these somethings gesture toward that which cannot be captured in language. They point toward that which cannot be pointed toward in a physical sense, toward that which is not precisely locatable and yet which is firmly felt to be present all the same.

Similarly, when Frost proclaims "Something there is that doesn't love a wall," when Wordsworth reaches toward a "something far more deeply interfused" that permeates all creation, or when W. S. Graham strives to capture on paper "something beyond any idea / Of pleasure," or even when Faulkner simply validates "a smell like rotting cucumbers and something else which had no name," we begin to appreciate the versatility and malleability of these ontological somethings.

When in *Giants in the Earth* Beret is driven insane by "something vague and intangible hovering in the air," when Mrs. Ramsay simply thinks of Lily's special quality as "a thread of something, a flare of something, something of her own," or when in *The Sacred Fount* we, along with the narrator, cogitate upon the "something ultimate" at the center of that Kafkaesque drawing room comedy, what is implicated in each case is precisely what cannot be said with regard to the topic under consideration. In each case, *something* is an indexical, keyed to a certain topic, that gestures outward to a sphere of meaning that can be registered but not directly communicated.

No doubt, some will object that the notion of verbal deixis is misapplied here because such phrases do not point toward anything "real," no isolatable or tangible object. But then what are these phrases doing? What purpose do they serve but to point toward what cannot be seen and to specify what must always remain unspecific because such things are by nature beyond the grasp of words. They are faint registrations upon a language apparatus that is not sensitive enough to plot them more exactly, directional markers in an unmapped world without compass points or fixed features. Yet they are phrases we cannot possibly do without, phrases that we habitually employ in our most profound cogitations. The fact that they are "empty" only increases their utility.

The range of this mere handful of examples already confirms the deictic properties of something, for all these various somethings do not refer to the same something. Rather, they simultaneously mask and emblem forth a wide range of unnameable sylphs that can be distinguished, even through they cannot be delineated individually. Two basic properties of deictic words involve a shifting of reference and a shifting of boundaries (Clark 89–90). In a statement like "I was born here," for example, "here" might denote "here in this room" or "here in Wisconsin" or "here in North America," depending on the context. The reference not only shifts from one thing to another, but it also shifts elastically in terms of that thing's boundaries. Similarly, "this" can designate "this dime" or "this water tower" or "this thunderstorm," from one context to another.

Although "something" may at first seem to designate an incorporeal and amorphous entity about which nothing more can be said, this is not completely the case. For even these ontological somethings gesture toward an unlimited range of *different* unnameable entities—that is, "something" shifts in reference and shifts its boundaries just as other deictic terms do. Insofar as absences are inevitably structured, even the sort of extremely rarefied structured absence signaled by "something" is shaped by discernible parameters that shift from instance to instance: Gretta's pose that becomes a "symbol of something," Faulkner's smell of "something else which had no name," and the "something rare and strange" for which John Marcher waits a lifetime do not refer to the same something. The smell without a name is not what Gretta is a symbol of, and neither of these ineffables is what John Marcher awaits. Nor are any of these somethings the same as Whitehead's something at the root of all religion, or Allston's something that is the essence of art, or the elusive something that Thomas Browne discerns within us.

Plainly, all these somethings are not the same something. All these gestures-in-default point mutely toward markedly different absent entities. And yet, as wonderfully various as they are, they do seem to occupy the same "sphere," namely that realm beyond language and the shaping and organizing categories of conceptual-rational thought made possible by language. Whether one wishes to credit or deny the validity of such momentary visions, one must at least agree that the contextual sense of these utterances is precisely that—carving out a portion from our talk and leaving instead a trembling blankness as a tribute to what we cannot get at with words.

As different as all these individual somethings are, there is, therefore, a family resemblance running through them. Having nothing necessarily to do with their subject matter or even with the various posited ungraspable "antecedents," the property in common is nothing more than the implicit affirmation that such wordless awareness is genuine. Visionary awareness and the possibility of transcendence are thus indirectly validated by allowing words to run in and out of blank zones of obvious "unknowing" that are nevertheless felt to be junctures of the highest significance.

Another common feature of deictic terms is that they usually come in mutually distinguishing pairs (here/there, this/that), and we might propose the contrast something/nothing in this regard. But the extremes to which these ontological somethings are pushed immediately begin to break down the implied contrast with "nothing" so that the difference between something and nothing quickly dissolves. Under sufficient pressure, something and nothing merge on the far side of the mind. Nothing becomes something, something nothing, when these words are pressed into service of embodying whatever it is we cannot discursively know.

This tendency becomes particularly evident in negative theology, where the affirmation of a registered nothing, of what lies beyond human comprehension, is paradoxically an encounter with an ineffable and nameless something. Negativity is thus adopted as the best means of bodying forth not a sheer nullity but rather an inchoate presence—a veiled or invisible something rather than a literal absence.

In *The Cloud of Unknowing*, for instance, an anonymous fourteenth-century mystical work, the very shortcomings of human reason make possible a state of higher enlightened "unknowing," which is figured as a "nothing" or a "blind nought" even though it is experienced as a positive fact:

> Let be this everywhere and this aught, in comparison of this nowhere and this nought. Reck thee never if thy wits cannot understand this nought, for surely I love it much the better. It is so worthy a thing in itself that they cannot understand it. This nought may be better felt than seen; for it is full blind and full dark to them that have but a little while looked thereupon. Nevertheless (if I shall trulier say) a soul is more blinded in feeling of it for abundance of ghostly light, than for any darkness or wanting of bodily light. What is he that calleth it nought? Surely it is our outer man and not our inner. Our inner man calleth it All. (McCann 91)

The sense of "nought" or "nothing" in this context is all but indistinguishable from the somethings employed by Whitehead, Browne, Joyce, or Lawrence. *The Cloud* author's "blind nought" is plainly a something, a positive quality or achieved state of awareness, and describing it as a nought is little more than an attempt to emphasize its incorporeal and unknowable aspects. In this regard we might note, following Henri Bergson, that while "nothing" may readily achieve a relational or contextual meaning, it is doubtful that it has any inherent existential validity. No matter how barren they may seem, our nothings, noughts, and néants never actually escape their own somethinghood. We are continually mistaking a nothing that is for a nothing that is not there, to paraphrase Wallace Stephens, and a nothing that *is* is really no nothing at all.

In his discussion of "the idea of nothing" in *Creative Evolution*, Bergson highlights the ways we fall into the easy delusion of believing that we can directly apprehend absolute nothingness. Inevitably, we thoroughly contradict such an assumption upon its very formulation by reifying such nothings, thus lending them a covert substantiality. To conceive of nothing, we must necessarily focus upon something, and such somethings are never void of all content, but necessarily are built of mind-matter with discernible attributes. As Bergson puts it, "we cannot imagine a nought without perceiving, at least confusedly, that we are imagining it, consequently that we are acting, that we are thinking, and therefore that something still subsists" (303).

The underlying reason for our persistent belief in the actual insubstantiality of our obviously substantial nothings, Bergson explains, is our predisposition to assume that "the full is an embroidery on the canvas of the void, that being is superimposed on nothing, and that in the idea of 'nothing' there is less than in 'something'" (302). Bergson not only takes exception to such a mind-set, arguing instead that "the full always succeeds the full" (307), but he goes on to demonstrate that there is actually *more* in the idea of nothing, as opposed to the simple affirmation of an object's existence.

In this sense, negation is not opposed to affirmation, but represents an "affirmation of the second degree" (313), being a secondary operation on an already preexisting affirmation of some kind. The fact that this secondary operation represents a denial, a subtraction, an erasure, does not make it any less a positive and active operation. As Kenneth Burke has observed, "You may or may not agree with Bergson when he says that we can't have an idea of nothing. But one thing is certain—any *image* you have of 'nothing' will necessarily be an image of *something*, otherwise it can't be an image" (169).

"Nothing" represents not the opposite of something, but its mirror-image, the selfsame thing perceived from the other side of the glass. As such, we might include "nothing" as another variety of default deixis and speak without paradox of an "ontological nothing" (a nothing that is), which is identical with an ontological something save that its unnameable nature is highlighted by approaching it from the negative, as in the passage from *The Cloud of Unknowing*.

From a Bergsonian perspective, therefore, "nothing" is but another variety of "something" that has undergone a marvelous sea-change. Consequently, if all our nothings are really somethings masquerading as less than what they are, then our ontological somethings can also be figuratively described as nothings insofar as we might want to accentuate their unnameable essence. Whereas "something" emphasizes the immediate actuality of the unnameable presence it gestures toward, "nothing" emphasizes its unnameable aspect to the point where the positive content of such a thought seems to vanish.

Such a characterization of our relationship to imagined voids and experienced nothingness, however, is directly at odds with what is probably a more widespread tendency to valorize our conjured nothings as instances of authentic emptiness in themselves. For example, regarding Rousseau's description of an objectless and unappeasable desire, Paul de Man observes that "one hesitates to use terms such as nostalgia or desire to designate this kind of consciousness, for all nostalgia or desire is desire for something or for someone; here, the consciousness does not result from the absence of something, but consists of the presence of a nothingness" (18).

But it is precisely this train of thought that Bergson shrugs aside as a mere "pseudo-idea" or "pseudo-problem." Though the abyss of death or the empty vastness of interstellar space may inspire a responsive dread or exhilaration at the prospect of endless nothing, human representations and conceptions of the void are themselves always full rather than empty, always possessing some positive content rather than being an instance of pure nullity. In this respect, de Man's distinction is more delusory than real: the "absence of something" is itself a nothing (the only kind we can know), and the "*presence* of a nothingness" is always a something and cannot be otherwise.

Fair is foul and foul is fair, one might say, and so our somethings run in and out of our nothings rather as warp and woof whose patterned entanglement weaves a seamless cloth of the frailest of yarn—over and under, under and over, the somethings above and the nothings under, but each as substantial as its twin.

Interestingly, Bergson's insistence that voids are always full rather than empty would strike a sympathetic response in the area of contemporary physics. After having scoffed for so long at the traditional wisdom that nature abhors a vacuum, particle physicists have in recent decades abandoned the idea that vacuums are truly empty. Vacuums, we are now informed, are positively seething with "virtual particles" that cannot be directly detected but whose existence is confirmed by their outward effects.

Rather than representing nothing, nullity, or emptiness, the "quantum vacuum," as Timothy Ferris explains, "is a seething ocean, out of which virtual particles are constantly emerging and into which they constantly subside" (352). Or, as Lawrence Krauss puts it,

> The vacuum of modern particle theory is a strange place indeed. From an unchanging "void" it has become an active arena out of which particles might be created or into which they might be destroyed. Just as light was supposed to excite waves in the aether according to Newton, we now envisage elementary particles to be excitations out of the vacuum state. That vacuum might even be the "source" of all matter in the universe. (41)

Krauss is well aware that some of the most ancient known cosmologies, like that espoused by Anaximander, are closer to the modern view than any intervening theory. Fritjof Capra's *The Tao of Physics* exhaustively explores such parallels, though he focuses exclusively on the affinities between ancient eastern mysticism and the world of modern physics. Capra observes,

> The distinction between matter and empty space finally had to be abandoned when it became evident that virtual particles came into being spontaneously out of the void, and vanish again into the void, without any nucleon or other strongly interacting particle being present. . . .
>
> The relation between virtual particles and the vacuum is an essentially dynamic relation; the vacuum is truly a "living Void," pulsating in endless rhythms of creation and destruction. . . . From its role as an empty container of the physical phenomena, the void has emerged as a dynamic quantity of utmost importance. (222–23)

Two short poems, Thom Gunn's "The Annihilation of Nothing" and Robert Frost's "For Once, Then, Something," can serve to demonstrate the literary significance of this something-nothing nature of void. Gunn's poem opens on a scene of Armageddon, most probably an ongoing nuclear apocalypse that rips the fabric of creation even while the poet looks on aghast:

The Annihilation of Nothing

Nothing remained: Nothing, the wanton name
That nightly I rehearsed till lead away
To a dark sleep, or sleep that held one dream.

In this a huge contagious absence lay,
More space than space, over the cloud and slime,
Defined but by the encroachments of its sway.

Stripped to indifference at the turns of time,
Whose end I knew, I woke without desire,
And welcomed zero as a paradigm.

But now it breaks—images burst with fire
Into the quiet sphere where I have bided,
Showing the landscape holding yet entire:

The power that I envisaged, that presided
Ultimate in its abstract devastations,
Is merely change, the atoms it divided

> Complete, in ignorance, new combinations.
> Only an infinite finitude I see
> In those peculiar lovely variations.
>
> It is despair that nothing cannot be
> Flares in the mind and leaves a smoky mark
> Of dread.
> > > > Look upward. Neither firm nor free,
>
> Purposeless matter hovers in the dark.

With the very first phrase, Gunn presents the paradox that soon becomes the focus of the entire poem: "Nothing remained." That some horrendous devastation has been loosed on the world, wiping out all that we hold most dear, is the most obvious and immediate sense of the statement; yet even here there are the seeds of contradiction. How can nothing, if it is truly nothing, *remain*? Can something be said to remain if it really isn't anything at all? This same paradox is carried over into the poet's recurring dream in which a "huge contagious absence lay." Once again, absence or nothingness is figured as an entity with measurable attributes. Moreover, this absence not only occupies space, but it somehow occupies *more* "space than space."

In the unspeakable tragedy and grief of the moment, the poet tries to take refuge in thoughts of nothingness and non-being, positively welcoming "zero as a paradigm"—the somehow comforting notion that underlying all things is a prior nothingness out of which everything has arisen and into which everything will return. But despite the total destruction seething all around, everything is not destroyed. The landscape remains and the atoms remain as numerous as before, but now floating free to join in "peculiar lovely variations." The poet is brought to the shocking revelation that he has mistaken the imagined power of nothingness, which he had thought "Ultimate in its abstract devastations," for the very different power of change and transformation that the cataclysm has unleashed. Matter is not destroyed but *conserved* through recombination. Even at the last extremity, there is no nothing, just transmogrified somethings.

Denied the allure of final and complete oblivion, the poet is forced to relinquish the oddly consoling and somehow compensatory thought that such unparalleled destruction will be followed by complete nothingness:

> It is despair that nothing cannot be
> Flares in the mind and leaves a smoky mark
> Of dread.

> Look upward. Neither firm nor free,
>
> Purposeless matter hovers in the dark.

What is left is not nothing but "purposeless matter," whose persistence specifically repudiates the possibility of nothing. Though Armageddon may wipe out humanity and even annihilate the earth itself, there will still not be nothing. The atoms and particles will persist. The cosmos will persist, and on a cosmic scale the destruction of one infinitesimal planet would be scarcely noticeable.

In one sense, the poem is an impossible poem. No poem or poet could survive the destruction it describes. Yet the "impossible" fact of its existence emphasizes, at least figuratively, that "nothing cannot be" and that all things will persist, even if strangely and terribly transformed. While the title, "The Annihilation of Nothing," may have seemed at first to presage a destruction so complete that it could only be conveyed by an intensifying double negative, the phrase actually turns out to refer, quite literally, to the annihilation of our fond ideas of nothing. In this respect, Gunn's poem is something of a "thought experiment" that explores the hypothesis of nothingness, which turns out for Gunn, as it had for Bergson, to be purely illusory.

Robert Frost takes a different, though complementary, approach in "For Once, Then, Something" where, rather than demonstrating the impossibility of nothing, the poet validates the existence of an inchoate something that cannot be better named. The object of the poet's search, the elusive end of his desire, exists as a glimmering awareness that cannot be further delineated and so must remain always unnamed. The poem opens with recollections of the poet gazing Narcissus-like down into wells, trying to see we know not what. Indeed, it is difficult to imagine what anyone might hope to see. Yet it is this dedication to an activity without clear purpose or likely reward that is indirectly figured as the paradigm of aesthetic endeavor:

> Others taunt me with having knelt at well-curbs
> Always wrong to the light, so never seeing
> Deeper down in the well than where the water
> Gives me back in a shining surface picture
> Me myself in the summer heaven, godlike,
> Looking out of a wreath of fern and cloud puffs.

> (276)

The Narcissus motif immediately suggests the impossibility of ever getting outside oneself or of seeing beyond the inexorable limitations of personhood. The mirrored surface reflects the observer's face and, rather like Plato's cave, allows only indirect observation of the outside world.

But the surface is occasionally translucent, especially during those rare moments when it is undisturbed, and at least once the poet did see down into the depths, glimpsing something beyond the mirror-image:

> *Once*, when trying with chin against well-curb,
> I discerned, as I thought, beyond the picture,
> Through the picture, a something white, uncertain,
> Something more of the depths—and then I lost it.
> Water came to rebuke the too clear water.
> One drop fell from a fern, and lo, a ripple
> Shook whatever it was lay there at bottom,
> Blurred it, blotted it out. What was that whiteness?
> Truth? A pebble of quartz? For once, then, something.
>
> (276)

As Richard Poirier has pointed out, such an unstudied and colloquial falling back on "something" is characteristic of Frost's poetry and a prime example of the way Frost is able to make "philosophical skepticism indistinguishable from the lilt of country talk" (*Renewal* 174).[1] Like the dynamic capacity of an empty vessel, that central image of Taoist thought, "something" accommodates an endless range of possible entities without favoring any particular meaning.

As with the previous examples of ontological somethings, Frost's something is a word to signal what words can never capture. Consequently, the poem celebrates that which eludes the poem, and the poet's final achievement resides precisely in his meticulously rendered and resonant failure. Though we cannot describe more exactly the nature of the something at the bottom of the well, the poem unapologetically affirms the actuality of that something—that ungraspable something that makes writing about what can't be written down so vitally important. Demonstrating that there are spheres of knowing unrecoverable in words by casting this insight into a styled structure, itself made of words, validates the existence of such wordless knowledge in a uniquely authoritative way.

In both Frost's and Gunn's poems, we have no way of knowing or naming exactly what it is that we are asked to focus upon, except perhaps to say that they appeal to states of mind beyond the edges of language. Frost's flickering "something" hidden in the shimmering depths, or Gunn's nonexistent "nothing" that the "purposeless matter" around him continually reproves, tacitly challenge the reader to grasp something not directly present but conjured up through the artistry of indirection.

All the various strategies examined thus far for throwing language into default, these calculated acts of unnaming, seem to actively conjure a state of dynamic "unknowing," to borrow the *Cloud* author's term. An almost aggressive campaign of unnaming leaves the object of attention unformalized, though richly and resonantly present—in fact all the more present for being unformalized. Such unknowing can surpass the limits of the known, at least momentarily, much as a flying fish is suspended awhile on wings above its native element.

So it is that Whitehead unnames "religion" by substituting a series of something-phrases as more adequate approaches to that supremely inchoate impulse, and Browne unnames the "soul" by substituting "something" as a more suitably nebulous analog to whatever it is that "soul" is felt to designate. In general, the settling upon "something" as the only adequate resource when tiptoeing along the outermost fringes of language stems from the realization that language itself, because of its necessarily schematic nature, conceals as much or more than it reveals.

By allowing vibrant mystery to be clothed in an opaque skin of certitude, the act of naming often falsifies as much as it clarifies, and the only remedy is to initiate a contrary process of unnaming. By merit of its unrivaled transparency, "something" often functions as a glass receptacle into which we can pour what we cannot say in order to observe it without obstruction.

Conclusion: The Dark Matter of Words and Worlds

The magnitude of the mystery is staggering. The great majority of the matter of the universe is utterly unknown, except through its gravitational effects. Yet through the gravitational field, it has shaped the way the universe has developed. It is as if physics has discovered the unconscious. Just as the conscious mind floats, as it were, on the surface of the sea of unconscious mental processes, so the known physical world floats on a cosmic ocean of dark matter.

—Rupert Sheldrake, *The Rebirth of Nature*

Certainly there is something poetic about a featureless fundamental essence.

—Lawrence Krauss, *The Fifth Essence*

The notion of a pervasive dark matter at the heart of the universe is endlessly suggestive. In our own day, the quest to understand the nature of this strange and exotic stuff is a prominent manifestation of what we do not know but which is definitely, verifiably there. Since it is something we can at least indirectly register by its measurable effects upon visible matter, the dark matter can be characterized as a "precise unknown" and also as a structured absence—the indirect evidence "structuring" the "absence," which is the unknown nature of the stuff itself.

By analogy, we can also speak of the dark matter of words, of the dark umbra enveloping a word's illuminating arc, as well as of the larger shadows permeating language in a more general sense. Our words ceaselessly implicate the wordless, just as what is beyond words inevitably leaves a telltale imprint upon language. Consequently, the full range and significance of our deepest utterances and our greatest literature depend upon a vital sense of what subsists beneath and beyond words while exerting a powerful influence over words.

Such a perspective on language and literature is very different from the more familiar notions of poststructural indeterminacy, deconstructive undecidability, and relativist non-referentiality, where language is seen as "always already" spiraling downward into a black abyss, ultimately incapable of signifying anything but the aporia of its own deadlocked nature.

Language is certainly able to signify. It exists only because it is able to refer to the world of human experience and convey to others meanings and messages of importance. If language was not successful, it would not exist. Such things are intuitively obvious to everyone, yet the dominant trend in literary criticism is to deny the ability of language to refer to anything outside itself. Words refer only to other words, we are told, and language is a self-enclosed, self-referential system with no exit. Language is necessarily schematic, and it is often plainly inadequate, but neither of these attributes render it "indeterminate." The fact that this schematic and inadequate medium can be manipulated in myriad ways to produce a felt sense of absence and a corresponding productive uncertainty is one of the most remarkable and interesting capacities of human communication.

In one sense, that which is beyond words must always remain beyond words, including these, and we will never succeed in rendering such inchoate awareness in material form. Still, it is the realization of the limitation of language that spurs us on to break its surface and to purposely weave into the fabric of words holes and openings that direct a reader's attention back to what words cannot say. Though inadequate to our deepest perceptions, words can effectively structure absences that require us to cope with something beyond the words on the page.

To overcome the impasse of inexpressibility, writers have fabricated devices and techniques that, through indirection, can at least partly speak the unspeakable, name the unnameable, and declare the unknowable. By exploiting the energy latent in the unfinished, by gesturing artfully toward what words miss, and by forging inexpressibility tropes anew, writers construct theaters in which the reader is made to participate in the richness of nonverbal realms of knowing and inarticulate spheres of being.

Through a wide variety of structured absences, readers are made to *feel* what words cannot touch and to experience sympathetically what our logical and discursive abilities cannot approach. At their most extreme, such negative techniques can initiate a heuristic process of unnaming, whereby the scaffolding of words and sentences is seemingly dismantled in favor of some less material but immensely more powerful form of awareness.

Such literary techniques are not the hothouse flowers of an aesthetics divorced from experiential reality; rather they correspond to the actual conditions of human existence. Our faculty of sight, for instance, is sensitive to only a very narrow range of wavelengths, and so we are blind to much of what transpires around us every moment of our lives. We know there are such things as the infrared and the ultraviolet and that they have measurable effects upon our lives and the world, and yet we cannot directly register such things. We are blind to much of the pageant of creation, and, most importantly, we are acutely aware of our blindness (though some people more than others).

The same is true of our other bodily senses. A dog's ear pricks alert, responding to some whistle beyond human hearing, or a raccoon pauses to sample the breeze, nostrils extracting olfactory information of a sort we cannot imagine, and we realize how much there is from which we are cut off. In terms of direct human experience, all these phenomena lie beyond our bodily limitations, be they ultrasonic sounds or radio waves, infrared radiation or super subtle scents. And so in human terms we encounter them as absences—as structured absences, since they are structured by their measurable effects within the human realm, as when we turn on a radio or use a dog whistle.

Innumerable forms of registered absence swarm around us on all sides, whether it is simply the *lack* of dandelions warning of the poison upon a modern chemical lawn or the *absence* of frogs that indicates some insidious pollution in a stream. Tracks in the snow and starlight inform us of things now departed, of the enduring mark of the absent past upon the present. It is only through silence that music assumes meaningful shape, and the manipulation of shadow and darkness upon a flat canvas brings color and form to life. Whether it be the missing arms of a statue or the missing movement of a symphony, whatever is pointedly absent can become the most crucial feature of a work of art—or of a physics experiment, an ecological survey, an astronomical chart, or a psychological profile.

Consciousness, at some level, is the result of molecular and neurochemical processes. The brain subsumes many diverse perceptual pathways feeding into numerous even more complex cognitive systems that give rise to innumerable states of awareness. This is obviously the concern of scientists, but literary theorists also need to become more aware of the degree to which the question of the nature of mind impinges upon the discipline.

Physiologically, the mind is made up of interconnected networks of neurons that spider web their way through the densely packed "wetware" in our heads. But it is not simply through neurons that the fire storm of cognition blazes. It is equally through the synapses, the gaps, the absences between the neurons without which the neuron could not function.

This emptiness, this absence, is at the core of consciousness, at the core of our conceptions and perceptions, just as an equally dynamic emptiness is the essence of the atomic structure of matter. The daily realization of our own being continually activates a vast orchestra of synapses, of dynamic absences, in order to be made present to itself. So it is not surprising that the aesthetic constructs of beings built upon emptiness, conceiving, perceiving, and experiencing through the perpetual activation of synaptic absences, should be infused with equally productive absences whose felicitous ministrations mysteriously convey back to us the realization of our own nature.

When René Daumal's uncategorizable novel *Mount Analogue* trails off in mid-sentence halfway through the fifth of seven projected chapters and leaves the reader stranded in the foothills along with an expedition that was to have ascended the mountain in order to gain access to a higher enlightenment, the unfinished state of the novel is not perceived as a flaw. On the contrary, when the reader is left to stare at the blank whiteness of the page, knowing that Daumal died of tuberculosis soon after penning that last sentence fragment, something almost unaccountably strange occurs. As in the case of Bruckner's Ninth Symphony, the fragmentary remains of this most singular of novels seems unerringly appropriate, perhaps even inescapable, given the inferred ambition of the novel to gain a direct (and presumably communicable) realization of a higher perception of reality. Beyond a certain point in the ascent, any discursive representation was bound to be counterproductive. Daumal no doubt realized this and would have devised some way to get around the problem, but fate spared him this trouble.

As it is, *Mount Analogue* leaves the reader facing sheer blankness—the inchoate twilight of death and dissolution—with intimations of a supreme enlightenment made more palpable for having again escaped our wide-meshed nets of language. As with Bruckner's Ninth, this absence is rendered dynamic and richly resonant by merit of its position within a larger structure, albeit fragmentary, that channels more energy into the absence then anything formally present could hope to bear. Daumal's valedictory blankness thus functions as a structured absence, the five strangely lit, nearly phantasmagorical, chapters carving out and shaping the contours of that inescapable, final emptiness.

Absence or fragmentedness in and of itself is not necessarily productive. Charles Dickens's unfinished novel, *The Mystery of Edwin Drood*, is not enhanced by being incomplete—which is also true of nearly all other works left accidentally unfinished. In Daumal's novel or Bruckner's symphony, however, as in the sculpture of Henry Moore or the *Venus de Milo*, the extant and accessible portion structures the inaccessible in a productive way. The conspicuous is thus able to relate the recondite.

Most of us have never wondered why the night sky is black. Beyond a certain age, most of us would probably not give the question a second thought. That the night is dark seems an absurdly basic fact: The sun goes down, the light departs, and so the sky at night must obviously be black. But it's really not as simple as that. Quite the contrary, the issue of why the night sky is black is one of the most fascinating and persisting mysteries confronting humankind—though this should not be confused with the problem of the dark matter.

In an unusual late essay entitled *Eureka: A Prose Poem*, Edgar Allan Poe focused attention upon this enigma, pointing out that if we do live in an infinite universe there should be no point in the heavens without a visible star. The sky at night should be ablaze with light, not merely peppered with a sprinkling of visible stars. Why, then, is the night sky black?

For generations, this basic question has perplexed scientists and strained calculation to the limit, recurring again and again as the frontiers of scientific knowledge have advanced. As Edward Harrison points out in his comprehensive study of the dark night riddle, Poe was essentially correct in hypothesizing that the darkness of the sky indicates that there are vast regions of the universe so distant that no light from them has yet had time to reach our planet. Within the areas that we now see as sheer darkness, there are really suns blazing and stars exploding, but our telescopes register nothing because the time it would take light to traverse the distance exceeds not only the lives of astronomers but the life of the galaxy itself.

The darkness of night, far from being an obvious fact we should take for granted, actually testifies to the staggering immensity of the universe. It is the silent trumpet fanfare of infinity most of us never pause to hear.

This riddle of the dark is another instance where absence proves just as significant as presence, where darkness proves more illuminating than light. As I have tried to show in this study, there is also a darkness within our books and between our words, an ambient and vitally significant blackness that we too often take for granted because, like the darkness of night, we are so accustomed to it.

Notes

•

Works Cited

•

Index

Notes

1. Seeing What Isn't There

1. Over the past decade, there has been a flood of excellent treatments of the dark matter issue ranging widely in terms of sophistication and specialization. Lawrence Krauss's *The Fifth Essence*, scientifically detailed yet highly readable, is probably the most generally recommendable. Equally compelling is Michael Riordan's and David Schramm's *The Shadows of Creation: Dark Matter and the Structure of the Universe* (NY: W. H. Freeman, 1991). In a more popular vein, John Gribbin's and Martin Rees's *Cosmic Coincidences: Dark Matter, Mankind, and Anthropic Cosmology* (NY: Bantam, 1989) is more unabashedly speculative about the implications of dark matter. Richard Morris is able to lucidly explain difficult scientific concepts in *Cosmic Questions: Galactic Halos, Cold Dark Matter, and the End of Time* (NY: John Wiley, 1993). Marcia Bartusiak's *Through a Universe Darkly* (NY: Harper Collins, 1993) provides a comprehensive treatment of the historical background.

2. For a good taste of the complexity and richness of Sanskrit poetics, see William Haney's *Literary Theory and Sanskrit Poetics*, S. K. De's *Sanskrit Poetics as a Study of Aesthetics*, the fascinating essays and translations in Andrew Schelling's *Twilight Speech: Essays on Sanskrit and Buddhist Poetics*, and René Daumal's two collections of essays *Rasa or Knowledge of the Self* and *The Powers of the Word*.

For an enchanting account of the Taoist poets of the T'ang era, see Edward Schafer's *Mirages on the Sea of Time: The Taoist Poetry of Ts'ao T'ang* and *Pacing the Void: T'ang Approaches to the Stars*. On the Sufis, see Idries Shah's series of books, especially *The Sufis*. For the Symbolist movement, see Arthur Symons's headwater study *The Symbolist Movement in Literature*, still the best work on the subject.

3. See, for instance, Peter Baker's useful *Deconstruction and the Ethical Turn*, Gary Wihl's rather labored *The Contingency of Theory*, Nicholas Royle's much more lucid *After Derrida*, and Jeffrey Nealon's closely argued *Double Reading: Postmodernism after Deconstruction* (Ithaca: Cornell UP, 1993).

4. See, for instance, Ajay Heble's *The Tumble of Reason: Alice Munro's Discourse of Absence*. Heble's otherwise insightful reading of Munro is unfortunately compromised by an uncritical assimilation of some of the more questionable tenets of poststructural and deconstructive theory regarding the nature of language.

5. Counterarguments to deconstruction (not to mention the counter- counterarguments) constitute a vast body of material under which many a library shelf sags. Other key studies would include Gerald Graff's *Literature Against Itself*, Umberto Eco's *The Limits of Interpretation*, M. H. Abrams' *Doing Things With Texts*, Ferry and Renault's *French Philosophy of the Sixties*, and Frank Kermode's "Prologue" to *An Appetite for Poetry*.

2. Orchestras of Shadow

1. Dericksen Brinkerhoff's *Hellenistic Statues of Aphrodite* contains many examples of less well-known statues surviving in fragmentary form. Exactly why the *Venus de Milo* has so enraptured the world is a question not easily answered. Certainly the mistaken early attribution to Praxiteles accounts for part of the original fervor. Martin Robertson feels that the reputation is largely based on "propaganda," but his bristling opinion that the *Venus de Milo*'s "mild merits hardly justify the figure's extraordinary reputation" (55) seems almost willfully petulant. For all his purple prose, Rodin's musings on this queen of fragments penetrates much more to the heart of the matter. In an odd way, the current debate over the intrinsic merits of the statue seems to go hand in hand with the unsolvable enigma presented by the fragmented form itself.

2. Marcia Allentuck's "In Defense of the Unfinished *Tristram Shandy*" discusses the *non finito* from a literary perspective, though she confines her focus to works that "the artist *intended* to leave unfinished" (147), excluding works that have come down to us in fragmentary form or those left incomplete at the time of the artist's death. Yet it seems obvious that, regardless of intention, fragmented and unfinished works can potentially engage a viewer through the same dynamics of absence as a work whose partialness was planned.

Eric Rothstein's more comprehensive "'Ideal Presence' and the 'Non Finito' in Eighteenth-Century Aesthetics" extends the discussion of the non finito to works that are "formally completed," yet still engage the dynamics of the unfinished through such things as the "deliberately laconic sign" (326) that enkindles a responsive "imaginative expansion of the text" (310).

For a discussion of the theory and importance of the literary fragment for the Jena group of early German Romanticists, including Friedrich

Schlegel's *Athenaeum* fragments and Novalis's *Grains of Pollen,* see Philippe Lacoue-Labarthe's and Jean-Luc Nancy's *The Literary Absolute.*

3. In his study of the short story, John Bayley also focuses on this same passage in "The Dead" as central to the story, commenting that the "story's mystery resides precisely in what its central participants, who stand so close to Joyce, cannot grasp" (*Short Story* 158).

4. This point appears several times in Cage's writing. In the 1958 "Composition as Process" he writes:

> These [ambient] sounds (which are called silence only because they do not form part of a musical intention) may be depended upon to exist. The world teems with them, and is, in fact, at no point free of them. He who has entered an an-echoic chamber, a room made as silent as technologically possible, has heard there two sounds, one high, one low—the high the listener's nervous system in operation, the low his blood in circulation. There are, demonstrably, sounds to be heard and forever, given ears to hear. [I have not reproduced the original line breaks used by Cage when reading this work with his *Music of Changes*] (23)

5. Keith Jarrett, who, like Hillier, has recorded and championed Pärt's music, shares this visionary sense of silence. He writes in his notes to *Spirits:*

> Silence is the potential from which music can arise. Music is the "activity-of-meaning" that is able to be actualized only because of silence. . . . There is a fine line between using technique and making music. We must be open to the spaces (silence) in order to fill them just right. We must see the spaces, inhabit them, *live* them. Then, the next note, the next move, becomes apparent because it is *needed.* Until it is apparent nothing should be played. Until it is known, nothing should be anticipated. (1)

6. These issues are explored with great subtlety in David Epstein's *Beyond Orpheus,* especially in his sections on thematic and rhythmic shape, and his remarks on phrasing and nuance. His chapter on musical ambiguity also explores the structural functions of uncertainty in musical compositions, an illuminating analog to the similar uses of uncertainty in literature.

7. In his *Flaubert and Kafka,* Bernheimer writes:

> His testamentary wishes regarding his works show a similar ambivalence. On the one hand, his request that Max Brod burn his manuscripts after his death seems to reflect a desire that his writings perish at the same time as his body, as if they were

an organic extension of that body. On the other hand, Brod was the person least likely to fulfill this request since it was precisely he who had most persistently encouraged Kafka to publish. (244)

Many other critics have expressed similar doubts about whether Kafka really wanted the manuscripts destroyed. Herman Uyttersprot's more traditional notion that Kafka "demanded that the manuscript be destroyed because he did not wish the public to see an incomplete work" (142) rings completely false. After all, Kafka himself had ample opportunity to destroy anything of his he wished.

3. The Wordless Blank and the Gift of Tongues

1. There are several excellent recordings of selections from Hildegard's *Symphonia armonie celestium revelationum*, which provide a far richer experience than merely reading the texts: *A Feather on the Breath of God* performed by Gothic Voices (Hyperion Records CDA 66039, 1982) is perhaps the best introduction.

The early music ensemble Sequentia has embarked on a magnificent complete cycle of Hildegard's work, of which they have now completed five volumes, including the complete *Ordo Virtutum* (Harmonia Mundi IC 165-99942/43, 1982).

The others are:

Symphoniae: Spiritual Songs (Deutsche Harmonia Mundi 77020-2-RG, 1985)

Canticles of Ecstasy (Deutsche Harmonia Mundi 05472-77320-2,1994)

Voice of the Blood (BMG Classics 05472-77346-2, 1995)

O Jerusalem (BMG Classics 05472-77353-2, 1997)

2. Rorty's wider position is grounded, of course, on a tenet typical of linguistic philosophy, namely that "only sentences can be true, and that human beings make truths by making languages in which to phrase sentences" (9). Truth, Rorty declares "is a property of sentences," and furthermore "since sentences are dependent for their existence upon vocabularies, and since vocabularies are made by human beings, so are truths" (21). Such a wholesale redefinition of "truth," which would render the word unintelligible to most thinkers and writers of the past three thousand years, highlights the degree to which language has usurped the seat of power.

Whether or not Rorty might acknowledge the reality of wordless cognition or prelinguistic consciousness in itself is a moot point, since he excludes such questions from the scope of his inquiry. To what extent are our sentences dependent on prelinguistic perception? To what degree is the resulting "truth" of a sentence therefore dependent on such wordless components of thought? A willingness to leave such questions unasked and unanswered is a major shortcoming of such a perspective.

The blatantly anthropocentric bias of Rorty's assumptions, as in a statement like "where there are no sentences there is no truth" (5), is discussed at length by Alexander Argyros in A *Blessed Rage for Order*, where Rorty is grouped together with other "social constructivists" like Thomas Kuhn. See also Paisley Livingston's *Literary Knowledge* for a thorough treatment of the shortcomings of "framework relativisms" like Rorty's.

In Rorty, we witness one example of a more general refusal to credit experiences that are perhaps familiar enough, but only dimly appreciated because of a prejudicial refusal to take full account of anything beyond what we can accommodate in words and discursive conceptualization.

4. The Prison-House of Language

1. Abrams goes on to repudiate this view in no uncertain terms:

> I believe not only that interpretation involves human beings at each end of a language transaction, whether spoken or written, but also that language can signify, and so bring to our attention, aspects of things that exist outside of language, even when those things are works of literature which themselves consist of signifying language. (Lipking 172)

2. George Steiner has suggested that philosophies might usefully be grouped according to those that assume language to be fundamental and those that, while recognizing the obvious shaping power of language, do not accord it primary significance:

> [O]ne can reasonably divide the history of philosophy between those epistemologies that stress the substantiality, the exterior verifiability and concrete objectification of human experience, and those that emphasize the creative or confining wholeness of their own means of statement—i.e., which see man reaching out to reality and inward to himself only so far as language (perhaps his particular language) allows. (*Extraterritorial* 74–75)

Steiner further traces the perennial idea that cognition is a function of language back through medieval scholasticism and to Peter Damian in the eleventh century (see "The Language Animal" in *Extraterritorial* and "Language and Gnosis" in *After Babel*). Each time the language-as-consciousness flag has been raised, it has been challenged (and refuted, I think) much as Steiner, Arnheim, Siebers, Abrams, Penrose, Nuttall, and so on have done most recently.

In *The Arts Without Mystery*, Denis Donoghue proceeds unapologetically on a thoroughly intuitive basis, but he is in essential agreement with the viewpoints expressed by Steiner, Powys, and Watts:

> It is reasonable to assume that there are experiences which lie so far beyond "nature"—however we elucidate that word—that words have never been found for them, and will never be found. It is also reasonable to make the same assumption of the experiences which lie beneath nature. It is impertinent to assume that there are words for every experience; if there were, music, sculpture, and silence would be redundant. I find it congenial to believe that there are moments at which language stands baffled, saying of what it has just said that that is not it at all, not at all. Such moments are congenial because they tell against the idolatry of language to which we are all, in some of our moods, susceptible. Knowing that language has done so much, we want to believe that it can do everything. (132)

In his monumental study, *The Act of Creation*, Arthur Koestler comes to much the same conclusion. After having discussed the obscure nature of sudden enlightenment (what Koestler calls the "Eureka Act"), in the course of which he reviews and extends the thesis put forward by Jacques Hadamard (see following note), Koestler warns against any exact equation between language and consciousness:

> Most of us were brought up in the belief that "thinking" is synonymous with verbal thinking, and philosophers from Athens to Oxford have kept reasserting this belief. The early Behaviorists went even further, asserting not only that words are indispensable to thought, but also that thinking is nothing more than the subliminal movements of the vocal chords, an inaudible whispering to oneself. Yet if all thinking were verbal thinking Einstein would not qualify as a thinker. In fact, the whole evidence points in the opposite direction. . . . the high aesthetic value which we put on visual imagery should not obscure the fact that as vehicles of thought, pictorial and other non-verbal representations are indeed earlier, both phylogenetically and ontologically older forms of ideation, than verbal thinking. (173)

In *The Limitations of Language*, Terence Moore and Chris Carling use the examples of face recognition and the language of wine tasting to make a similar point. Plainly, the direct gustatory experience of wine is not mediated or shaped by language, though it certainly does confer knowledge. As the authors vividly demonstrate, our often rather desperate attempts to describe a wine's precise qualities can lead to rather outlandish coinages, such as "goaty," "ragged," "autumnal," or "inky," which in themselves can communicate little or nothing to anyone who has not already tasted the wine. Rather than serving as a positive description, such groping language often serves more to signal the failure of words to adequately address immediate and distinct nonverbal knowledge.

Likewise, each of us can instantly recognize thousands of faces, yet we would be hard-pressed to explain how we can do this. "Language is linear," Moore and Carling explain. "Words have to come out one after another, marks on a page arranged in lines, successively. Much of our perception, on the other hand, is holistic, non-linear. Trying to describe a face in words amounts to forcing non-linear visual awareness into a linear device" (91). We might add here that trying to describe a face, to convey its full and unique singularity through language, is just one instance where our appeals to inexpressibility would be immediately recognized as valid and familiar. Koestler's remarks and the example of face recognition also call to mind Jacques Maritain's meditation on the wordless substratum—the realm of "trembling inchoation"—existing prior to and engendering verbal articulation. But such examples and citations could go on forever.

Perhaps the example of gravity may prove instructive. Gravity is itself insubstantial and invisible, and its full nature still lies beyond science. But just as celestial galaxies are born of this immaterial force that organizes and shapes swirling masses of stardust into highly complex planetary systems, so too do our most fugitive impulses and wordless motions of spirit seem capable of generating airy worlds upon a latticework of words.

In this manner, poets and writers are able to render the inchoate and invisible at least partly visible—the partiality of their success confirming both the reality of wordless states as well as the limited nature of language. As Liu Hsieh might have phrased it, the subtle art of manipulating words allows us access to the realm of the recondite through the portal of the conspicuous.

3. Hadamard's classic study of 1945, *The Psychology of Invention in the Mathematical Field*, is a wide-ranging and thought-provoking refutation of what he sees as the perennial fallacy besetting epistemological inquiry—the assumption that the structures supplied by language are necessary for thought. See especially the chapter on "Discovery as Synthesis" and the section entitled "Words and Wordless Thought."

As with Arnheim, Hadamard focuses mainly on the role of "concrete representations other than words" (71) such as mental images, whereas Penrose (as well as Einstein, George Steiner, and Ann Chalmers Watts) are equally concerned with mechanisms of thought and modes of consciousness that are essentially representationless. Hadamard also discusses the controversy of the late 1880s that centered on Max Müller's contention that thought is not possible without words and therefore consciousness must derive from language. In *The Origin of Language*, G. A. Wells provides a more thorough treatment of Müller and his contemporaries in the context of a reappraisal of Condillac's theory of language. Arnheim's essay on "The Myth of the Bleating Lamb" in *Toward a Psychology of Art* (Berkeley: U of California P, 1966) traces the current variety of "linguistic determinism" back to Herder while sharply criticizing the excesses of "word-struck theorists."

For Roger Penrose's theory of consciousness, see also his more recent *Shadows of the Mind*.

4. See Mark Turner's two books, *Reading Minds* and *The Literary Mind*, and Ellen Spolsky's *Gaps in Nature: Literary Interpretation and the Modular Mind*. Spolsky focuses on the "gaps in human cognitive structure" that inevitably result from the modular nature of the brain. Her main focus is on how the modular mind relates to different, often antagonistic, schools of literary criticism. She does not specifically discuss gaps in literary works or the role of textual absences.

See also Alexander Argyros's *A Blessed Rage for Order*, Frederick Turner's brilliant essays collected in *Natural Classicism*, and F. Elizabeth Hart's essay on "Cognitive Linguistics."

5. In an essay exploring Kristeva's critique of Lacan, Shuli Barzilai comments, in full agreement with Kristeva, that

> To insist on the primacy of language is, therefore, to fail to account for preverbal and nonverbal elements that escape the safety net of language, that cannot be subsumed under the Saussurian sign. It is to fail to account for areas of aesthetic and, in particular, literary creation situated beyond signification and meaning. (296)

6. The discrepancy between the circumscribed orbit of the word and the wordless trajectories of music is a primary focus of David Epstein's *Beyond Orpheus*. Cautioning readers to remain constantly aware of the inescapable distortion accompanying any discursive attempt to illuminate a radically non-discursive medium, he notes:

> Ultimately these concerns about musical expression may never be answered in the verbal manner that some would hope for.

For the question itself is framed at variance with the realities of musical communication. Whatever "expression," values, or personal interior world is communicated by music, however compellingly it is communicated, it is communicated through a medium—sound and time—that is unique, intrinsic unto itself and incapable of translation. Were this not so, we should long ago have seen more success in the many attempts to relate musical essence through metaphor, poetic description, analogy, and image. (11)

Here, we have what amounts to an appeal to inexpressibility, an appeal rigorously argued and experientially grounded in a thorough and closely argued manner. "More than any other act of intelligibility and executive form," writes George Steiner, "music entails differentiations between that which can be understood, this is to say paraphrased, and that which can be thought and lived in categories which are, rigorously considered, transcendent to such understanding" (*Real Presences* 18–19).

7. In his revaluation of the issue of mimesis, which often overlaps suggestively with aspects of Tobin Siebers's discussion of the ethics of criticism, A. D. Nuttall is in complete agreement with Siebers:

The philosophers who opt for language rather than consciousness as ontologically fundamental eagerly inhale the new atmosphere of suprapersonal rules and conventions as if its very impersonality somehow conferred substance, but a rule which obliges no one and relates to no material circumstance external to itself is quite as vacuous as the most fugitive and private mental image. (45)

On this topic, Alexander Argyros remarks that "contrary to what many language chauvinists might believe, it is quite clear that the mind avails itself of a congeries of information-processing techniques—linguistic, to be sure, but also visual, musical, olfactory, somatic, etc." (293). Argyros further observes that "it is unlikely that the mind uses only one strategy to store, manipulate, and create information; every indication that we currently have suggests that the brain is highly redundant, so I suspect that its ideas are stored as prototypes, abstractions, and lists, as well as structural, functional, and associative descriptions" (293).

It is tempting to conjecture that the material truth behind our claims to inexpressible knowledge might derive from this very redundancy and interconnectedness between various areas and functions of the brain. The palpable sense of a knowledge that can find no adequate expression in words may be born of the inexorable fact that no amount of interconnectedness within the brain can make the functions themselves fully interchangeable.

8. James T. Jones's *Wayward Skeptic: The Theories of R. P. Blackmur* makes a convincing case for the central importance of Blackmur's thought in contemporary literary theory. Jones points out that a major reason for Blackmur's current neglect is the misguided perception that Blackmur engaged in "applied" or "practical" criticism rather than something more systematically theoretical.

The critical assessments and memoirs collected in *The Legacy of R. P. Blackmur* include Edward Said's perceptive "The Horizon of R. P. Blackmur" as well as W. S. Merwin's moving memoir "Affable Irregular," which concludes with Merwin wanting to thank Blackmur most for

> confirmations that have survived him, among them a tenacious esteem not for the human alone but for the inchoate in humanity, as it struggles inexplicably to complete itself through language. In the purity of impure human language, in language as the vehicle for the unsayable. A faith in empty words. (Cone 176)

5. *Language as Gesture*

1. Of course, Blackmur's ideas regarding language and language-as-gesture evolved over the decades. In "Language and Gesture" (1942), Blackmur tends to talk of gesture as an unacknowledged ingredient in language, an essential component, but one that can be isolated from other constituents. By the time of "The Language of Silence" (1955), gesture is no longer a mere component of language but is nearly synonymous with it—the other constituents now being seen more as elements or side effects of gesture. Ultimately, the wordless motion of gesture residing in words is figured as silence, and silence becomes the root of meaning.

Though Blackmur's theories regarding the element of gesture inhabiting the written word conceive of gesture primarily in a figurative and analogical sense, Blackmur also makes clear the reinforcing ties with our uses of gesture in a literal sense. Obviously, Blackmur's characterization of language as gesture is indebted to some degree to the fertile speculations regarding the relationship of spoken language and physical gesture that occupied linguists in the decades prior to Blackmur's essay.

For example, Sir Richard Paget's influential study, *Human Speech*, traces the possible evolution of spoken language from bodily gesture in great detail (see especially 126–75). Starting from the widely-held intuition that the earliest form of human communication was through physical gesture, Paget hypothetically sketches, sometimes with wildly fanciful leaps of logic, how the biological mechanisms for enunciating certain sounds, sound-emotions, syllables, and proto-words might have evolved from cruder, non-verbal gestures.

Ultimately, Paget proposes that there is, at least in certain instances, a recoverable though imperfect relationship between the sound / movement and the sense / response in human communication—a suggestion that would not sit well with many contemporary linguists or literary theorists for whom the distance between the signifier and signified must always be absolute and arbitrary. But this idea would find congenial reinforcement in, for example, Robert Frost's "sound-of-sense" theory of poetics. In any case, the point here is simply that such discussions regarding gesture do have some bearing, if only an indirect one, on Blackmur's aesthetic theories.

In *The Origin of Language*, G. A. Wells provides a bracing reconsideration of Condillac's theory of language, focusing especially on the indispensable role played by gesture both in the rudimentary stages of language development and less obviously in its higher evolution. David Hayman's "Language of / As Gesture in Joyce" explores both Joyce's fascination with gesture and with "words as repositories of gesture," as well as Joyce's use of gesture in his own works. Joyce's theory that, as Hayman characterizes it, "all art, all expression, has its origins in the primitive need to express simple emotions, in gestures which adhere as hieroglyphs even to the sophisticated work" (210–11) anticipates later studies like Sir Richard Paget's. Hayman also discusses Joyce's interest in Abbé Marcel Jousse's theory that "language was derived from and still conceals gesture" (212).

For an interesting extension of these matters into the semiotics of gestuality and gesticulation in its widest sense, see A. J. Greimas's "Toward a Semiotics of the Natural World" in *On Meaning* (Minneapolis: U of Minnesota P, 1987).

Mikhail Bakhtin's notion that language must be studied both on its own terms and also according to "the impulse that reaches out beyond it," the "living impulse toward the object," also embraces the idea of gesture and seems especially resonant with Blackmur's outlook:

> Discourse lives, as it were beyond itself, in a living impulse toward the object; if we detach ourselves completely from this impulse all we have left is the naked corpse of the word, from which we can learn nothing at all about the social situation or the fate of a given word in life. To study the word as such, ignoring the impulse that reaches out beyond it, is just as senseless as to study psychological experiences outside the context of that real life toward which it is directed and by which it is determined. (292)

George Steiner's definition of literature as "the maximalization of semantic incommensurability in respect of the formal means of expression" (*Real Presences* 83), is also reminiscent of Blackmur's concept of language-as-gesture in that both emphasize the tendency of literary works to heighten the non-verbal aspects of meaning inherent in words. "A sentence always means more," Steiner insists, and here the sense of "more" is directly allied to what Blackmur defines as the element of gesture working through words.

2. See William Shullenberger's insightful essay on "'Something' in Wordsworth" in *Ineffability: Naming the Unnamable from Dante to Beckett*, a valuable collection of essays edited by Peter Hawkins and Anne Howland Schotter.

8. "For the Snark Was a Boojum, You See"

1. The excellent edition of *The Hunting of the Snark* edited by James Tanis and John Dooley, which includes Martin Gardner's "The Annotated Snark," presents the complete series of Holiday's illustrations, including his preliminary drawing of the Boojum that Carroll banished.

9. Uncertainty vs. Inderterminacy

1. The further development of Saussure's pioneering conception of the sign and of the conceptual categories inexorably formed by systems of signs lies not in the path followed by deconstruction, but rather in the direction taken by ethnolinguists like Edward Sapir or the unclassifiable Benjamin Lee Whorf, who explores how differences in language precipitate differences in culture, perception, and values. George Lakoff's *Women, Fire, and Dangerous Things* is perhaps the most lucid and strikingly original vindication and refinement of both Saussure's and Whorf's explorations of the ways language "segments," colors, and determines our sense of reality. Mark Turner's *Reading Minds* brilliantly outlines an approach to literary studies based on a "cognitive rhetoric" grounded in a deeper appreciation of the conceptual metaphors at the root of language.

10. Absence and "Structured Absence"

1. Dolores Lucas's limited but still useful study, *Emily Dickinson and Riddle*, does not, unfortunately, comment at length on this poem. It does, however, give a good account of the extent of Dickinson's manipulation of riddling techniques, as well as their wider epistemological implications.

11. The Spectrum of Structured Absences

1. Though Nystrand uses "impaction" and "rarefaction" as a method of analyzing errors in written communication, his citations from Edith Sitwell, Lewis Carroll, Jonathan Swift, and others show that he is well aware that what would be seen as errors in "plain" writing often be-

come masterful techniques in the hands of authors such as James, Woolf, or Faulkner.

2. See Gregory R. Wegner's essay on "Hawthorne's 'Ethan Brand' and the Structure of the Literary Sketch" for a good treatment of the genesis of the story and the critical controversy surrounding it. Wegner argues convincingly that "Ethan Brand" is a self-sufficient literary sketch into which Hawthorne has intentionally injected little touches to make it seem a fragment of a larger work.

3. It is suggestive to compare Burke's notion with what a Taoist abbot told John Blofeld during his wanderings across China in the years before the second world war: "void is the painter's greatest asset, in that whatever is sharply defined is thereby limited, whereas what is merely hinted at or left void in a picture is infinitely suggestive" (*Secret* 121). For the abbot, if not for Burke, the manipulation of suggestive vagueness is not limited to language alone but can also be exploited in visual art.

12. Ciphers and Halos

1. See David Hayman's *Re-Forming the Narrative* for a thorough consideration of parataxis, especially in the context of modernism.

2. I have borrowed the term "nesting" from Ragnar Rommetveit's *On Message Structure*. Rommetveit characterizes communication as a progressive "nesting" of new information within a previously negotiated "temporarily shared social reality," so that "what is initially unknown to the listener is made known to him in terms of a progressive expansion and modification of an actual or intersubjectively presupposed shared social world" (95). This "progressive nesting of information" assumes a particular pattern integrally related to what is being communicated, and this particular pattern is the structure of that message.

In the case of a structured absence nested within another structured absence, the temporarily shared social reality established by the first structured absence must be seen as *intentionally uncertain*—a situation in which the author has intentionally negotiated an imbalance of some sort. Any subsequent nesting of structured absences within this already problematic shared social reality obviously represents a calculated strategy on the part of the author to heighten the imbalance and disorientation experienced by the reader.

15. Unnaming the World

1. See also Poirier's chapter on "The Reinstatement of the Vague" in *Poetry and Pragmatism*, which includes an extended consideration of Frost's use of "something" as well as a reading of this poem.

Works Cited

Aarsleff, Hans. *From Locke to Saussure*. Minneapolis: U of Minnesota P, 1982.

Abrams, M. H. *Doing Things with Texts*. NY: Norton, 1991.

Adams, Robert. *Nil: Episodes in the Literary Conquest of Void During the Nineteenth Century*. NY: Oxford UP, 1966.

Allentuck, Marcia. "In Defense of the Unfinished *Tristram Shandy*: Laurence Sterne and the *Non Finito*." *The Winged Skull*. Eds. Arthur Cash and John Stedmond. Kent: Kent State UP, 1971.

Allston, Washington. *Lectures on Art and Poems*. 1850. Gainesville: Scholars Facsimiles & Reprints, 1967.

Ammons, A. R. *Garbage*. NY: Norton, 1993.

———. "A Poem Is a Walk." *Claims for Poetry*. Ed. Donald Hall. Ann Arbor: U of Michigan P, 1982.

Argyros, Alexander. *A Blessed Rage for Order: Deconstruction, Evolution and Chaos*. Ann Arbor: U of Michigan P, 1991.

Arnheim, Rudolf. *Visual Thinking*. Berkeley: U of California P, 1969.

Auden, W. H. "Concerning the Unpredictable." Introduction. *The Star Thrower*. By Loren Eisely. NY: Harcourt, 1978.

Austen, Jane. *Pride and Prejudice*. 1813. NY: Penguin, 1982.

Bachelard, Gaston. *The Philosophy of No: A Philosophy of the New Scientific Mind*. Trans. G. C. Waterson. NY: Orion, 1968.

Baker, Peter. *Deconstruction and the Ethical Turn*. Gainesville: UP of Florida, 1995.

Bakhtin, Mikail. *The Dialogic Imagination*. Trans. Caryl Emerson and Michael Holquist. Austin: U of Texas P, 1986.

Baring-Gould, William. *The Annotated Mother Goose*. NY: Bramhall, n.d.

Barnes, Djuna. *Nightwood*. NY: New Directions, 1961.

Barzilai, Shuli. "Borders of Language: Kristeva's Critique of Lacan." *PMLA* 106.2 (Mar. 1991): 294–305.

Bayley, John. *The Short Story: Henry James to Elizabeth Bowen*. Brighton, Sussex: Harvester, 1988.

Benjamin, Walter. *Illuminations*. Trans. Harry Zohn. NY: Schoken, 1969.

———. *Reflections*. Trans. Edmund Jephcott. NY: Harcourt, 1978.

Bentley, E. C. *Trent's Last Case*. 1913. NY: Harper, 1978.

Bergson, Henri. *Creative Evolution*. Trans. Arthur Mitchell. Westport: Greenwood, 1977.

Bernheimer, Charles. *Flaubert and Kafka*. New Haven: Yale UP, 1982.

Bickerton, Derek. *Language and Human Behavior*. Seattle: U of Washington P, 1995.

Blackmur, R. P. *Language as Gesture*. NY: Harcourt, 1952.

———. *Outsider at the Heart of Things*. Ed. James T. Jones. Chicago: U of Illinois P, 1989.

———. *Poems of R. P. Blackmur*. Princeton: Princeton UP, 1977.

Blofeld, John. *Taoism: The Road to Immortality*. Boston: Shambhala, 1985.

———. *The Secret and the Sublime: Taoist Mysteries and Magic*. NY: Dutton, 1973.

Bloom, Harold. *Ruin the Sacred Truths: Poetry and Belief from the Bible to the Present*. Cambridge: Harvard UP, 1989.

Borges, Jorge Luis. *Labyrinths*. Eds. Donald Yates and James Irby. NY: New Directions, 1964.

Brinkerhoff, Dericksen. *Hellenistic Statues of Aphrodite*. NY: Garland, 1978.

Bromfield, Louis. *The Strange Case of Miss Annie Spragg*. NY: Frederick A. Stokes, 1928.

Brontë, Charlotte. *Jane Eyre*. 1847. London: Penguin, 1987.

Browne, Sir Thomas. *Religio Medici*. *Sir Thomas Browne: Selected Writings*. Ed. Sir Geoffrey Keynes. Chicago: U of Chicago P, 1968.

Bruffee, Kenneth. "Collaborative Learning and the 'Conversation of Mankind.'" *College English* 46.7 (Nov. 1984): 635–52.

Brunn, Emilie Zum, and Georgette Epiney-Burgard, eds. *Woman Mystics of Medieval Europe*. Trans. Sheila Hughes. NY: Paragon, 1989.

Bryant, Mark. *Riddles: Ancient and Modern*. NY: Peter Bedrick, 1984.

Burke, Edmund. *A Philosophical Enquiry into the Origin of Our Ideas of the Sublime and the Beautiful*. 1759. Ed. J. T. Boulton. NY: Columbia UP, 1958.

Burke, Kenneth. *Language as Symbolic Action*. Berkeley: U of California P, 1973.

Butor, Michel. *Passing Time*. Trans. Jean Stewart. London: Jupiter Books, 1965.

Cage, John. *Silence*. Middleton: Wesleyan UP, 1961.

Capra, Fritjof. *The Tao of Physics*. 3rd ed. Boston: Shambhala, 1991.

Carlyle, Thomas. "Sir Walter Scott." *Critical and Miscellaneous Essays*. Centennial Memorial Edition. Vol. 4. Boston: Dana Estes, 1892.

Carroll, Lewis. *The Hunting of the Snark*. Ed. James Tanis and John Dooley. Los Altos: William Kaufmann, 1982.

Cassirer, Ernst. *Language and Myth*. Trans. Susanne K. Langer. NY: Dover, 1953.

Cather, Willa. *My Antonia*. Boston: Houghton, 1918.

Chopin, Kate. *The Awakening*. 1899. NY: Bantam, 1981.

Clark, Eve. "From Gesture to Word: On the Natural History of Deixis in Language Acquisition." *Human Growth and Development*. Eds. Jerome Bruner and Alison Garton. Oxford: Clarendon, 1978. 85–120.

Clark, James, and John V. Skinner. *Meister Eckhart: Selected Treatises and Sermons*. London: Faber, 1958.

Cleary, J.C., ed. and trans. *A Tune Beyond the Clouds: Zen Teachings from Old China*. Berkeley: Asia Humanities P, 1990.

Colish, Marcia L. *The Mirror of Language: A Study in the Medieval Theory of Knowledge*. Rev. ed. Lincoln: U of Nebraska P, 1983.

Collis, John Stewart. *The Vision of Glory: The Extraordinary Nature of the Ordinary*. NY: George Braziller, 1973.

Cone, Edward, Joseph Frank, and Edward Keeley, eds. *The Legacy of R. P. Blackmur: Essays, Memoirs, Texts*. NY: Ecco, 1987.

Conrad, Joseph. *Heart of Darkness*. 1902. NY: Norton, 1963.

———. *Lord Jim*. 1900. NY: Bantam, 1981.

Cooper, James Fenimore. *The Pathfinder*. 1840. NY: Modern Library, 1952.

Curtius, Ernst Robert. *European Literature and the Latin Middle Ages*. 1953. Trans. Willard Trask. Princeton: Princeton UP, 1967.

Daumal, René. *Mount Analogue: A Novel of Symbolically Authentic Non-Euclidean Adventures in Mountain Climbing*. Trans. Roger Shattuck. Boston: Shambhala, 1992.

———. *The Powers of the Word: Selected Essays and Notes 1927– 1943*. Trans. Mark Polizzotti. San Francisco: City Lights, 1991.

———. *Rasa or Knowledge of the Self: Essays on Indian Aesthetics and Selected Sanskrit Studies*. Trans. Louise Landes Levi. NY: New Directions, 1982.

De, S. K. *Sanskrit Poetics as a Study of Aesthetics*. Berkeley: U of California P, 1963.

de Man, Paul. *Blindness and Insight*. NY: Oxford UP, 1971.

Derrida, Jacques. *Of Grammatology*. Trans. Gayatri Spivak. Baltimore: Johns Hopkins UP, 1976.

———. *Writing and Difference*. Trans. Alan Bass. Chicago: U of

Chicago P, 1978.

Dickinson, Emily. *The Poems of Emily Dickinson*. Ed. Thomas H. Johnson. Cambridge: Harvard UP, 1968.

Donoghue, Denis. *The Arts Without Mystery*. Boston: Little Brown, 1983.

Dreiser, Theodore. *Sister Carrie*. NY: Penguin, 1983.

Eco, Umberto. *The Limits of Interpretation*. Bloomington: Indiana UP, 1990.

Eliot, George. *Middlemarch*. Middlesex: Penguin, 1976.

Eliot, T. S. *The Music of Poetry*. Glasgow: Jackson, 1942.

Ellis, John. *Against Deconstruction*. Princeton: Princeton UP, 1989.

Emerson, Ralph Waldo. *The Collected Works of Ralph Waldo Emerson*. Ed. Robert Spiller and Alfred Ferguson. Vol. 2. Cambridge: Harvard UP, 1979.

Epstein, David. *Beyond Orpheus: Studies in Musical Structure*. Cambridge: MIT Press, 1979.

Faulkner, William. *As I Lay Dying*. 1930. NY: Vintage, 1964.

———. *The Bear*. *Three Famous Short Novels*. NY: Vintage, 1961.

———. *Light in August*. 1932. NY: Vintage, 1972.

Ferris, Timothy. *Coming of Age in the Milky Way*. NY: William Morrow, 1988.

Ferry, Luc, and Alain Renaut. *French Philosophy of the Sixties*. Trans. Mary H. S. Cattani. Amherst: U of Massachusetts P, 1990.

Fielding, Henry. *Miscellanies by Henry Fielding, Esq*. Ed. Henry Knight Miller. Vol. 1. Middletown: Wesleyan UP, 1972.

Flaubert, Gustave. *Madame Bovary*. Trans. Mildred Marmur. NY: New American Library, 1964.

Fontenelle, Bernard le Bovier de. *Conversations on the Plurality of Worlds*. 1686. Trans. H. A. Hargreaves. Berkeley: U of California P, 1990.

Forster, E. M. *Aspects of the Novel*. NY: Harcourt, 1955.

Frost, Robert. *The Poetry of Robert Frost*. Ed. Edward Connery Latham. NY: Holt, 1967.

Gleick, James. *Chaos: Making a New Science*. NY: Penguin, 1987.

Gödel, Kurt. *On Formally Undecidable Propositions*. NY: Basic, 1962.

Goodheart, Eugene. *The Skeptic Disposition in Contemporary Discourse*. Princeton: Princeton UP, 1984.

Goodrich, Lloyd. *Albert Pinkham Ryder*. NY: Braziller, 1959.

Graff, Gerald. *Literature Against Itself: Literary Ideas in Modern Society*. Chicago: U of Chicago P, 1979.

Graham, W. S. *Collected Poems, 1942–1977*. London: Faber, 1979.

———. *Selected Poems*. NY: Ecco, 1979.

Gunn, Thom. *Moly and My Sad Captains*. NY: Farrar, 1973.

Hadamard, Jacques. *The Psychology of Invention in the Mathematical*

Field. 1945. NY: Dover, 1954.

Haines, John. *The Stars, the Snow, the Fire: Twenty-Five Years in the Northern Wilderness*. St. Paul: Graywolf P, 1989.

Haney, William S. "Deconstruction and Sanskrit Poetics." *Mosaic* 28.1 (Mar. 1995): 119–41.

———. *Literary Theory and Sanskrit Poetics*. Lampeter: Edwin Mellen, 1993.

Hardy, Thomas. *The Return of the Native*. 1878. NY: Pocket Books, 1973.

Harrison, Edward. *Darkness at Night: A Riddle of the Universe*. Cambridge: Harvard UP, 1987.

Hart, F. Elizabeth. "Cognitive Linguistics: The Experiential Dynamics of Metaphor." *Mosaic* 28.1 (Mar. 1995): 1–23.

Hartman, Geoffrey. *Criticism in the Wilderness*. New Haven: Yale UP, 1980.

Hawkins, Peter, and Anne Howland Schotter, eds. *Ineffability: Naming the Unnamable from Dante to Beckett*. NY: AMS, 1984.

Hawthorne, Nathaniel. *The Celestial Railroad and Other Stories*. Ed. R. P. Blackmur. NY: Signet, 1963.

Hayakawa, Samuel. *Language in Thought and Action*. NY: Harcourt, 1949.

Hayman, David. "Language of/ As Gesture in Joyce." *Ulysses: Ciquante Ans Aprés*. Ed. Louis Bonnerot. Paris: Didier, 1974. 209–22.

———. *Re-Forming the Narrative: Toward a Mechanics of Modernist Fiction*. Ithaca: Cornell UP, 1987.

———. *Ulysses: The Mechanics of Meaning*. Rev. ed. Madison: U of Wisconsin P, 1982.

Heble, Ajay. *The Tumble of Reason: Alice Munro's Discourse of Absence*. Toronto: U of Toronto P, 1994.

Herring, Phillip. *Joyce's Uncertainty Principle*. Princeton: Princeton UP, 1987.

Hildegard of Bingen. *Scivias*. Trans. Bruce Hozeski. Sante Fe: Bear, 1986.

Hillier, Paul. "Arvo Pärt—Magister Ludi." *The Musical Times* (Mar. 1989): 134–37.

Hirsch, E. D. *Validity in Interpretation*. New Haven: Yale UP, 1967.

Hobson, J. Allan. *The Chemistry of Conscious States: How the Brain Changes Its Mind*. Boston: Little Brown, 1994.

Hofstadter, Douglas. *Gödel, Escher, Bach: An Eternal Golden Braid*. NY: Vintage, 1980.

Holiday, Henry. "The Snark's Significance." *The Academy* 29 Jan. 1898: 128–30.

Hopkins, Gerard Manley. *Poems and Prose of Gerard Manley*

Hopkins. Ed. W. H. Gardner. Harmondsworth, Middlesex: Penguin, 1983.

Ingarden, Roman. *The Literary Work of Art*. Evanston: U of Illinois P, 1973.

Iser, Wolfgang. *The Act of Reading*. Baltimore: Johns Hopkins UP, 1978.

———. *The Implied Reader*. Baltimore: Johns Hopkins UP, 1974.

Jackendoff, Ray. *Consciousness and the Computational Mind*. Cambridge: MIT, 1987.

———. *Patterns in the Mind: Language and Human Nature*. NY: Basic, 1994.

Jakobson, Roman. *Language in Literature*. Eds. Krystyna Pomorska and Stephen Rudy. Cambridge: Belknap, 1987.

James, Henry. *The Figure in the Carpet and Other Stories*. Ed. Frank Kermode. NY: Penguin, 1986.

——— *The Portable Henry James*. Ed. Morton Dauwen Zabel. NY: Penguin, 1983.

———. *The Sacred Fount*. 1901. NY: Grove, 1979.

———. *The Turn of the Screw*. 1898. *The Aspern Papers and The Turn of the Screw*. NY: Penguin, 1984.

———. *The Wings of the Dove*. 1902. Harmondsworth, Middlesex: Penguin, 1986.

James, Philip, ed. *Henry Moore on Sculpture*. London: MacDonald, 1966.

James, William. *The Varieties of Religious Experience*. 1902. NY: Longmans, 1935.

Jarrett, Keith. *Eyes of the Heart*. ECM Sound Recording, 1976.

———. *Spirits*. ECM Sound Recording, 1985.

Jones, James T. *Wayward Skeptic: The Theories of R. P. Blackmur*. Chicago: U of Illinois P, 1986.

Joyce, James. "The Dead." *Dubliners*. 1914. NY: Penguin, 1984.

Kafka, Franz. *The Trial*. 1925. NY: Schoken, 1968.

Kawin, Bruce. *The Mind of the Novel: Reflexive Fiction and the Ineffable*. Princeton: Princeton UP, 1982.

Keats, John. *Selected Poems and Letters*. Ed. Douglas Bush. Boston: Houghton, 1959.

Kemmett, Bill. "Love Poem." *Yankee* (Feb. 1990): 127.

Kermode, Frank. *An Appetite for Poetry*. Cambridge: Harvard UP, 1989.

Koestler, Arthur. *The Act of Creation*. NY: Macmillan, 1964.

Konner, Melvin. *The Tangled Wing: Biological Constraints on the Human Spirit*. NY: Holt, 1982.

Krauss, Lawrence. *The Fifth Essence: The Search for the Dark Matter of the Universe*. NY: Basic, 1989.

Kristeva, Julia. "Within the Microcosm of 'The Talking Cure.'" *Interpreting Lacan*. Eds. Joseph H. Smith and William Kerrigan. New Haven: Yale UP, 1983. 33–48.

Lacoue-Labarthe, Philippe, and Jean-Luc Nancy. *The Literary Absolute: The Theory of Literature in German Romanticism*. Trans. Philip Barnard and Cheryl Lester. Albany: SUNY, 1988.

Lakoff, George. *Women, Fire, and Dangerous Things*. Chicago: U of Chicago P, 1987.

Lao-tsu. *Tao Te Ching*. Trans. Gia-Fu Feng and Jane English. NY: Vintage, 1972.

Lawrence, D. H. *Fantasia of the Unconscious and Psychoanalysis and the Unconscious*. Harmondsworth, Middlesex: Penguin, 1977.

————. *The Rainbow*. 1915. NY: Penguin, 1976.

————. *St. Mawr* and *The Man Who Died*. NY: Vintage, 1953.

Lipking, Lawrence, ed. *High Romantic Argument: Essays for M. H. Abrams*. Ithaca: Cornell UP, 1981.

Liu Hsieh. *The Literary Mind and the Carving of Dragons*. Trans. Vincent Yu-chung Shih. Hong Kong: Chinese UP, 1983.

Livingston, Paisley. *Literary Knowledge*. Ithaca: Cornell UP, 1988.

Lucas, Dolores Dyer. *Emily Dickinson and Riddle*. Dekalb: Northern Illinois UP, 1969.

Maritain, Jacques. *Creative Intuition in Art and Poetry*. NY: Pantheon, 1953.

Marks, Elaine, and Isabelle de Courtivron, eds. *New French Feminisms*. Amherst: U of Massachusetts P, 1980.

McCann, Abbot Justin, ed. *The Cloud of Unknowing and Other Treatises by an English Mystic of the Fourteenth Century*. London: Burns Oates, 1952.

Merwin, W. S. *The Drunk in the Furnace*. NY: MacMillan, 1960.

Moore, Henry. *Henry Moore: My Ideas, Inspiration, and Life as an Artist*. San Francisco: Chronicle Books, 1986.

Moore, Terence, and Chris Carling. *The Limitations of Language*. NY: St. Martin's, 1988.

Müller, F. Max. *The Science of Thought*. London: Longmans, 1887.

Natoli, Joseph. "Tracing a Beginning Through Past Theory Voices." *Tracing Literary Theory*. Ed. Joseph Natoli. Chicago: U of Illinois P, 1987.

Newman, Barbara. *Sister of Wisdom: St. Hildegard's Theology of the Feminine*. Berkeley: U of California P, 1987.

Nuttall, A. D. *A New Mimesis: Shakespeare and the Representation of Reality*. NY: Methuen, 1983.

Nystrand, Martin. *The Structure of Written Communication*. NY: Academic Press, 1986.

———, ed. *What Writers Know: The Language, Process, and Structure of Written Discourse*. NY: Academic Press, 1982.

Otto, Rudolph. *The Idea of the Holy*. Trans. John W. Harvey. 2nd ed. NY: Oxford UP, 1970.

Ozick, Cynthia. "Science and Letters: God's Work—and Ours." *The New York Times Book Review* 27 Sept. 1987: 3, 51.

Paget, Sir Richard. *Human Speech*. NY: Harcourt, 1930.

Pärt, Arvo. *Tabula Rasa*. ECM New Series Sound Recording, 1984.

Penrose, Roger. *The Emperor's New Mind: Concerning Computers, Minds and the Laws of Physics*. NY: Penguin, 1991.

———. *Shadows of the Mind: The Search for the Missing Science of Consciousness*. NY: Oxford UP, 1994.

Perry, Walter. *Greek and Roman Sculpture*. London: Longmans, 1882.

Picard, Max. *The World of Silence*. Chicago: Henry Regnery, 1952.

Poe, Edgar Allan. *Eureka: A Prose Poem*. *Edgar Allan Poe: Poetry and Tales*. NY: Library of America, 1984.

———."Ms. Found in a Bottle." *Edgar Allan Poe: Poetry and Tales*. NY: Library of America, 1984.

Poirier, Richard. *Poetry and Pragmatism*. Cambridge: Harvard UP, 1992.

———. *The Renewal of Literature: Emersonian Reflections*. New Haven: Yale UP, 1988.

———. *A World Elsewhere: The Place of Style in American Literature*. 1966. Madison: U of Wisconsin P, 1985.

Polanyi, Michael. *Personal Knowledge*. Chicago: U of Chicago P, 1958.

———. *The Tacit Dimension*. NY: Doubleday, 1966.

Powys, John Cowper. *The Meaning of Culture*. NY: Garden City, 1941.

———. *Wolf Solent*. 1929. NY: Harper, 1984.

Pynchon, Thomas. *The Crying of Lot 49*. NY: Bantam, 1967.

———. *V*. 1963. NY: Bantam, 1977.

Rilke, Rainer Maria. *Rodin*. Trans. Jessie Lemont and Hans Trausil. 1919. NY: Fine Editions, 1945.

Robertson, Martin. *A History of Greek Art*. London: Cambridge UP, 1975.

Rodin, Auguste. *Venus: To the Venus of Melos*. Trans. Dorothy Dudley. NY: B. W. Huebsch, 1912.

Rölvaag, O. E. *Giants in the Earth*. Trans. Lincoln Colcord and O. E.

Rölvaag. 1927. NY: Harper, 1965.

Rommetveit, Ragnar. *On Message Structure.* NY: John Wiley, 1974.

———. *Words, Meanings, and Messages: Theory and Experiments in Psycholinguistics.* NY: Academic Press, 1968.

Rorty, Richard. *Contingency, Irony, and Solidarity.* Cambridge: Cambridge UP, 1989.

Rothstein, Eric. "'Ideal Presence' and the 'Non Finito' in Eighteenth-Century Aesthetics." *Eighteenth-Century Studies* 9.3 (Spring 1976): 307–32.

Royle, Nicholas. *After Derrida.* Manchester: Manchester UP, 1995.

Saussure, Ferdinand de. *Course in General Linguistics.* Eds. Charles Bally and Albert Sechehaye. Trans. Wade Baskin. NY: McGraw Hill, 1966.

Schafer, Edward H. *Mirages on the Sea of Time: The Taoist Poetry of Ts'ao T'ang.* Berkeley: U of California P, 1985.

———. *Pacing the Void: T'ang Approaches to the Stars.* Berkeley: U of California P, 1977.

Schaller, Susan. *A Man Without Words.* NY: Summit, 1991.

Schelling, Andrew. *Twilight Speech: Essays on Sanskrit and Buddhist Poetics.* Calcutta: Punthi Pustak, 1993.

Shah, Idries. *The Sufis.* NY: Anchor, 1971.

Sheldrake, Rupert. *The Rebirth of Nature: The Greening of Science and God.* London: Century, 1990.

Siebers, Tobin. *The Ethics of Criticism.* Ithaca: Cornell UP, 1988.

Smith, Patti. *The Coral Sea.* NY: Norton, 1996.

Spanos, William, Paul Bové, and Daniel O'Hara, eds. *The Question of Textuality: Strategies of Reading in Contemporary American Criticism.* Bloomington: Indiana UP, 1982.

Spolsky, Ellen. *Gaps in Nature: Literary Interpretation and the Modular Mind.* Albany: SUNY Press, 1993.

Steinberg, Danny. *Psycholinguistics: Language, Mind and World.* NY: Longman, 1982.

Steiner, George. *After Babel: Aspects of Language and Translation.* NY: Oxford UP, 1975.

———. *Extraterritorial: Papers on Literature and the Language Revolution.* NY: Atheneum, 1971.

———. *Language and Silence.* NY: Atheneum, 1967.

———. *On Difficulty and Other Essays.* Oxford: Oxford UP, 1978.

———. *Real Presences.* Chicago: U of Chicago P, 1989.

Sterne, Laurence. *The Life and Opinions of Tristram Shandy.* Baltimore: Penguin, 1967.

Story, William Wetmore. *Poems*. Vol. 2. Boston: Houghton, 1900.

Sutton, Denys. *Triumphant Satyr: The World of Auguste Rodin*. NY: Hawthorn, 1966.

Symons, Arthur. *The Symbolist Movement in Literature*. 1919. NY: Dutton, 1958.

Taillander, Yvon. *Rodin*. Trans. Anne Ross. NY: Crown, n.d.

Thompson, Lawrence, ed. *Selected Letters of Robert Frost*. NY: Holt, 1964.

Thoreau, Henry David. *Walden*. 1854. Columbus: Charles E. Merrill, 1969.

Tobin, Frank. *Meister Eckhart: Thought and Language*. Philadelphia: U of Pennsylvania P, 1986.

Turner, Frederick. *Natural Classicism: Essays on Literature and Science*. NY: Paragon, 1985.

Turner Mark. *The Literary Mind*. NY: Oxford UP, 1996.

———. *Reading Minds: The Study of English in the Age of Cognitive Science*. Princeton: Princeton UP, 1991.

Uyttersprot, Herman. "*The Trial*: Its Structure." *Franz Kafka Today*. Ed. Angel Flores and Homer Swander. Madison: U of Wisconsin P, 1958.

Watts, Ann Chalmers. "Pearl, Inexpressibility, and Poems of Human Loss." *PMLA* 99.1 (January 1984): 26–40.

Webb, Mary. *The Golden Arrow*. 1916. Garden City: Doubleday, 1984.

———. *Precious Bane*. 1924. Notre Dame: U of Notre Dame P, 1980.

Wegner, Gregory R. "Hawthorne's 'Ethan Brand' and the Structure of the Literary Sketch." *The Journal of Narrative Technique* 17.1 (Winter 1987): 57–66.

Wells, G. A. *The Origin of Language: Aspects of the Discussion from Condillac to Wundt*. La Salle: Open Court, 1987.

Welsh, Andrew. *Roots of Lyric*. Princeton: Princeton UP, 1978.

Wheelwright, Philip. *The Burning Fountain: A Study in the Language of Symbolism*. Rev. ed. Bloomington: Indiana UP, 1968.

Whitehead, Alfred North. *Adventures of Ideas*. 1933. Cambridge: Cambridge UP, 1947.

———. *Science and the Modern World*. 1925. NY: MacMillan, 1962.

Whorf, Benjamin Lee. *Language, Thought, and Reality*. Ed. John B. Carroll. NY: John Wiley and MIT P, 1959.

Wihl, Gary. *The Contingency of Theory: Pragmatism, Expressivism, and Deconstruction*. New Haven: Yale UP, 1994.

Winn, James. *Unsuspected Eloquence: A History of the Relations Between Poetry and Music*. New Haven: Yale UP, 1981.

Wittgenstein, Ludwig. *Tractatus Logico-Philosophicus.* Trans. D. F. Pears and B. F. McGuiness. London: Routledge, 1969.

Woolf, Virginia. *The Common Reader.* London: Hogarth, 1984.

———. *The Second Common Reader.* NY: Harcourt, 1932.

———. *To The Lighthouse.* 1927. NY: Harcourt, 1955.

Wordsworth, William. *Selected Poems and Prefaces.* Ed. Jack Stillinger. Boston: Houghton, 1965.

Zhang, John Zaixin. "Free Play in Samuel Richardson's *Pamela.*" *Papers on Language and Literature* 27.3 (Summer 1991): 307–19.

Index

Timothy Walsh's poems, short stories, and essays have appeared in numerous literary magazines and journals. He earned his Ph.D. in English at the Univerity of Wisconsin–Madison, where he taught for a number of years and now works as a senior advisor. He is currently at work on a novel.